I

This book is

R

fo

FROM

FROM HULL TO HELL AND BACK

An Autobiography

Lee Crooks
with Vince Groak

Scratching Shed Publishing Ltd

First published by Scratching Shed Publishing Ltd in 2011
Registered in England & Wales No. 6588772.
Registered office:
47 Street Lane, Leeds, West Yorkshire. LS8 1AP

www.scratchingshedpublishing.co.uk

ISBN 978-0956252685

Unless stated otherwise, all photographs are from the
personal collections of Lee Crooks

A catalogue record for this book is available from the British Library.

Typeset in Warnock Pro Semi Bold and Palatino

Printed and bound in the United Kingdom by
L.P.P.S.Ltd, Wellingborough, Northants, NN8 3PJ

Contents

Hessle Road vi

Acknowledgements vii

Foreword *by Peter Sterling* 9

1.   Love Will Tear Us Apart 13
2.   There in Black and White 35
3.   Testing Times..87
4.   Captain Crooks..124
5.   Wests Life 153
6.   Marching on Together? 164
7.   Castleford Calling...181
8.   Sidesteps and Dummies 191
9.   A Gottle o' Geer 213
10. The Party's Over 233
11. Made in Hull 257
12. Is Pat on the Bus?...271
13. On the Right Path 291
14. Crossing the Divide...302
15. Back to the Future...318

Hessle Road

"Hessle Road, Hessle Road, I am proud of Hessle Road.
When folks ask where I come from, my head it is not bowed.
I say I come from good old Hessle Road.

I miss the bonfires in the street. I even miss the bullies,
Sat'day trips round Boyes's and the prams outside of Woolie's.
I miss those bobbers' clogs at two, that very fishy smell,
Langham and Eureka, and Picky Park as well.

I miss those little gardens with sooty coloured roses,
Little kids with wellies on, with yellow snotty noses.
I miss those shotgun weddings, those little corner shops,
Playing football in the street and getting chased by cops.

I miss those brave young fisher kids, coming home to shore,
Spending all their money, then going back for more.
I even miss Criterion—a very quiet pub—
And a little lass from Subway Street our kid put in the club.

I miss Sat'days at the Boulevard. we always used to win,
With the Drake twins, Tommy Harris, Mick Scott and Tommy Finn,
Loose forward Johnny Whiteley—the finest in the land—
And the best-behaved supporters, we were there on Threepenny Stand.

There was Havelock and Gillett Street, West Dock and Boulevard.
They're pulling them all down now. It's hitting people hard.
They've left it all behind them, and on to Bransholme strode,
But I bet they don't forget the laughs, the tears on Hessle Road.

I remember what me dad said, when I was leaving home
To fend for meself and start a family of my own.
He said, "I brought you up, son, but nowt to me is owed.
Just remember where you come from. You're a kid from Hessle Road."

Words: Pete Smith

Acknowledgements

Lee

My thanks to Peter Sterling, Garry Schofield, Colin Maskill, Franky Punchard, Arthur Bunting, Mike Page, Richard Crooks, Vince Groak and David Howes.

This book is dedicated to my mam and dad... for all the things I didn't do.

To my four kids - Emma, Stuart, Megan and Ben - and grandkids Sonny, Beau and Georgia. You make everything worthwhile.

Vince

To my mam and dad and sister, Joanna; To Chubs, Fewy, Big Lee, Little Lee, Neilo and Steve for making Friday nights enjoyable regardless of the result, and to Lee Crooks for the enormous privilege of sharing his story with me.

To Claire, of course, for never doubting that this book would one day be finished, and to Dylan; one day, my boy, one day. I love you both.

*

Foreword
by Peter Sterling

Lee Crooks is directly responsible for affording me one of the greatest thrills of my rugby career.

As a child, my father always used to wake me up in the wee small hours to watch Test matches between Australia and Great Britain at Wembley. So from an early age I had a burning desire to one day set foot on the hallowed turf.

In April 1985, Hull FC played Castleford in the Challenge Cup semi-final at Headingley. The winner, of course, would go through to the final to be played at that magical venue. But with time almost up and Cas leading by six points, we were in a bit of trouble. Suddenly, we managed to score a try and give ourselves the chance of an unlikely replay.

Displaying nerves of steel close to the sideline, Lee calmly potted the conversion and kept our hopes alive. History shows we beat Castleford comfortably in the replay and went on to appear in one of the most exciting games ever to be played beneath the old Twin Towers.

I wasn't surprised that Crooksy made that kick look so

easy because his prodigious talent was a leading attraction in persuading me to travel 12,000 miles to join the Airlie Birds the previous season.

Our paths had first crossed during the 1982 Australian Kangaroo Tour in which we both made our Test debuts. Lee was still only nineteen when he was chosen by the Lions' selectors for the first game in Hull. His selection certainly piqued interest in our camp because he was viewed as the kind of individual who could cause us some problems. Respected local judges had assured us that he was a youngster with plenty of skill but that he also possessed a relatively short fuse.

After he missed the Second Test through injury, we were able to take advantage of his fiery nature in the final game when some well-placed sledging drew a reaction and led to him being sent off. Despite this dismissal he had already demonstrated that a marvellous career was underway. Over the ensuing years the mental side of Lee's game developed to match his physical influence and he became a professional's professional.

Three of his twenty seasons in the top grade were spent Down Under where he is still regarded fondly as one of the truly great English imports to have graced our competition. The fact that he was a traditional 'pommy' front-rower from a bygone era made him an immediate crowd favourite and a particularly dangerous proposition on the paddock.

Not since Brian Lockwood had our game seen the kind of crafty ball-playing ability so often associated with English prop forwards and, sadly, not since Lee have we seen it again.

While that high-profile meeting with Castleford obviously made an impression on my life, it is actually a run-of-the-mill club game the previous year that sums up the Lee Crooks I will always remember.

On an awfully bleak night at the Boulevard we took on Leigh in a match that we were expected to win easily and, although we ultimately did so, the game took place in freezing conditions. Snow fell throughout and the ground was an unforgiving surface that burnt the skin upon contact. To be honest, Australia had never looked so good.

I believe that I managed to go through the full eighty minutes without being tackled and went into the sheds happy with the win and pleased to be physically unscathed.

This was put into perspective when I sat next to Crooksy and looked down at his knees. They were a bloody red mess; the top layer of skin long gone from continual contact with the frozen surface I had tried so hard to avoid.

It hadn't been a cup final and victory had never been in doubt, but Lee had played with the same intensity and desire that he would have done if it had been a Test Match.

He embarrassed me that night and I made a promise that I would never again look to take the comfortable route.

Due to the tyranny of distance I don't get to catch up with my former teammate as often as I would like these days but, with the rugby league world being what it is, I always look to see how my old mates are getting on. The last time I heard from Lee, he was spreading the gospel in Serbia.

I am extremely proud to call Lee Crooks a mate. The same pride I felt every time we took the field of battle together.

Peter Sterling, May 2011

1

Love Will Tear Us Apart

When Hull FC sold me to Leeds in 1987, they received more money than any club had ever got for a rugby league player. My hometown club had fallen on hard times and were skint. They needed the brass. Leeds were a rising force, bristling with ambition and with cash to burn. I wasn't the only top player they signed that summer; just the most expensive.

Most players in the same position would have been excited and even grateful but when the directors of Leeds, with great pride and arrogance, rolled me out in front of the TV cameras on that June afternoon, I would rather have been anywhere in the world but Headingley. I had never been more miserable in my life and, rather than celebrate the hefty signing on fee, the pay rise and the opportunity to join one of the biggest clubs in the country, I just wanted to get away to drown my sorrows.

Once the formalities were over, I drove a few miles down the road to Rothwell to meet up with Garry Schofield. The interview I had given at Headingley that afternoon had been shown on BBC *Look North*; Schoey had seen it and had found it quite amusing. He told me he'd never seen anybody look so pissed off. We had a few beers and he tried to cheer me up but it didn't work. It hadn't been my decision to leave Hull and I was too upset to try and pretend I was happy about it.

A couple of weeks earlier, I had been in Sydney playing for Balmain Tigers when I was told I had to fly home to sign for Leeds. I'd been back in England a few weeks while the deal was finalised and, in that time, there weren't many days when I didn't have a beer to try and cheer myself up. Since most of my (now ex-) Hull team-mates were on holiday, I was pretty lonely and spent most days searching for people to go drinking with. To make matters worse, before I had flown out to Australia, I'd given up the lease on my flat in Hull so I had nowhere to live either. I crashed wherever I could; on the floor of mates' houses, in hotels, in pubs, in my car. I don't think I spent more than two nights in any one place.

I would disappear for days on end. Occasionally, someone would get worried that they hadn't heard from me for a while and would ring around trying to track me down. It was a thankless task; I could have been anywhere. Anywhere that sold beer that is. Schoey once went looking for me and traipsed around most of the pubs in Castleford before he finally gave up. He ended up getting pissed himself and landed in bother with his missus as a result!

When the time came for me to go to Headingley for the medical, I turned up with a hangover and was told that I had a very high level of alcohol in my blood. I told them that that wasn't remotely surprising since I'd been drinking non-stop for a fortnight.

I couldn't care less what they thought of me and, if anyone at Leeds was concerned about how I was feeling, they never really showed it, certainly not to me. I had to go back a few days later to do the medical again and, this time,

I was unveiled to the press as the world's most expensive player. As I stood there posing for photographs holding a Leeds RLFC scarf above my head, I couldn't believe how I had come to be in such a situation.

For the answer, I had to go back a couple of years.

*****

By 1985, I wasn't the same bloke who had burst onto the rugby league scene five years earlier. The success I enjoyed at the start of my career had gone to my head in many ways. And who could blame me? I was captain of my hometown club; the team I supported as a boy and the one I had always dreamed of playing for. The team I led onto the Wembley pitch for that now famous Challenge Cup final in 1985 contained legends of the game; Steve 'Knocker' Norton, Peter Sterling, Dane O'Hara, Gary Kemble, Garry Schofield and James Leuluai, to name a few.

Not only was I one of the key players in the Hull side, I was as close to being a regular in the Great Britain team as I would ever be. Later in the year, I single-handedly saved a Test series against New Zealand with a man-of-the-match performance and a last-minute penalty kick from the touchline. It had seemed, for five years or so, that everything I touched turned to gold and I felt that I could do no wrong.

I'd always had a big ego but there was no doubt that, by 1985, it had started to turn to arrogance; a characteristic that I have always hated in other people. When I first broke into the team, I was by far the youngest member and I suppose that my occasional indiscretions were sort of laughed off. If I ever got into trouble, there was always someone there to help me out and I guess I started to take that for granted. Gradually, I became more and more selfish in my attitude and behaviour.

From Hull to Hell and Back

It was ironic really because I used to pride myself on not letting my success go to my head. For years, my first wife Janet and I spent most of our time with her family and friends, having family parties and talking about rugby league in social clubs around Hull. I had celebrated my eighteenth and twenty-first birthday parties, as well as my engagement, in the Charleston Club just down the road from the Boulevard. All of our families had been there and it was very down-to-earth and normal.

When Janet and I moved to Hessle in 1983, we put a little more distance between us and her family and I started to spend less time with them and more time with my team-mates. It never got to the stage where I was out every night by any means, but there was never a shortage of opportunities to go out drinking and, inevitably, it started to drive a wedge between Janet and myself.

Janet and I had married when I was very young and I probably missed out on a lot of the things that a typical seventeen or eighteen-year-old might get up to. By the time I was twenty-one, I started to think about what I had supposedly lost and, I guess, started to act like the teenager I had never really been.

Ironically, at the same time, I had become one of the senior players at Hull FC and, as captain, they needed some maturity from me to help turn around the club's fortunes because, after the 1985 Cup final, everything at Hull began to go downhill very quickly.

After the Bradford City stadium fire in 1985, the club had been forced to shut down the Boulevard's famous wooden Threepenny Stand. When we started the following season at home to Widnes, there was no atmosphere in the ground and it affected us on the pitch; we put in a very poor performance and were hammered.

It was a miserable season. Rovers knocked us out of both

the Yorkshire Cup and the Challenge Cup, we were humiliated at St Helens in the John Player Trophy and the tour game against New Zealand was a bloodbath. Five years earlier, we had played the touring Kiwi team and, although we had lost, the club and its fans had made such an impression on the tourists that four of them went on to sign for us. In November 1985, we lost again and I was one of five players sent off in a bad-tempered game.

While we were struggling on the pitch, there were also lots of rumours about the club's financial problems. The prize money wasn't coming in any more and the crowds were well past their peak. Meanwhile, the club still had a large squad and a massive wage bill. When the directors were faced with having to make ground improvements, they just didn't have the money. There were major problems just around the corner, although I had no idea at the time how those problems would come to affect me.

*****

Just before Christmas of 1985, we headed over the Pennines for what ought to have been a fairly easy game against Swinton. But it didn't turn out that way; they got stuck into us, stopped us from playing and we lost.

We knew we had underperformed badly and everyone was gutted on the bus journey home but we were still in the top half of the league and nobody was panicking. Certainly, none of us had any idea of the plotting taking place on the directors' bus. Chairman Roy Waudby called an emergency board meeting for later that night. At the meeting, he asked for a vote of no confidence in Arthur Bunting as coach. Apparently, it was strongly opposed by some directors but Roy invariably got his own way and, the next day, it was announced that Arthur had been sacked.

Roy and Arthur hadn't seen eye to eye for quite a few years. As a teetotaller, Roy had never felt comfortable when Arthur encouraged his players to go out together. He never really understood why sportsmen liked to have a beer to help them bond and relax. While the team was successful, there was no real challenge to Arthur's methods but, once our results started to slip, Roy was quick to blame it on what he saw as a lack of discipline.

Arthur broke the news to us at training the next day and, to a man, none of us could believe it. Even though our form had been poor by our own standards, we hadn't thought for a minute that Arthur might get the sack. We all went to the Norland pub for a drink, but we didn't know what to say to him, nobody was able to make sense of what had happened. I guess you just never know, until it's too late, that you're past your peak, either as a team or an individual. At that time, we still thought we were the best team in the competition and that we would bounce back. But we were wrong and it never happened.

Arthur's biggest strength had always been his ability to get the best out of his players. He was the best man-manager that I ever played under but, with the benefit of hindsight, he had probably got as much out of some players as he was going to. One of the accusations against Arthur was that he allowed the team to grow old together without bringing in enough younger players. Arthur was well aware that he sometimes needed to move players on but whenever he decided to let somebody move they just didn't want to go. The atmosphere at Hull was so special that nobody wanted to leave. At one point, Arthur struck a deal with York for them to sign Sammy Lloyd, but Sammy said he'd rather retire than play anywhere else and refused to go. It proved very hard to break up the team and some of the older players stayed longer than they probably should have.

Arthur wanted to be ruthless and bring in younger players but it didn't quite happen.

Instead of easing young players into the team gradually, as he had done with me, he suddenly found that he had to bring lots of them in all at once. Jon Sharp, Alan Tomlinson, Neil Puckering, Andy Dannatt and Paul Eastwood were all good players but they were all dropped in at the deep end at once. It wasn't their fault they lacked the experience to deal with the pressures of playing at a club that was expected to win trophies every season. So Arthur was fired and Ken Foulkes took charge for the rest of the season. It didn't improve our results and 1985-86 fizzled out badly.

Just before the new season began, Len Casey took over as coach. Compared to Arthur, Len was a novice and it had only been a year since he finished playing, but Roy Waudby thought Len would bring in the discipline he felt we lacked. In the event, Len's management style was too much of a contrast to Arthur's and for some of the older players, it was a change too far. The players also felt a lot of loyalty to Arthur and Len had a tough start. His playing style had always been very competitive and his style of management was just as aggressive. We made an inconsistent start and, by November, Len was already struggling to get the best out of us. We started to suffer the kind of heavy defeats that seem to happen when all is not well. It certainly wasn't the kind of form we wanted to take into a fixture against the Australian touring team.

Four years earlier, we had almost beaten the 1982 Invincibles and Peter Sterling had been so impressed that he chose to join us for two years, but the way we approached the fixture in 1986 said a lot about the team we had become. It was a brutal game, quite similar to the Tour game against the Kiwis the year before, with fights breaking out at regular intervals. Garry Jack later complained that, while he was trying to break up a fight that had spilled over the touchline, he had been assaulted by a middle-aged Hull woman who had hit him with her umbrella. Three players were sin-binned but the fan was never brought to book! The Aussies beat us 48-0 and, after the game, Sterlo said that if he ever came back to play in England then it wouldn't be with Hull FC. I was embarrassed.

Len Casey had lots to offer the game but his style of man-management wasn't getting the best out of us. Len put the fear of God into his players and I think some of the younger ones were intimidated. Mind you, although I didn't think he was right for the club at that time, I still had a lot of respect for Len as an individual. He certainly tried to help me out as my marital problems got worse.

After a big argument with Janet one night, I went out on the piss with a couple of players from the colts team. We were daft enough to go out down Hessle Road where I was sure to be spotted. Inevitably, someone decided to tell Len what I had done and, the next day when I turned up to play, he took me to one side for a chat.

I was expecting to get a bollocking and, to be honest, I didn't care. I was bang to rights and so I never bothered to deny it or offer an excuse. I just told him that I'd had a row with the missus, felt sorry for myself and decided to go out. Len had been through the same kind of situation himself a few years earlier and knew exactly what I was going through. Rather than come down heavy on me, he offered me some advice. "If you're ever going to do something like that again, don't do it in Hull. Go somewhere else where it's quiet," he told me.

It wasn't what I was expecting to hear. Len wasn't soft by any means - he'd be more likely to thump a player than let them off the hook - but I guess Len wanted to show me some sympathy and he certainly didn't want to put my back up as he needed me to play. I was touched by the gesture but, to be honest, I needed someone to reign me in. The last thing I needed at that stage of my life was someone to cut me some slack.

Arthur Bunting had been like a father figure to me and he knew exactly how to handle me. When he left the club, I probably needed to take more responsibility for myself and, I'm ashamed to say, I wasn't able to. If I had been happier at home, it might have all been different but the cracks in my marriage to Janet were getting wider and there's no doubt that it was affecting my career.

I had met Janet when I was just fifteen and she was twenty-one. At that time, the age difference didn't matter to either of us; I was quite a mature teenager and we enjoyed doing the same things. As far as I was concerned it was a brilliant relationship and I just wanted to do the normal things most people do when they meet the right person; get married, buy a house and start a family. For five years or so, it all went to plan. Our kids, Emma and Stuart, arrived and we were very happy bringing up our family. I had everything I could possibly want; success as a rugby player, great mates who I went into battle with every week, and my own family. It was perfect, but it didn't last.

Like a lot of men, I wanted to have my cake and eat it. I loved Janet and worshipped the kids and I wanted to have a satisfying home life. On the other hand, I also wanted to go out whenever I felt like it and we all know that those two options aren't compatible. Nevertheless, it didn't stop me trying for a while and I began to spend more and more time away from home as the temptation to get drunk and go to parties grew greater and greater.

I had my own way of explaining my behaviour. I always felt that drinking with my team-mates was part and parcel of being a sportsman. It was the reward we earned for the hard work that we put in on the training field every week. I never thought that my drinking could do any serious harm and I probably felt that I was entitled to do as I wanted since it was my success that had given us the lifestyle we enjoyed. Besides, I was a Great Britain international and the captain of Hull FC. Didn't that mean I could get away with what I wanted?

The situation came to a head around Christmas of 1986. I had a big argument with Janet and was all set to storm out of the house. I had two pay packets sat on the mantelpiece, one of them had only a few pounds left in it, but the other contained over four hundred quid. I grabbed that one and left the house. I headed for the Albion pub where I knew the landlord, Andy Stephenson, quite well. It was the last Friday before Christmas and the pub was soon filling up with the lasses from the local factories. Most of them knew who I was and it wasn't long before I was chatting them up and having a laugh.

By then, I was spending a lot of time with my team-mate Steve 'Knocker' Norton and so, once I had decided that I was going to stay out all night, I asked Pauline, the landlady, to ring 'Knocker' and get him to come and join me. I'd spent whatever cash I'd had in my pocket and so I dug in my jacket pocket for the wage packet that I'd brought with me, but once I opened it up I realised that I'd picked up the wrong one and it only had about a tenner in it. I was gutted and it put me in a really bad mood. Knocker turned up eventually but, by then, I was hammered so he just took me back to his house where I could sleep it off.

By the start of 1987, I knew that my relationship with Janet had broken down and I made the very tough decision to leave her. Although my mind was made up, it proved to be very difficult to make the break as I just couldn't bring myself to leave my kids. There were days when I would convince myself to leave and there were others when I was just as determined to mend the relationship and make it work.

One night, I headed for training determined to come straight home afterwards since I had my driving test the next day. On the way to training, I stopped off to order an Indian takeaway which I planned to pick up later and take back home to Janet.

It was Knocker's testimonial season that year and, after training, some of the players were getting ready to go to one of his functions. Since I had decided not to go out, I offered to give them a lift but, once we got to the pub, I decided to pop in just for one. As soon as I walked in, I noticed that Knocker's sister, Karen, was there. I had always got on well with Karen and, to be honest, I fancied her like mad.

After a shandy, I had a beer, then another and, eventually, Knocker, Karen, me and half the team stayed up drinking most of the night. At some point during the evening, something clicked between Karen and me. I think the feeling was stronger from my side, certainly at first, but, looking back, that night was the first time I started to think that I might have a future with Karen.

The following morning, I had to sit my driving test. I called my driving instructor and asked him to meet me at the test centre. He stopped by at my house to pick up my provisional licence and paperwork and Janet insisted on coming to meet me as well. When he finally turned up I couldn't believe it when I saw Janet and the kids in tow. Janet wanted to know where I had been all night and it all ended up in a big row.

Years earlier, the club had arranged for me to have a sponsored car and I had driven around in it for a long time without a proper licence. Because of that, I thought I was perfectly roadworthy but, as everyone knows, passing your test is quite different to being able to drive. I didn't do too badly on the practical and it all came down to how well I knew my Highway Code.

The examiner showed me a load of cards and asked me what they meant. I was doing okay until we got to the last one - some dotted white lines on the road. I had no idea and could only guess. I think I got it wrong first time but he gave me a second chance. I kept getting it wrong and he continued to give me clues until eventually I got it right. It wasn't until much later that I found out he was a massive Hull FC fan and, at the time, I just assumed that it was normal procedure to give clues. Anyway, I was a bit surprised when he told me that I had passed my test.

I was chuffed to bits and in the mood to celebrate so I went to meet one of my team-mates, Carl Sanderson, in the pub. Karen was there again, we all had a few drinks and, to be honest, I just wanted to spend as much time with her as possible. She needed to get back to Wakefield and the pub that she ran with her partner, so we all drove over there to celebrate me passing my driving test. I ended up staying there all day and, after that, I never really went home again. Nor did I ever pick up that Indian takeaway.

*****

Leaving Janet and the kids was the hardest thing I ever did in my life and it wasn't the end of the story by a long way. It was a momentous decision and it tore me apart to leave my kids, but I didn't think I could be happy if I stayed.

I moved out early in the New Year into a flat in the centre of Hull. I tried to get on with my life but I didn't find it easy. It was bad enough being away from the kids but the flat was grotty, dark and miserable. I had no furniture to speak of and I blagged curtains and stuff from wherever I could get them. I had a friend who worked in a launderette and she helped me furnish the flat with whatever oddments she could nick from work. None of my curtains matched and the bedding and cushions were straight out of the 1970s, but at least I had my own place.

I did what most blokes do in that situation; I went on the piss. I always knew that on Tuesdays and Thursdays I could have a beer with the lads after training and, at weekends, there were always plenty out and about. Whenever I had the chance, I headed for Wakefield or Castleford in the hope that I might cross paths with Karen. Castleford had also become the home of what would become known as 'Mad Monday' or 'The Monday Club'.

Monday afternoon drinking has always been a tradition around Castleford. I think it stems from the mining industry for some reason. As a result, the pubs were always busy at the start of the week and I could always find someone that would join me for a pint.

I would usually drive over from Hull and meet Knocker in The Horse and Jockey where there would be plenty of people having a drink and a laugh. I loved it; everyone knew me, there was plenty of banter and lots of beer. I could forget all about Janet and the kids and enjoy the male company. I never knew what was likely to happen or where we would end up, and that was the main attraction. One year, one of my old team-mates from my time playing in Australia was playing for Oldham and he decided, on the spur of the moment, to throw a party at his local pub. He rang us up in the Jockey, we jumped in someone's car and drove over the Pennines to join the party. On another occasion, I walked into the Jockey to see Knocker, who told me 'It'll be a laugh, tonight, Crooksy. Woodsy's coming over.'

Paul Woods was part of the Hull team when I first joined the club. By the mid-80s, he had retired but he remained a real character and quite an intimidating bloke when you first set eyes on him. Knocker wanted to see how all the locals reacted when Woodsy arrived so he never told them that he was expecting a visitor. When Paul arrived, the pub went quiet as all the locals sized him up. He wasn't particularly big but he had a look about him, did Woodsy.

Once they realised that Paul was a mate of ours, everyone relaxed and we had a cracking night. Around nine o'clock, Woodsy decided that he fancied going to Hull for a drink. I had drunk the least and so I was roped into driving. Knocker thought better of it so Woodsy, myself and a guy called Squirrel (a Jockey regular) drove over. On the way, we decided that we would head for Henry's nightclub, quite a dodgy place but one that was guaranteed to be fairly lively even on a Monday night.

As I spun my car around and pulled up in front of the club, the bouncers recognised us straight away and ushered us in. Squirrel was an oddball, though. He had a withered, deformed arm and a terrible habit of spitting every thirty seconds, which he couldn't stop himself from doing even inside the nightclub. After a couple of warnings, one of the bouncers asked him to leave, which was quite ironic since the club was a real shithole and there was far worse than spit soaked into the carpets at Henry's. Reluctantly, Squirrel left but kept trying to get back into the club. He was causing the bouncers some real grief and one of them came over to me and Woodsy and asked us to sort him out. I suppose we ought to have taken him home or tried to find somewhere else to go but really there was nowhere else open and we were having a good night, so I bundled him into the back of my car, locked the doors and went back into the club, leaving him banging on the inside of the windows.

Once we finally left Henry's there was only my one-bedroom flat left for us to go to, so that's how I came to spend the night under a pink and orange duvet with Paul Woods, while Squirrel slept on the floor under a beige curtain.

*****

Around that time, Len Casey decided that he needed to get the players together for a bonding session to boost morale and so he decided to take us all to Spain for a week. Len wanted to clear away any doubts his team might have had about him but if he had hoped to stamp his authority on the players during that trip, it didn't really work out that way. It was just an extended piss-up punctuated by the occasional training session. Knocker spent most of the time at the hotel bar while the rest of us spent the majority of the week trying to keep away from Andy Dannatt who had brought a bag of firecrackers with him and thought it was hilarious to throw them at anyone he came across.

A couple of the lads stayed out all night on one occasion and turned up for training the next day still wearing their party clothes. Everyone braced themselves for Len to go mental but he just let it pass. Len had been going nuts about the pair of them but, once they turned up, he never said a word. I couldn't figure Len out. He seemed to avoid confrontation more often than not and, by the end of the week, I was certain that I wasn't going to enjoy playing for him as much as I had for Arthur.

A number of the directors weren't happy with the sacking of Arthur either and there was quite a bit of turmoil for a while, with several directors deciding to stand down from the board. Throughout it all, though, there was no doubt in anyone's mind that Roy Waudby remained the most powerful man at the club. Roy had a real presence and rarely failed to get his own way. Nevertheless, things weren't going well and as he started to show his frustration at what was going on he had me squarely in his sights.

By the end of March 1987 relegation was a real possibility. At home to Warrington, we found ourselves thirty points down at half-time and, during the interval, Len had started throwing the teacups around when Roy walked in. The room went silent as Roy, normally quite composed, started getting stuck into the players: 'You're an embarrassment' he told us. 'You're not fit to wear the shirt'. It was one of those pointless outbursts that serve no purpose except to make Roy feel a bit better.

Few people ever spoke back to Roy and so he would have felt confident in saying whatever he liked. Then he turned to me. 'And you ought to spend less time in the pub and more time on the training pitch,' he said. It was a cheap shot. Everyone in the room knew that Roy's accusation wasn't too far off the mark. I was drinking far too much and losing the plot. With the club in danger of going down, Roy was entitled to expect that his best players would help to turn things around. Nevertheless, he shouldn't have said that to his captain under those circumstances and there was no way that I was going to allow him to humiliate me in front of the team. With all eyes on the pair of us, I turned on him and told him to 'fuck off'.

I doubt that anyone at the club had ever said that to Roy and he went ballistic. Len and one or two of the players tried to shepherd Roy out of the room before one of us lashed out further but Roy had time to make it very clear that I would regret speaking to him in that way. After he left, the dressing room went quiet. Everyone was shocked at what had happened, particularly at what I had said to the chairman. After the game, the colts' coach Dave Elliott told me that I should go and find Roy and apologise to him.

I had calmed down a bit by then but still felt annoyed

that he had come in and yelled at us. My apology wasn't exactly heartfelt.

'Mr chairman,' I said, as I walked into the boardroom. 'I've been told to come and apologise, so here I am.'

His acceptance wasn't very genuine either. He made it clear that he had a long memory and would not forget what had happened.

I've always had a complicated relationship with people in authority. Over the years, I have worked under some people that I have had massive respect for. In the coming pages, I will tell you about my relationships with Arthur Bunting, Malcolm Reilly and Darryl van der Velde. Each of them had something that meant I would do anything they asked. I believed in them. They were honest and straight in their dealings with me and I was loyal to them as a result.

On the other hand, I have clashed horribly with people I haven't had respect for, and I will tell you about those incidents as well. I've no time for people who are dishonest or use their position to get their way, without feeling that they have to explain themselves. That may be a naive view but I can't help it. I just expect leaders to lead by example and to show integrity and honesty.

I had respect for Roy Waudby but his behaviour that day wasn't worthy of a man in his position and it wasn't in my nature to keep my mouth shut and accept it. I made my peace with Roy a few years later but, at that time, I had made a powerful enemy and I would come to regret it.

*****

Things didn't get much better for the team after the Warrington defeat and we went into the Easter weekend needing to win at least two of our last three games in order to stay up. When Rovers beat us at Craven Park on Good

From Hull to Hell and Back

Friday, we were on the brink of relegation. We went to Wakefield desperate for a win and showed that we were still capable of putting in a performance when it mattered. Garry Schofield had a blinder, scoring four tries as we won easily. Two days later, we faced tougher opponents in the form of Widnes and, again, had to win to stay up.

I hadn't been playing well but knew that I needed to put in a big performance if we were going to avoid the drop. It was unthinkable that we could go down so soon after being the top team in the country but there was no use moaning about it; we just had to get on with it and get a result. Thankfully, we beat them comfortably but it was a disappointing end to a season. It was an emotional occasion too and the players gave a lap of honour of the Boulevard pitch more out of relief than any sense of achievement. I was glad to put the season behind me and looked forward to getting away from it all and heading off to play for Balmain. But, by the time I flew down under, I was in a bad place.

Although it had been my decision in the end, I never stopped agonising over leaving Janet. I missed the kids like mad and kept thinking that I ought to have stayed in my marriage for their sakes. As a parent, I wasn't sure that it was right to put my own happiness ahead of my children's. I kept telling myself that it was for the best in the long run and, while I wrestled with those doubts, I tried to put my life back into order.

As soon as I had decided to leave Janet, I began to pursue Karen. I always looked forward to seeing her, but nothing seemed to go smoothly for us. One night, we had been to one of Knocker's testimonial events in Hull and were heading back to his house in North Ferriby on the outskirts. I was driving and Karen sat up front with me, while a bloke called Dave, who worked at her pub, sat in the back. Dave was a big bloke, the kind of jolly fat guy that it's hard to dislike, so I didn't mind giving him a lift even though I would have preferred to be on my own with Karen. We were just out of Hull when Dave decided that he needed a pee, so I pulled over to the side of the road while Dave got out and climbed over the crash barrier to go in the bushes. While he was gone, I was seized by the moment and decided this was my chance to make my move on Karen.

With Dave pissing away merrily into the bushes, I grabbed Karen, told her I was crazy about her and snogged her. I think she was a bit startled but she didn't put up much of a fight which I took to be a good sign. No sooner had I got Karen in a clinch then we heard an almighty scream. I turned around, expecting to see Dave being attacked but he had disappeared. I could hear some moaning and groaning and then I heard Dave shout my name, 'Lee, Lee, I'm down here.' The daft bastard had lost his footing and fallen down the embankment. He was laid at the bottom unable to move.

'For fuck's sake, Dave,' I said, 'what are you doing down there?' It would have been funny if I wasn't so desperate to be on my own with Karen, but there was no way I could leave Dave to himself or he'd have died of hypothermia. I managed to climb twenty feet or so down the hill to reach him but he must have weighed twenty-five stone. As soon as I got him half way up the hill, one of us would lose our footing and end up back at the bottom again. It didn't help that Karen was stood at the top laughing like hell at us both.

The next few months were a blur. Before long, Karen had left her partner and we were able to spend most of our time together, but it was far from easy. I loved spending time with Karen but I was still upset about leaving Janet and the kids. There were many days when I felt that I had made a mistake and decided I would go back to them, which obviously hurt Karen a great deal.

Most of my family and friends felt that I had made a

massive mistake. My mam, in particular, hated Karen with a passion and was constantly involving herself in our relationship. Even Arthur Bunting tried to persuade me to go back to my family. I swayed one way and the other for months which not only screwed me up but hurt Karen, Janet, the kids and everyone else that knew us. It was a nightmare.

So when the time came to go to Australia to join up with my new team at Balmain, I looked forward to making a clean break and decided to ask Karen to travel with me. I hoped that a few months in Sydney with Karen would bring us closer together and stop me from going totally off the rails in Australia.

At first it was great, but it didn't take long before I started to miss the kids. I felt guilty being with Karen while they were at home missing me. In those days, I didn't really know how to deal with disappointment or unhappiness and so I found myself a bit of a soulmate in Benny Elias and went on the beer. Understandably, Karen wondered why the hell I had flown her to Australia only for me to go out on the piss with someone I barely knew.

One day she confronted me about it. I told her that I had made a big mistake and that I shouldn't have left the kids. She had heard it all before but probably wasn't expecting to hear it while we were on the other side of the world. If that was what I wanted, she said, then she was going home. I should get Janet and the kids to come out to join me. It seemed bizarre but, for a while, that was what I decided to do.

*****

Karen flew back to England in an absolute state and I was left on my own to further drown my sorrows. I had hoped that I could get myself sorted out if I was playing well for Balmain. I'd worked really hard to get myself fit hoping to give a good account of myself and I'd made a reasonable start to my time there picking up a couple of man of the match awards. The press were starting to write some positive things about me and the team did okay in the first three games I played in. But it all started to go wrong when the Balmain chief executive, Keith Barnes, called me into his office to say that there was a problem with my contract and that Hull FC wouldn't let me play any more games. It made no sense; why would I have flown to the other side of the world just to play three games? I knew that something was amiss but still had no idea what the problem was.

I called Len Casey and asked him what was going on and it was then that he dropped the bombshell I never thought I would hear; Hull FC had sold me to Leeds.

I have no idea how I reacted on hearing the news. I spent much of the next three years trying to recover from it so I had no reason to replay the moment over and over again. I do recall shouting and screaming down the phone at Len, calling him every name I could think of. It made sense now. Hull didn't want me playing any more games for Balmain in case I got injured which would stop my move to Leeds.

I can't recall whether Roy Waudby told me to my face or over the phone but I didn't really need an explanation from anyone. I was well aware that the club was desperate for the money they could get from selling me. The deal had been done and there was no going back. The fee - £150,000 - was a world record. As much as I could understand why Hull needed to sell me, it wasn't part of my career plan. I didn't want to leave Hull. I wasn't just a player, I was a fan and I wanted to play for Hull for the rest of my career. I felt as though everything was slipping away from me; Arthur Bunting had left the club and so had Knocker. I'd split up with my wife and left my kids and now Hull FC were telling me that I couldn't play for them.

From Hull to Hell and Back

And so the road that took me to Headingley was well sign-posted. But if the main motivation for my move came from Hull's financial predicament, the urgency behind the deal came from the imminent changes that were about to be made to the rules governing players' contracts. At the time, players had absolutely no employment rights at all; we 'belonged' to the club that registered us and they could sell us to whoever they wanted. It was called a 'feudal' system but was actually more like slavery when you think about it.

Anyway, there were rumours that the rules would be changed and that players who moved after the rule-change would have more rights. Hence players moving before the new law came into force would be more likely to command a big transfer fee.

Hull knew that if they were to sell anyone to help them out of their financial predicament, it had to be soon. Given that I was one of only two star players left at the club, and that Garry Schofield had never publicly embarrassed the chairman, that man had to be me. If my head had been straight during the previous season, I would have probably seen it coming. There wouldn't have been much that I could have done about it, but it wouldn't have been such a shock.

2

There in
Black and White

On the field behind where we lived, me and my mates would play rugby for hours on end. We would play three-a-side, two-a-side and, when everyone else had gone in and it was dark, I'd carry on playing on my own. I was thirteen and the scenario in my head was nearly always the same; I would pretend I was playing for Hull FC in the Challenge Cup final. With the game hanging in the balance and just minutes to go, the ball would come to me. I would use my sidestep and pace to get away from the imaginary defenders and score a try underneath the posts to win the Cup for Hull FC. With no one watching and the shadows lengthening, I'd jump in the air to celebrate before eventually making my way home, having a bath, saying 'goodnight' to my mam and going to bed to dream about it all over again.

Five years later, on May 19th 1982, with three minutes to go in the Challenge Cup final replay, Hull FC held a narrow 13-9 lead over Widnes. With Hull on the attack, Charlie Stone drove the ball in and was tackled ten yards out in front of the posts while, behind those posts, over fifteen-thousand Hull FC fans were counting down the seconds to the final hooter.

As Charlie got back to his feet to play the ball, I found myself at acting-half. When I spotted a gap in the Widnes defensive line, I had to pinch myself that I wasn't dreaming and that this was for real. Charlie had spotted it as well and, being the seasoned old pro that he was, he hurried to play the ball, leaning gently into his marker as he did so, taking him to one side and away from the line that Charlie knew I would be taking. That marginal advantage was all I needed to make a dash from the acting-half position. With half-a-yard head start on the square marker, I had gone past him before he could do anything about it. Defenders came in from both sides but the line was already coming up fast and my momentum was strong. There were arms all over me but I stayed on my feet, shrugged them off as best I could and just kept going for that line. When I knew the line was close enough I threw myself forward with the ball in front of me.

It felt like a dream but this was really happening. It wasn't on a school playing field either; it was Leeds United's Elland Road in full view of over forty-thousand supporters. I managed somehow to stay on my feet as I scored and instinctively jumped in the air. I knew we would win now. Even Widnes couldn't score two tries in the time left. We had won the Cup and I had scored the winning try. It was unbelievable and everyone was going crazy. Clive Sullivan was first to reach me. He gave me a big hug as I stared into his big toothless grin. Everyone piled in after that; Craney, Toppo, Tony Dean. We had won the Cup!

It was well after last orders on that Wednesday night when we arrived at the Garden Gate pub in Hunslet to celebrate. There had been lots of beer and champagne in the winning dressing room and we had been in no hurry to leave the ground. The locals had all stayed behind and an army of our fans followed us down the road from Elland Road to join in the party.

I wish I could describe how it felt but it is very difficult to put into words. It was only just over two years since I had left school. I couldn't take it all in and it's only by looking back that I can begin to understand how I came to be in the Garden Gate that evening.

*****

I might never have picked up a rugby ball if my parents hadn't decided to move house. In 1971, my mam and dad, Bert and Joan, moved their two boys, myself and my younger brother, Richard, from Hull's Orchard Park Estate to the Willerby Road area of west Hull.

Two years later, aged ten, I left primary school and started at Ainthorpe Juniors where the PE teacher had the idea of starting a rugby league team. He held an assembly one day during which he asked whether any boys were interested in playing the game. I didn't know anything about rugby but I was quite keen to try something different so I put my hand up. The teacher picked out twenty boys and told them to come to a training session. I was the last to be picked but it was soon obvious that I had natural ability. I took to the game straight away and scored a try during the first training session. I wasn't the only one who found that they could play the game. The whole team clicked and that group of boys was to form the nucleus of the team I would play with for the next six years.

In my second year at junior school, I was chosen to play for the Hull schools under-11s. This was the first time I was selected for a representative side and how pleased I was that someone had watched me play and been impressed enough to select me for a higher level. I always got a buzz from recognition wherever and whenever it happened. The Hull schools team was a strong unit in 1975 and we made it to the Yorkshire Schools Cup final that year. Each year, the County Schools Cup final was played as a curtain-raiser to the Challenge Cup final. Unfortunately, it was the turn of the Lancashire schools in 1975 and we missed the chance of playing at Wembley.

At thirteen, I left Ainthorpe and moved up to Sydney Smith High School. Most of my rugby playing team-mates moved with me at the same time but, because the school only offered rugby union to its pupils, it looked like the team would be broken up and that I would stop playing the game. Fortunately, an ex-Hull FC player, Brian Hambling, had a son that had played for Ainthorpe and he decided to do something about it. At the time, BARLA was relatively new and was looking for teams to take part in its junior leagues. Brian decided to set up a youth club team based at Ainthorpe school. Most of the old school team signed up, along with one or two other lads from the area and the Ainthorpe Amateur Rugby League under-14 team was born. Since most of us were only thirteen, we took some real hammerings in our first season. When we scored our first try - sometime in mid-season - we celebrated like we had reached Wembley. Brian was a very good coach though. He kept us motivated and we all continued to play the game, learning all the time. The following season, we played against boys our own age and more than held our own.

At Sydney Smith, my PE teacher, Mr Hudson, was aware of my ability and asked me if I would play rugby union for the school. I agreed and ended up playing scrum-half! In that position, I was very rarely tackled and I was more than happy not to be playing in the pack. Rugby union scrums have always terrified me.

My experiment with rugby union only lasted a year and I was pleased to play league again for Hull schools under-16s the following year, a season when I was also selected for the Yorkshire and England schools teams even though I was a year younger than everyone else. In my last year at Sydney Smith, I was finally able to persuade Mr Hudson to form a rugby league team at the school. Most of the Ainthorpe ARL side went to Syd Smith anyway so it was more or less the same team. In our first and only season, we made it all the way to the final of the Yorkshire Schools Cup where we played Castleford High at the Boulevard. That was a real thrill; I was a passionate Hull fan by then. The Cas team hadn't been beaten for years but we turned them over that day. I even kicked a drop-goal. Colin Maskill played for Cas High that day and still reminds me of it, as does the future referee Russell Smith, who also played for Cas.

As a youngster, my life revolved around rugby league. I would play every Saturday and Sunday and, when I wasn't turning out for either of my teams, I was playing with my mates in a field somewhere. I learned the game instinctively, trying new things all the time, becoming aware of what it was all about, developing my strengths and honing my skills. I played against older lads as well and loved it. If I tried something a bit flash, I'd get a smack which would hurt but it never put me off; I just learned not to do it again or to be more subtle or crafty. I learned more about how to play the game in those fields, working it all out in my head, than I ever did from a coach. When I began to play rugby at school and at Ainthorpe youth club, I started to receive coaching in the basic skills of the game. That added some improvement but I already knew instinctively how to play. When I turned professional, people marvelled at the lines and angles I would run. They would wonder how I learned to do that. I couldn't tell them; I had just figured it out.

From Hull to Hell and Back

If we are ever to beat the Australians again on a regular basis, we have to give young players the freedom to learn the game instinctively in the way that I did. Youngsters need to have game time in which to practise their skills. It is all well and good coaching the technicalities but the lads then need time, without the pressure of results or the fear of failure, to put them into practice and gain confidence. Good amateur coaches will recognise that and build it into training schedules. In general, though, there isn't enough understanding of the importance of young players having appropriate game time.

*****

I remember Ainthorpe coming up against a team from Widnes in the under-16s Cup. It was clear as soon as we stepped on the pitch that our opponents had brought in some ringers. They were massive, most of them clearly over sixteen; half of them had beards! Most of my team-mates started moaning and telling Brian that he ought to complain but I didn't think there was any point. I just told the lads that we had to get on with it. I don't know why I saw it differently; perhaps I relished the challenge or maybe I honestly thought that our complaints wouldn't get us anywhere. Even then, I knew I was a bit different to my team-mates.

But, no matter how much I was developing as a player for Ainthorpe or for Syd Smith, I don't ever recall anyone suggesting that I was good enough to play professionally. Although I knew I was good at the game, I didn't think I was that good and so I just assumed that I was playing the sport for pleasure and nothing more than that.

Throughout my early interest in rugby league, my dad was always there to watch and support me. Dad was originally from London and didn't know anything about the game but that didn't stop him coming to watch wherever I played. Mum wasn't much bothered about what I was up to and never came to see me or asked how I had got on. As a consequence, neither of them talked to me about whether I might have a future in sport. As confident as I was in my own ability, I hadn't translated that confidence into any thoughts that I was good enough to emulate the blokes that I saw each week playing for Hull FC. They struck me as bigger and stronger. They looked like real men rather than the boys I was up against. Maybe it was just the way that rugby players looked in the late 1970s; heavy men with wild hair and even wilder sideburns and beards. If they didn't have big hair, they would usually be bald. And, bloody hell, they aged badly! Even though they were only in their early thirties, Vince Farrar, Keith Boxall and Alf Macklin looked like they were in their fifties. No wonder I felt professional rugby league was a world away from me.

Nevertheless, I was doing very well in the amateur game and, in the spring of 1980, was selected to captain the England Schools team on a tour of France.

No one in my family or close to me had ever played sport at international level so the whole scenario was completely new. Even so, playing for my country was just an extension of what I had been doing for the last couple of years. After representing Hull and then Yorkshire, playing for England was just the next step. Even now, when I look back, I don't recall any fuss being made of me or anyone else at that time. Sport had a much lower profile back then and, if anyone did achieve some success, so what? In Hull in the late 1970s, you learned not to be a big head or think about showing much in the way of ambition.

So, probably a bit underwhelmed, I joined the touring squad for France. I felt quite at home; not only were there lots of Hull lads in the team, I also knew most of the kids from Oldham, Castleford and Swinton as well. As soon as we left the M62 heading south, the squad started to divide into three cliques - the Yorkshire lads, the Lancashire lads, and those - like me - who had enough confidence to mingle with anybody. Although we were representing our country, it felt just like a school trip. We travelled everywhere by bus, stayed in dormitories, slept in bunk beds and got up to all of the usual pranks that teenage boys will do when they are not being supervised very much. Much of it was prompted by one group of lads daring another group to do something daft, such as shaving off someone's eyebrows and so on. The more bored we got, the more extreme the dares became. One lad would do just about anything for a dare and, I mean, anything. Someone challenged him to drink some sperm. He agreed and, after a couple of lads had done their business in a cup, he mixed it with something alcoholic and drank it. None of us could think of anything to top that and so we got a bit fed up of that particular way of passing the time.

Of course, most of the lads just wanted to get drunk and chase French girls but we were all confined to a hostel under curfew which meant we couldn't get up to too much mischief. I was quite strong-minded, though, and one night when I couldn't get to sleep, I decided to go out and have a look around the area. Having got myself out of the first floor window, I managed to shin down a drainpipe and earn my freedom. Once I'd got out, I didn't have much idea what to do, so I just went for a bit of a walk until I found a bar. I didn't know what to order but I saw a bottle of Pernod behind the bar which reminded me of someone back in Hull who drank it. It seemed quite exotic and appropriate to drink in France so I had a couple of glasses but I didn't like the taste of it all that much, soon got bored and decided to break back into the dormitory none the worse for wear. While I was never afraid of wandering off for an adventure, it was actually quite rare for me to do it alone. I usually liked to have someone with me to keep me company, carry me home or take some of the blame if I got into trouble.

On the pitch, it was a successful tour and we won all three games. It was a good one for me personally and I was chosen as joint-player of the tour despite getting injured in the final match. I needed to be stretchered off and I was mortified when the Yorkshire coach, Les Clarkson, brought his daughter, Julie, onto the pitch to help carry me off. Julie must have good strong genes, though. Her married name is Burgess and she has four big sons who nowadays play rugby league for Leeds, Bradford and South Sydney.

After the final match, there was a reception for the touring team at Lézignan Town Hall. It was quite a formal affair and we were seated around long dining tables with a French lad placed between each English boy. The hosts had put several bottles of wine on our table and we soon got into a drinking competition with the French, but while they were sipping their drinks, we knocked ours back with gusto. Even at sixteen, I already enjoyed the odd drink back home and so I didn't miss out on the opportunity to get tucked into the free wine on offer. Much to everyone's amusement, I got myself into a real state. But it wasn't much fun for me. I spent most of the three-hour bus journey back to our hotel being sick into a plastic bag.

*****

I didn't go back to school after I came home from France. If you were sixteen years old and weren't sitting any exams you were allowed to leave at Easter, so that's what I did. I guess it was a disappointing end to my time at school because I had actually shown quite a lot of potential when I started there. I had been in the top set for most subjects and would have been entered for 'O' Levels and possibly gone on to do 'A' Levels if I had stayed the course. I wasn't keen on some subjects, such as maths, economics or physics, but I enjoyed history, English and, of course, PE. I was quite a hard working lad who generally kept out of trouble and got on with playing my sport. By my last year, I was quite well known around the school because of my success at rugby. For that reason, it was generally assumed that I was the 'cock' of Syd Smith, a strange honour given to the best fighter at the school. In actual fact, I don't think I ever had to fight anyone to be granted that title, but it did lead to one or two challenges being laid down and I remember when one lad came forward to announce he wanted to take me on.

I didn't care whether or not I was the cock of the school and I had no reason to want to fight anybody. Nevertheless, peer pressure meant that I had to and so a scrap was arranged. I have no idea how those kind of school fights were organised but, by the end of the day, everyone in the school had been informed of what was going on and where the fight would take place. Except the teachers. It was incredible how it happened. Don King could have learned a lot from the fight promoters at Sydney Smith. Anyway I won, which kind of settled that particular issue.

In my final year, I was made a prefect. I was a popular lad and, in spite of my occasional prize-fighting, not a bad role model either. But, by the second half of the year I had lost interest in school completely. I suppose I just grew out of it. I was going out with Janet by then and spending most of my time with her family, who were all much older than me. School just became irrelevant. I couldn't even blame my lack of motivation for school on my obsession with rugby league. I just wasn't interested and left as soon as I could.

Not that I had any idea what to do next. Nobody had discussed my career options. There wasn't much use of the word 'career', to be honest. That would have suggested that there was a plan. Instead, kids like me would just aim to get a job and hope to hold onto it. If I had given any thought to my prospects I wouldn't have looked much further than picking up some work on Hull Docks. Or, given the state of the fishing industry in Hull at that time, I might have looked to follow my dad and get a job driving a lorry.

That said, just before leaving school I did have a career's interview with a woman who plainly didn't give a toss. When she asked what I wanted to do with my life, I told her, with a straight face, that I wanted to be a butcher. I said that I'd heard you didn't need qualifications to become a butcher and figured there would always be a demand for meat. In reality, I didn't know what I wanted. I applied for all sorts of jobs but nobody seemed keen to offer a job to a sixteen-year-old lad with no qualifications. They were lean times in Hull in 1980, even for people with more to offer than me, so I had few prospects of meaningful employment that summer. And then, out of the blue, came the telephone call that changed my life.

*****

It was a Tuesday, just after tea time. I was at Janet's house, watching TV. The phone rang and Janet's dad, Arthur, got up to answer it.

It was for me, which wasn't unusual as I spent so much time there. Arthur said the caller was Brian Holwell, coach of the Hull schools team. That wasn't unusual either, so I picked up the phone, wondering what he wanted. However the voice on the other end of the phone wasn't Brian's at all, although it was vaguely familiar.

'Hello, Lee, it's Arthur Bunting,' said the voice. I was stunned. Although my first thought was that someone was winding me up, the voice did sound like that of the Hull FC coach. I don't think I said a word, so Arthur carried on talking. 'I didn't want anyone to know it was me until I had chance to speak to you directly, Lee,' he said. 'I want to ask you to come down to the Boulevard tonight to speak to me and some of the directors.' There was a slight pause. 'We'd like to sign you.'

I have no idea what I said in reply. I was stunned and probably garbled some nonsense, but basically told Arthur that, of course, I would go.

The call had come completely without warning. I hadn't been for a trial at the club or anything like that. I had no idea they were even aware of me let alone that they had seen me play. Janet's dad suggested I ought to ring my Ainthorpe coach, Brian Hambling, and ask him to go down to the ground with me. They were all as shocked as me and, while we waited for Brian to arrive, I tried to calm myself down.

It took no more than ten minutes to get to the Boulevard and, before I knew it, I was in the boardroom. It was a very formal meeting, with the chairman, Charles Watson, at the head of the table, as I recall. Charles told me they had been keeping a very close eye on me (news to me), that they were well aware of how good I was and that they wanted my signature. He also said that they were going to offer me more than they had ever offered a sixteen-year-old player before. I thought I was dreaming. I couldn't believe what I was hearing. Less than an hour earlier, I had been sat in front of the telly and now I was in contract talks with the Challenge Cup finalists, Hull FC.

The deal they were offering was quite complicated. The amount of money I was to receive would be dependent on my playing a certain number of games for the club as well as earning international honours. I didn't take in the detail. I'm not even sure if I was listening properly. I was just trying to let the words sink in. I couldn't believe I was hearing the chairman of Hull FC saying: 'There will be another two thousand pounds if you play for Great Britain'. Play for Great Britain? I played for Ainthorpe! It was surreal. I left the talking to Brian, who actually told the chairman that he felt the club was trying to get me on the cheap. I would have signed for nothing so I was grateful to have Brian by my side; he managed to get me a bit more money.

Brian drove me back to Janet's house and I told her family everything. It was one of those 'winning the lottery' moments. I had been given unbelievably good news and we were all shocked and delighted but not really sure how to react or what to do next. I can't even remember whether I called my own parents to tell them.

Over the next few days, it began to sink in and, although I was obviously very excited, I had to remember that, although I had been offered a professional contract, it wasn't a proper job. Rugby league was a part-time sport and few people - if any - could make a full-time living from the game in the early 1980s. While I had been given a couple of thousand pounds up front, there was no guarantee that I would ever play for the club's first team and, if I didn't, I wouldn't get a penny more than that. As soon as the initial fuss died down, nothing changed. I went back to mucking around with my mates and hanging around with Janet. There wasn't any immediate impact; I wouldn't actually start training with Hull FC until the following season.

But then, just a few days after I had been to see the Hull board and still just a couple of weeks after I'd left school, Brian got a phone call from Roger Millward, the player-coach of Hull Kingston Rovers. Roger asked if I would meet him about possibly signing for Rovers. I had no interest at all in playing for Hull FC's bitter rivals but Brian suggested that we ought to at least go and see them and find out what they had to say. So we went down to Craven Park and met some of the Rovers directors, as well as Roger Millward.

'We know that Hull have spoken to you,' said Roger, 'and we know you're a big Hull FC supporter, but we want to sign you.' He then offered to double Hull's offer. I was gobsmacked. Brian checked that they were aware of just how big the Hull offer had already been. They said that they were and that they were still prepared to double it. Now it was Brian's turn to be gobsmacked.

I don't recall what was said at the time. I think we told Roger that we would go away and think about it, and then I went straight outside and burst into tears. 'I don't want to sign for these,' I told Brian. 'Hull FC want to sign me and I want to play for them.' It sounds romantic and naïve to suggest that the money didn't matter. To an extent, of course it mattered. But it didn't matter enough to persuade me to play for another club when I had the opportunity to play for the team I loved.

Over the past couple of years I'd become used to people telling me I was a good player. I was accustomed to winning man of the match awards most weeks and knew there weren't many players of my age as good as I was. But I certainly never thought that two of the biggest clubs in the game would get into a bidding war over me.

Having so much money on offer certainly didn't do me any harm and it probably gave me the confidence I needed once I began playing professionally, but I was still struggling to come to terms with the dilemma that the team I wanted to sign for had offered me half as much as the red and white bastards (as I would have referred to them at the time).

Brian told me not to worry about it. He knew that the deal I had agreed with Hull wasn't binding. Although I had agreed to its terms, I was still only sixteen and I couldn't officially sign professional terms with anyone until my seventeenth birthday, which was still five months away. So we went back to the Hull FC board and spoke to director, Mike Page. Mike said that he was aware of what Rovers had offered, but he reminded us that we had already agreed a deal with them. Mike, who is a good friend of mine now, was adamant that there would be no increase to their offer.

Of course, they were trying it on a bit but I didn't like all the hassle and just wanted to get a deal sorted out. I would never have signed for Rovers but I found the whole situation frustrating and kept wondering why Hull weren't prepared to pay me as much as Rovers. Throughout my career, I never really appreciated my own value and would often sell myself short in contract negotiations. Perhaps the seeds of self doubt were sown right at the very beginning when Hull FC hesitated to increase their offer to me?

Nothing was resolved at that meeting and we agreed to speak again later. Brian was convinced that Hull FC would eventually match Rovers' offer but I wasn't so sure and it still occupied most of my thoughts over the next few days. In truth, I didn't have much else to think about as my day to day life consisted of not very much since I wasn't exactly rushed off my feet with exam revision.

With my future still undecided, I went on holiday with Janet and her family to a caravan in Flamborough, on the North Yorkshire coast. The plan was to go for a week but I had to come back early for the Hull schools presentation evening on the Friday night. I was aware that someone from Hull FC had been trying to get hold of me while I was away and when I got back on Friday afternoon, I'd only been in the house a few minutes when there was a knock on the door. Somehow Arthur Bunting had found out I was home and he and Peter Darley, a Hull director, told me the board had reconsidered and were now prepared to match Rovers' offer. That was exactly what I wanted to hear. I had no hesitation in signing there and then. I had spent the week wondering what was going to happen and hoping that Hull would come up with a better offer. Brian had assured me that Hull would and, although I had some doubts, he had been right. My main emotion was relief that it had all been ironed out.

Although the deal was everything I wanted, it caused Brian Hambling and myself to fall out briefly. He had stayed busy while I was on holiday and spoke to Widnes, who were prepared to offer me even more money. Brian was keen to get the best deal, no matter where that might be. I wasn't interested in going anywhere else, though. 'I don't want to play for Widnes, Brian. I want to play for Hull,' I told him. 'They've offered me what Rovers have offered, I've signed and that's the end of it.'

With the deal sorted, I went to the presentation evening. Arthur and some directors came along as well and they used the event to announce my signing to the press. I signed what they called schoolboy terms, which meant I was pledged to them once I reached seventeen. I had my photograph taken with Arthur in a brand new grey Hull FC sweater. I couldn't have been more pleased and proud of myself.

But there was a flipside; the signing cost me my membership of St Andrews Social Club. I'd always looked older than my years and I'd managed to convince them that I was old enough to become a member. When the club steward read in the paper that I was only sixteen, he barred me. I wasn't allowed back for another couple of years.

*****

Not only did I sign for Hull FC that spring, I landed my first job. With unemployment rising fast, the directors wanted to make sure I had something to occupy myself with, so they got their heads together and agreed that I should work for

Arthur Bunting's painting and decorating business. I had no real ambition to become a decorator and suspect that Arthur had no real need for one either, but the club did a deal with him and probably paid most of my wages. The plan was that I would start an apprenticeship with Arthur that September and, until then, I was told to turn up for work at the Boulevard to spend some time on the groundstaff.

The speed of events was dizzying. I had only left school a few weeks earlier and here I was preparing to start work at the Boulevard, the place I spent my Sundays cheering on my heroes. And what a time to be there. Hull FC had just beaten Widnes in the semi-final of the Challenge Cup and, the week after I signed for the club, they were due to take on Hull KR in the first-ever all-Hull Cup final. You can imagine what the atmosphere was like.

Although I didn't see any of the players or have any involvement in the build-up to the game, I didn't miss out on the sense of occasion around the place. I remember being there when all the wives and girlfriends (nobody used the term WAGS at that time) arrived, ready to catch their own coach down to London for the weekend. It had been twenty years since the club last made it to Wembley so it was a very big deal.

Of course, I went to the game as well. I travelled down to London on the Saturday morning with Janet and her family. We went on a day trip; down and back in a single day. Like the many hundreds of other coach parties that travelled from Hull that day, ours was made up of a mixture of Hull FC and Hull KR fans, some of them from the same family. The rivalry was intense but the atmosphere was friendly. There was great banter and huge anticipation of the occasion and the game. Neither side had appeared in a Wembley Cup final since the 1960s so few of the fans had ever experienced anything like it. Apparently, Hull was a ghost town that day, particularly after 3pm when the game kicked off and everyone who wasn't in London was in front of a TV. I threw myself into it. I wore my full Hull FC kit and had my hair dyed black and white. Almost everyone else was wearing red and white or black and white plastic bowler hats that had been given away by one of the national newspapers. At every service station we called at, there were hundreds of supporters singing 'Old Faithful' or 'Red Red Robin'. I remember walking up Wembley Way and seeing it awash with red, black and white. I had never seen anything like it. As kick-off drew nearer, we took up our spots in the upper tier at the Hull end of the stadium. We were late getting in and could only find standing space right at the very top of the terrace. We were so high up that the far side of the pitch was obscured by the roof but we were swept away by the excitement and atmosphere of the occasion. In those days, you learned as much about how the game was going from the noise and sway of the crowd around you than you did from actually watching the action on the pitch.

In spite of the hype, the game didn't really live up to the occasion. Rovers scored a try in the first half and managed to stay in front throughout. We lost 10-5 and I was as gutted as anyone could be. The journey home was miserable, made worse by having to watch the celebrations of the Rovers fans on our bus. I didn't think it was possible to be so disappointed ever again.

So, even though I had already signed for Hull and had spent the previous week working at the Boulevard, I'd travelled to Wembley as just a normal supporter. In truth, I had signed to play for the Hull colts team, as the junior professional team was then known. The first team was a million miles away and for that reason, I still only felt the same connection to the club as I had all season.

After the Cup final, there was a gloomy atmosphere

around the Boulevard but the reserve team - the 'A' team - still had a couple of games left to play before the season ended. There was nothing much to play for but Arthur decided that it would be a good opportunity to give me my first run out in a black and white shirt. I was still only sixteen so I have no idea whether I was classed as a professional or not; nor can I remember whether I got paid. It wasn't important to me; I was just delighted to be getting a chance to show what I could do on a bigger stage. If you can say that about a reserve team fixture on a Tuesday night in Batley.

I didn't know anyone in the team very well so I sat on my own on the bus journey down the M62. Most of the other lads, I think, just assumed I was there for the ride and weren't expecting me to play, so they were quite surprised when they saw my name on the team sheet. I seem to recall that I took Carl Sanderson's place. Carl is a couple of years older than me and had been in the team for a year or so and he wasn't best pleased. Keith Hepworth was also at the club then and was a key figure in the 'A' Team. Heppy was in his late thirties at the time and had been playing long before I was born. He had played many times for Great Britain and was a real legend of the game.

When we arrived at Mount Pleasant, I couldn't take my eyes off Heppy. It only took him five minutes to get changed but then it took another half an hour to strap himself up. I couldn't believe someone could wear so much strapping. It looked as though, if he had taken it all off, he would have fallen to pieces. I had rushed through my own preparations and got myself changed and strapped up with more than an hour to kill before kick-off.

As we came out of the dressing room, Keith gave me the pre-match team talk that he'd probably given to a generation of cocky young forwards: 'Tackle anything that comes near you, son, and don't touch the fucking ball!'

From Hull to Hell and Back

Ten minutes into the game, someone passed me the ball and, ignoring Heppy completely, I made a line break down the left-hand side. I was half in the clear and, as someone tackled me from behind, I popped out a pass for our left-winger Steve Dennison. But Steve had decided not to back me up and was yards behind me, watching as the ball went to ground and dribbled into touch. I was quite pleased with the break I'd made and annoyed that Steve hadn't backed me up. Heppy, on the other hand, had only seen the ball roll into touch and had chased sixty yards down the pitch to bollock me. 'I told you not to touch the fucking ball,' he screamed.

My response surprised me. In spite of it being my first game in a Hull shirt and being faced down by a man of Heppy's stature, my first thought was: 'Silly old bastard. Who are you to tell me what to do?' I knew my strengths were all about what I could do with the ball. There was no way that I could ignore my instincts just to keep him happy.

Even at a young age, I felt that I knew how to play. The game changed a lot during the seventeen years that I played professionally but there wasn't much about my game that changed in that time. I had learned how to play by playing for hour after hour after hour. I learned instinctively that rugby is essentially a game in which the players strive to control the space around them. Whoever makes the best use of that space invariably has the best chance of winning. No-one taught me that; I developed my understanding through trial and error and by having the freedom to try things out and make mistakes. If I ran into a space that wasn't there, I would often end up on my arse and so learned not to do it again. If I dared to pop out an impossible pass and lost the ball, I would look like a prat but that didn't matter. I would just be a bit more careful next time. By the time I made my debut at Batley, I already had 75 per cent of the knowledge and skills I would ever have. That gave me the confidence to ignore Heppy and just play the game as naturally as I had for Ainthorpe or Sydney Smith.

Looking back, even playing hopscotch, which I loved as a kid, helped me. I enjoyed trying to maintain my balance over a short obstacle course and get to the end. When you think about it, hopscotch is quite similar to some of the drills that coaches put players through nowadays and, although I didn't know it at the time, I was developing some of the agility that helped me to become a professional player.

While I had confidence in my instincts once I stepped onto the pitch, I didn't have much of a clue about how to prepare for a game, so I was always very keen to learn about that aspect. I watched the senior players going through their routines in training and before a match. Much of what I saw became part of my own routine over the years.

All in all, I was a very willing learner and always keen to learn some of the technical aspects of my new job. I would spend hours, after training, with Hull's goal-kicker Sammy Lloyd, trying to learn how he got so much power behind the ball. I was never a natural goal-kicker and wasn't very good at all when I first started playing the game but, through practice and watching Sammy who was one of the finest kickers of his day, I ended up quite accomplished. I studied Sammy carefully and took some ideas on board while, ultimately, doing what was right for me. When I think back, it surprises me just how confident I was.

*****

The week after my debut in the 'A' team I was back at the Boulevard, where I spent the rest of the summer doing a bit of painting here and there, sweeping up and basically getting in everyone's way. The Hull Lada Vikings speedway team was based at the Boulevard at the time and they had some of the world's best riders racing for them. The day after race night, it would be our job to clean the mud and dirt off the terraces, while their team manager, Brian Larner rode around on a tractor-cum-roller repairing and flattening the track that ran around the pitch. One of my colts team-mates, Kenny Jackson, was also on the groundstaff and we would try to amuse ourselves by finding different ways to piss Brian off, such as racing the tractor around the track while Brian chased after us, calling us all the names under the sun. It was a great laugh and I didn't much care if we got into trouble; I knew I was only passing time until my apprenticeship started in September when I could do some real work.

The first team players returned for pre-season training in August and, for the first time I met the players I had idolised from the Threepenny Stand. I was a bit over-awed by being on the same training field as them, especially Knocker, who was my favourite. I was quite a shy kid and didn't say much to any of them at first. I just wanted to get on with training so I could show them what I could do.

Training was pretty advanced for its day. Arthur was always looking for ways to give his team an edge and had travelled to Australia and America several times to study different techniques. He brought lots of ideas to the game and we were one of the first teams in England to use weight training in a significant way. He was a great tactician who would spend hours studying our opponents and was very well connected in the amateur and professional games. More than anything, he was a supreme man manager and developed a great team spirit so that most of the players actually enjoyed training.

As soon as training was over, all the players went to the supporters' club bar just outside the Boulevard ground to have a drink together. It hadn't always been that way. When Arthur first arrived in 1978, he hadn't been impressed with the team spirit and told them he wanted them all to go for a drink after a game together, even if they didn't drink beer. It soon worked. Within a few weeks the players were mixing together away from games and training; even the wives started to socialise with one another. When Knocker joined the club later that year, Arthur found himself a willing ally. While Arthur was the brains of Hull FC, Knocker became its heart and soul. Between them they ensured that team spirit was very healthy by the time I joined.

I couldn't believe my luck in the bar after my first training session. All the players were there; I remember seeing Clive Pickerill, Charlie Stone, Vince Farrar and John Newlove arguing like hell over whose round it was - and they were only drinking orange juice. I decided I would drink whatever the other younger players were drinking, which was usually Coke or fruit juice.

Although the first team players were hugely respected by the younger lads, there was no sense of 'them and us'. Arthur and Knocker went out of their way to ensure that everyone was treated equally and that nobody acted in a way that was detrimental to our camaraderie. The only time that first team players pulled rank was when they decided at which point a new player could use the first team changing room to prepare for training. Everyone but the first team players would change for training in the away team's dressing room at the Boulevard. Even if you had made some first team appearances, that's where you changed until Arthur decided that you were ready to use the first team dressing room. It was a huge accolade and everyone took it very seriously. There were some real cocky characters in the Hull colts team but nobody dared to step into the first team dressing room until they had been invited. If we wanted to use the physio's room behind their dressing room, we had to walk all the way around the back of the stand and enter through a separate door. Small things make clubs great and, for me, once I was allowed into the first team dressing room, I thought of it as an almost sacred place. I was a member of the Hull FC first team and it was a huge honour.

At one of my earliest training sessions, Arthur asked Knocker to look after me and kind of take me under his wing. Given the way things were to turn out, some might think it was a mistake to ask him to keep tabs on someone as impressionable as I was but, in truth, Knocker only ever had a positive influence on me. He had a far greater effect on the fortunes of Hull FC than most people imagine.

I knew that Knocker was our team's best player, but soon realised he was also its undisputed leader on and off the field. Once I'd broken into the first team, I saw that it was Knocker who decided where and when the team would go for a beer after a game. Once we were there, everything revolved around him too. His was an infectious personality and I loved being around him. Knocker was also the hardest trainer at the club by some distance. Like most of the team, he liked a drink now and again but would always punish himself the next day. He would spend hours in his gym or run for miles in order to burn the alcohol out of his system. That kind of attitude is something I have seen repeatedly from the best rugby league players and it was an important lesson so early in my career.

I also got lessons in how players should treat each other, as well as club staff. Nobody was bigger than the team and no one got a big head. I fell short of those standards once or twice and was quite rightly chastised by my team-mates if I did. I once threw a cupful of powdered milk at our bus driver, Tony Sutton, who was pissing me off. Tony and all the other support staff were seen as equals by the players, so my misdemeanour smacked of arrogance for which I was given a major bollocking. I also overstepped the mark in ripping the piss out of Paul Rose when he joined the team from Hull KR. I kept calling him a red and white bastard which annoyed some of the other blokes and I got a dressing down for that as well.

*****

Even though I had begun to train alongside the first team, my first year at the club saw me playing mainly for the colts. We had an exceptional side for several years, barely losing a game in 1980-81 on our way to a League and Cup double. Our Cup final was played as the curtain-raiser to the Challenge Cup semi-final. The big occasions seemed to bring out the best in me and I won the Jim Challinor Trophy as man of the match in front of a big crowd of St Helens and Hull KR fans at Headingley.

Even though I was one of the youngest colts, my team-mates knew I was important to their success, so whenever I had something to say they tended to listen. The coaches, Dave Elliott and Nick Trotter, made me captain and I soon felt that I had become team leader on and off the field.

Like me, everyone was a diehard Hull FC fan long before they signed for the club, massively proud to be playing in the black and white hoops. Team spirit was great. After a game on a Saturday afternoon, all the players would go out for a drink. We'd start off in The Eagle, from where we'd head to The Bean and then, eventually, The Kingfisher. We had some terrific times in those pubs, all within shouting distance of the Boulevard. At the end of the night, the landlord of The Kingfisher would ring the bell and call 'last orders' but it would take him another hour or so to clear us. We'd usually end up standing on the tables singing 'Old Faithful' until he could finally throw us out. It was a black and white pub through and through. On the rare occasion that a Rovers fan wandered in, they tended to keep their mouths shut and hope nobody noticed. After a derby in the early 1980s, one Rovers fan came in and started taunting the Hull FC fans, ignoring everyone who told him to shut up. In the end, someone picked him up and threw him through the window, which I suppose was one way of shutting him up. Violence was very rare but there was more than a bit of other dodgy activity. You could buy pretty much anything you wanted in there. I once got my mam a microwave for Christmas.

*****

I took to colts rugby pretty well and was soon being selected to play for the 'A' team. It was quite a big step up and much more physical than the colts competition had been. Though it wasn't easy, I adjusted fairly well; I was already a reasonable size and I had developed an aggressive style of play which meant that I was able to look after myself, even in the first few games.

After just a few games in the 'A' team, I became aware that Arthur Bunting was already thinking of handing me my first team debut. I knew I had made a bit of an impression but I was still quite surprised when I overheard Arthur chatting in the supporters' club bar after training one night. He was discussing with Tim Wilby, a first-team player, how well I'd been playing. Arthur remarked that it wouldn't be long before I was ready. I heard Tim, who was never short of an opinion, pushing Arthur to pick me. Arthur evidently wasn't too sure and it wasn't until six weeks later, at the end of November, that I played my first game for Hull FC.

Hull FC had made an inconsistent start to the 1980-81 season and perhaps Arthur felt that his older players needed a break, or maybe he genuinely felt that I could do a better job than some of them. I don't know the reason but, as we began to pack up at the end of training one Thursday night, Arthur wandered over and told me he was going to give me a run out at home to Salford that Sunday. I tried not to show too much excitement but inside I was bursting. As a young player, it's never a complete shock when you are selected for your debut; you build up for it and hope it will happen one day. Nevertheless, I was thrilled and felt very, very proud of myself. The next three days were a total blur but, once it sunk in, I started to have the occasional panic at the prospect of playing in front of a crowd that would be well over ten thousand in an important First Division league game.

After training, I rushed around telling everyone. My parents and Janet's family, of course, were delighted and very proud that I'd made the first team at such a young age. At the time, I was the second youngest player to turn out for the club and there was an extra bit of media attention as a result. I remember turning up to meet my brother, Richard, as he left school that week. I was on my bike and, when I turned up at the school gate, there was a bit of excitement as a bunch of Richard's friends rushed over to see me give my brother a croggy home. I felt like a bit of a star, even if only to a group of thirteen-year-old boys.

I don't remember much about the day of the game itself, except not knowing what to do with myself as I kicked around the house for a couple of hours before setting off for the Boulevard. I remember the weird feeling as I arrived at the ground and entered through the 'Players and Officials' gate rather than the regular turnstile I usually paid to go through. I felt a bit self-conscious and wondered whether anyone would recognise me or ask who I was as I headed to the dressing room around the back of the terrace that they called the 'Best Stand' at the Boulevard.

I had never used the first team changing room before, not having yet been invited into the first team's inner sanctum.

I didn't have my own bench space and I remember that I didn't have a clue where to sit or what to do. It didn't take long to figure out that, on match days, everyone sat in order of their shirt numbers so I found myself sat between Charlie Stone and Sammy Lloyd, with Knocker just one space down to my left. Everyone arrived an hour before kick-off but there wasn't much to do. The space was small and there just seemed to be lots of blokes stamping around and doing their own thing. Most of them changed into their shorts first and waited to go through to the adjoining room to get strapped up. Paul Prendiville was arsing around making lots of noise but everyone seemed to be ignoring him so I did the same. The minutes seemed to pass too slowly and so I took my time and changed methodically, taking my cue from my older team-mates, and trying desperately to look composed.

I should have felt at ease. There was always a warm reception for a debutant from the first team players. They were an experienced group; the average age would have been around 28 or 29 and so they were all mature enough to know how important it was to help a younger player settle into their new environment. They had also seen enough of me in training to know how much it meant to me to be playing for my hometown club. I had quickly settled in at the club and, after just a few weeks of training with the first team, I had turned a few heads when I'd given Knocker a bollocking for not passing the ball to me when I wanted it. They were impressed and a little bit amused by me, I think, and I expect they were keen to see how I would react when one of the Salford forwards gave me a whack to welcome me to first team rugby.

Fifteen minutes or so before kick-off, Arthur took his place on the steps that led up to the shower area, from where he had an elevated view of the rest of the room. Arthur kept his pre-match pep-talks as brief as he could, but I have no idea what he said. I probably wasn't even listening to him at the time. I had my own thoughts to cope with and just wanted to get out there and get on with it.

Taking the field for the first time was an amazing experience. For most of the players and fans, it was just another game, but for me it was all very special and dramatic. I tried to shut out the noise and atmosphere that was a feature of any match at the Boulevard. I remember the pitch being very muddy. It was always that way and that suited our big pack, so Arthur would tell the groundsman: 'Keep watering it, keep watering it'.

The heavy pitch didn't really suit my own style of play but, nevertheless, I don't think I looked out of place. We won the game and, as we left the field to the cheers of the crowd, I was confident it wouldn't be the last time I played for the first team. I had never dreamed I might be good enough to play professional rugby league but, on that muddy pitch at the end of November, and just a few months after my seventeenth birthday, I began to realise that not only was I good enough to play for Hull FC, I was probably good enough to achieve just about anything I wanted.

*****

By November, I had begun working full-time for Arthur. I was enrolled as an apprentice painter and decorator and would spend a couple of days each month at Park Street College in Hull, learning the skills of the trade. I learned all sorts; spray painting, sign writing and so on, but, most of the time I would be at work, learning on the job. Arthur would send me out all over Hull and East Yorkshire with the rest of the blokes who worked for him.

After I'd broken into the Hull team, I still spent most of my time with Janet's family and so I rarely met anyone that

From Hull to Hell and Back

I didn't already know. Working for Arthur, however, put me into lots of situations where I would meet people that I didn't know, but who felt that they knew me. In most cases, I could sense people looking at me and telling their mates who I was. Often, they would say something. It was usually kind, but not always, especially if they were Rovers fans.

Not long after I made my debut for Hull, I was sent off to paint the inside of Rosen's shoe factory on Hessle Road. The place was full of over two hundred middle-aged women, many of whom knew who I was as soon as I walked in. After word circulated that a Hull player was in the building, they wound me up no end. For the whole time I was there, they ripped the piss out of me in the way that only middle-aged Hull women can.

I completed my apprenticeship and would have been able to earn a living as a painter and decorator but I never saw it as a job I wanted to do for life. It wasn't because I was determined to be a professional rugby player either because it was barely possible to make a living out of the game. If you were asked what you did for a living, you wouldn't say that you were a rugby league player, because that wasn't an occupation in 1980. You'd say you were a painter or a docker or a miner. The difference between the rest of the Hull team and me was that I didn't even bother to say I was a painter.

Nevertheless, I continued to work with Arthur, on and off, for several years, as did some of the other players at the club, such as Carl Sanderson, Trevor Penrose and Gary Peacham. We did lots of work for Rosen's, which was owned by one of Hull's directors. One day, we were painting their offices when Gary had an accident with a tin of paint, spilling it all over the floor. It made a right mess but I noticed that it had actually only damaged half-a-dozen carpet tiles.

We got our heads together and tried to figure out how we could replace the tiles. Someone noticed that there was a huge safe in the corner of the office, covering at least a dozen tiles. If we could shift the safe, we could probably slide out the tiles from underneath it and swap them with the tiles that were damaged. Gary was relieved and after throwing away the damaged tiles the four of us set about trying to move the safe. It took us over an hour to get it to budge only to find that it was sitting on bare floorboards - there were no tiles underneath it. We pissed ourselves and started to think about how we could explain where the floor tiles had gone and why the safe was laid on its side.

I never really took the job very seriously but the money wasn't bad. I think Arthur used to pay me about forty quid a week which, on top of the money I got from my original signing-on contract and appearance money for the colts, 'A' team or first team, meant that I was earning far more than most other seventeen-year-olds in Hull at that time. I felt quite well off and had no problem spending it either.

One day, when I was on my way home from work, a nice Yamaha 185cc trials bike caught my eye. It cost £750 and I wanted it. The next time I went by, I had the money with me and went in. The dealer asked if I'd ever ridden a motorbike before, so the big-time-Charlie in me said: 'Of course I have'. Actually, the biggest thing I'd ever been on was a little Honda-fifty and, when I got it outside, I couldn't even get it started. In the end I had to leave it outside the showroom while I rang Janet's brother-in-law to help me get it started.

*****

I only played five first team games during the 1980-81 season, so I was hardly a regular. Of course, I wanted to be in the first team every week but I was well aware that - at seventeen - time was on my side. In actual fact, my career was already way ahead of most others my age, but I was still thought of primarily as a colts player and that was proven when I was selected for the Great Britain Colts side in a two-match series against France. We drew the first game at Headingley in January and travelled to France the following month to play the second game in a place called Cavaillon.

At the time, I felt that we had a strong GB Colts team but we were beaten in France and so lost the series. It was my second trip to France after touring with the schoolboys team the year before and I loved it, particularly the freedom to do what we wanted while we were away. We got away with murder on some of those trips. I remember a group of us walking through the town square when someone decided that the square's fountain would look a whole lot better if we were in it. When Keith England ran out of team-mates to throw into the fountain, he stopped a passing car, pulled out the driver and threw him in. We thought it was hilarious. God knows how we got away with it.

I suppose that, looking back, the whole colts competition just wasn't professional enough and lacked intensity. Very few of that GB Colts team went on to play at the highest level and I suspect that was one reason why we fell so far behind the Australians; we just weren't producing enough good young players. At Hull FC, we totally dominated the league and won most of our games easily and yet very few of the Hull team made it either.

I loved those brief trips away from home and always came back to Hull with a smile on my face, ready to get stuck into the day-to-day routine of club rugby. By mid-March, the first team faced a fixture pile-up and Arthur let it be known that he would be calling on all of the players in his squad so that the first teamers could be rested for a couple of the games. That was good news and I played in quite a few games towards the end of the season, including the final league game at Bradford Northern when I was called up at the last minute after a senior player was dropped for breaking the curfew at the team hotel the night before.

Bradford needed to beat us for an outside chance of winning the league title providing that Warrington also lost. Deep into the second half, we were winning narrowly and we sensed that Bradford had just about given up on the title. Suddenly, the tannoy announcer told the crowd and players that Warrington were losing; the Bradford players were lifted and it was like playing a completely different team. They pushed on in the final twenty minutes and won both the game and the title.

Although we finished seventh, we managed to reach the final of the Premiership Trophy where we were set to play Hull KR again. In spite of a few first team appearances, I never made the first team and played in the curtain-raiser against Rovers colts in our own Premiership final. We won and I got the man of the match award. It was to be my final appearance for the colts team. I didn't know it at the time, but I was destined for greater things the following season.

Rovers won the senior final 11-7 and, although the scoreline looks close, that's only because we scored a late try to close the gap. In reality, Rovers dominated. Hull had matched them in the forwards, but Rovers blew us away with their pace in the backs, led by the likes of Roger Millward, Mike Smith and Steve Hartley. It highlighted a weakness in the Hull team which Arthur and the directors were desperate to get sorted and which would be to my advantage. The team would be rebuilt with greater skill, flair and pace; qualities that I hoped I had shown often enough to make a real impact.

And, while my career was moving on rapidly, I also decided to get married. Janet and I had become engaged a couple of years earlier and, with me earning some decent money, it just seemed the right thing to do. As you'd expect, it was a Hull FC wedding. The page boys were in black and white. Janet's brother, my colts team-mate Andrew, was best man. We held the reception in The Priory pub and it was a bloody good do, with lots of my Hull team-mates turning up as well. By then, we had also taken out a £7,000 mortgage (costing twenty-five quid a month) and bought a house on Perth Street West, less than a mile from the Boulevard.

Just over a year after leaving school, I was a professional rugby league player and married man with a mortgage. I wasn't even eighteen until the start of the following season. As that campaign got nearer, there was only one more thing I wanted; a regular first team place.

*****

The rebuilding of the first team began as soon as the season ended. During the summer of 1981, Kevin Harkin, David Topliss, Mick Crane and Trevor Skerrett all joined, while the legendary Clive Sullivan also returned from Hull KR. That wasn't the end of Arthur's recruiting.

At the start of the previous season, Hull had played the New Zealand touring team at Hull City's Boothferry Park in front of a large and noisy crowd. The game left such an impression on the touring players that, later in the tour, the Hull director Dick Gemmell, who was also part of the Great Britain management team, was able to sign Dane O'Hara and Gary Kemble. Gary asked if Hull might also be interested in signing his mate. When he found out who that was, Dick jumped at the chance: James Leuluai.

No coach can ever be certain that new players will settle or that lots of new signings will gel into a team. The players Arthur signed during that close-season were all very high quality but they were also very well chosen. They created a balance within the squad and gave Arthur what he had wanted since taking over as coach; competition for places.

There is nothing like competition. I learned the hard way during my own brief experience as a head coach that if you have a small squad, you have to do exceptionally well to get the best out of them on a regular basis. If you have a large squad, as we did in 1982, it creates a challenge within the team and, off the back of that, brings out the best in the players. The signings also showed Arthur's intention to play more expansive rugby. We'd relied too much on Knocker to make things happen. Now we would have several players who could create gaps and lots who could exploit them.

At the same time as Arthur was rebuilding his squad, the Boulevard itself was being prepared for a new era. For some years, Hull FC had shared the Boulevard with the Hull Lada Vikings. Having a speedway track around the ground meant that the pitch was quite narrow. However the Vikings now had notice that the track was going. During that summer, the pitch was duly widened, which allowed us to play a more open style of rugby. The pitch itself was also dug up and re-laid. For years, it had turned into a mudbath in mid-season, but after new drainage systems were in place it was ready for Hull's new stars to play on top of, rather than through.

The transfer activity created an air of optimism around the place, but some of the blokes who'd been there a while might have been apprehensive about what the future had in store. We had around thirty players at the club at the time and most of them would have had first team aspirations. Yet only fifteen could play every week. Nevertheless, Hull FC played forty-five games during that 1981-2 season and forty-six the following year, so every member of the squad had the chance to make a contribution and everyone who took the field, however briefly, knew that they had played some part in our success. Everyone shared in the success as well. We all celebrated together after every victory and the entire squad would travel to the many cup finals we appeared in.

From Hull to Hell and Back

I was only slightly worried. The only real danger to me was Mick Crane who, although he was a totally different type of player, would add competition for the back-row places. So I was very pleased to kick the season off in the starting line-up and even happier that we made a good start. After half a dozen games or so, we were top of the league as we prepared for one of our biggest games of the season; a home fixture with Castleford.

That week, Dane O'Hara and James Leuluai had arrived in Hull and had been taken on a tour of the Boulevard to get used to the place. The last time they had been in the city, they'd played in front of a packed house at Boothferry Park, just down the road. The atmosphere and noise had helped to clinch their signings but nobody had explained that wasn't where Hull normally played. When they stepped out at a deserted and unrecognised Boulevard on a Tuesday morning, Dane turned to James and said: "Shit, we've signed for the wrong team, mate!"

Come the weekend, packed with over sixteen-thousand fans, the ground looked totally different. It was a real carnival atmosphere as Dane and James, together with Gary Kemble, were introduced to the crowd. We won 42-24, easily our highest scoring game of the season. It whet everyone's appetite for the rest of the year and beyond.

Now that I was a first-team regular, I began to look forward to some of the bigger fixtures on the calendar, such as the New Year derby against Hull KR. Nobody needed to tell me how important that particular fixture was; I had been watching them as a fan for years and I knew how electric the atmosphere would be.

The winter of 1981-82 was shocking and we didn't play a single game for six weeks in the run up to the derby. My form had been good prior to the break and I just hoped Arthur would remember that when he came to pick the team to play Rovers. Fortunately he did and I was chosen to line up against our arch enemies at the Boulevard.

The game was even more highly charged as both sides had made it through to the John Player Trophy final which was due to be played three weeks later. Arthur Bunting had always prepared me for big games by telling me I should get stuck into my opponents before they could get stuck into me. I tended to focus my attention on whichever of my opponents had the reputation for being the toughest or hardest. I would then single them out to give them a smack. Old pros hated getting a cheap smack from a young kid and I knew that I could get under their skin. In this case, the opponent I ear-marked was Len Casey.

Casey had started playing in the sixties and was proud of his 'Iron Man' nickname. Some might have called him dirty, but he was also a very good player who had played plenty of times for Great Britain and would pose a big threat to us if we didn't get on top of him. My strategy was to force him to lose concentration by giving him a whack early on so that he would be more concerned with trying to take his revenge on me than following Roger Millward's game plan.

The tactic worked to perfection. I had an opportunity to smack Len early in the game, which I did, and he then spent the rest of it trying to take my head off. It was hilarious. My team-mates knew what was going on and they kept winding Len up, which made him even angrier. We won, too, which earned us the bragging rights for at least another three weeks. When the final hooter sounded and the players started to shake hands, I noticed Casey making a beeline for me. I wasn't afraid of a dust-up with Len, but I wasn't stupid either. I made sure I had a couple of big blokes in black and white jerseys stood near me as Len came over. I braced myself for what was to come and made sure that I never took my eye off him. As he got within range, he stuck out an arm, grabbed my hand, shook it hard and said: 'Well done son, you got one over on me there'. I was still only eighteen years old but every time I successfully faced down an opponent of Len's stature, I grew in confidence.

I found myself in a very similar situation the following year, this time with the notorious Australian hard man, Les Boyd. After the First Test at Boothferry Park, where I had made my Great Britain debut, there was a reception for both teams at a hotel on the outskirts of Hull. During the game, I'd landed more than a few shots on my opponents, particularly Boydy, and noticed how much it wound them up. As I nipped out of the reception to use the toilet I suddenly found myself face to face with Les, nobody else in sight. I froze and felt the hairs on the back of my neck stand up. I had no idea how he would react and, for a moment, really thought that he might give me a smack. Instead, he gave me a huge grin, shook my hand and told me what a great game I had played. As well as relief, I was impressed that he could so easily forget the cheap shots I had thrown at him on the pitch.

*****

After the derby, the weather affected our fixtures again. We only played one more game before the John Player final at Headingley. It was the club's fourth Cup final in just over two years and all of them had been against Rovers, but it was my first and I looked forward to it with massive expectation.

The club always made sure its players were properly prepared for big matches. Whenever we reached a semi-final or a final, or whenever there was a particularly important league game, the team was sent into camp at a hotel near the ground. We stayed in some very nice places and the fact that we were treated well probably had a big impact on our confidence and preparation. For the final of the John Player

Trophy, we checked into the Granby Hotel in Harrogate the day before. Everyone knew the drill; it rarely changed in Arthur's time as coach. We trained as soon as we arrived and then sat down for our evening meal, after which Arthur announced who would be playing. I was delighted to be told that I was in the team; my first cup final for Hull FC.

After the final team meeting of the night, Arthur would tell us all to go off and have a drink together. He felt that it was far more beneficial for us all to be together on that last night than to be tucked up in our rooms. It became common practice that we would go out and have a pint on the night before a big game. Nobody - as far as I can recall - ever abused that freedom and even those that didn't drink would come along to enjoy a few laughs and some camaraderie. It was a great way to prepare. I felt relaxed and confident as we headed back to our hotel.

We trained again in the morning and had some lunch before boarding the coach to the ground. Anyone who has ever been to a cup final as a supporter knows how exciting it is, especially as you approach the stadium. I can only say that, as a player, you can magnify that a hundred times and, for me, playing for the team I loved, I was completely beside myself. Once the team bus approached the ground, we could see the thousands of supporters heading to the stadium and milling around outside the pubs and takeaways. If they noticed the bus, they would wave their flags and cheer us on. I loved it but I was also very nervous and apprehensive; partly because the occasion was so big, but there was also a bit of fear that I might do something stupid to lose us the game and let down all of those supporters. In 1980, Sammy Lloyd had missed some goal-kicks at Wembley and nobody ever forgot it. This time, I would be on goal-kicking duty and fear was never far away from my thoughts.

There was a record crowd of over twenty-five-thousand

squeezed into Headingley; the atmosphere was incredible. As we kicked off, the noise was deafening from all sides of the ground. I had an early chance to put us ahead when we were given a penalty. As I lined up the kick, the Hull fans went silent but the Rovers fans tried to put me off by making as much of a racket as they could. I tried to shut it all out and was relieved to see the kick sail between the posts to give us a 2-0 lead. There wasn't much in the game until the half hour when Ronnie Wileman scored a try that will go down in Hull FC history.

After Mick Crane was tackled on the halfway line, Ronnie went in at acting-half and spotted that the Rovers' defence wasn't in position. He urged Mick to play the ball as quickly as possible and, as soon as he had the ball in his hands, he dummied to his left and shot into a gap down the touchline. Ronnie was in the clear and managed to outpace Rovers fullback, George Fairbairn, and go fifty yards before scoring in the corner. It was a stunning try and none of us could believe what he had done. Arthur had brought players from all over the world to score length-of-the-field tries and here was our hooker going in from the halfway line.

Knocking over the conversion gave us the momentum we needed to go on and win. There were no other tries in the game and my goal-kicking was instrumental in keeping us in front. When the hooter sounded for full-time the Hull fans in the stadium went crazy, myself included. Hundreds of our supporters poured onto the pitch to celebrate with us. After collecting the trophy, we attempted a lap of honour before heading to the sanctuary of our dressing room. We never bothered with anything like stretching down in those days, we tucked straight into the beers until we were changed and could go up to join our families in the bar.

It was always quite difficult to get friends and family into any kind of bar after a cup final, and it became a game of cat and mouse between the players and the venue's staff. They wanted to keep the numbers limited to sponsors, directors and so on, while we wanted to get as many mates and members of our families in as possible. We usually won. There were always ways to get people in and I remember that Janet was there in the Headingley bar with most of her family. After we left the ground we stopped off for a few drinks on the way home before the team bus took us back to Hull. The city centre has always been a lively place on a Saturday night. With thousands of returning FC fans still celebrating it was buzzing when the team bus pulled into town. Ronnie Wileman was already well lubricated and no one was able to get the trophy out of his hands, even when he started to wave it out of the window at all the Hull fans. I don't know where we ended the night, although I'm sure somewhere would have given us a lock-in.

On the Monday, the first-team squad and officials flew off to Spain for a mid-season break, warm-weather training and, to be honest, a bit of a piss-up to celebrate. Arthur was very keen on these short breaks and had convinced the club directors to stump up for them. The timing wasn't good for me though. Janet was pregnant, so it wasn't appropriate for me to be jetting off to Spain with the lads. While my team-mates enjoyed themselves in the sun, I trained with the 'A' team in the January gloom.

*****

The bad winter meant that a fixture backlog was inevitable but it didn't seem to matter at first as we kept on winning. We lost only one game throughout February and March and made it through to the Challenge Cup semi-finals. For the second time in a couple of months, thousands of Hull fans poured into Headingley, this time to see us take on

Castleford for the right to meet Widnes at Wembley. We went in as overwhelming favourites, but we always seemed to have tight games against Cas and only just managed to scrape through, 15-11.

With a cup final on the horizon, the biggest challenge was to maintain our focus on our challenge for the league title. With less than four weeks left of the season, we still had to play eight league games. Amazingly, seven were away from home. We clocked up hundreds of miles going back and forth over the M62 two or three times a week. Despite the fixture backlog, we kept on winning to put pressure on the league leaders, Leigh. As the final week approached, the title was in our own hands. We had a tough but winnable game at Fulham, followed by games against St Helens and Widnes. If we won all three, we would be the champions.

The Fulham team were a wily bunch of old pros, most of them northerners who'd been tempted down to London out of curiosity. But they knew the game inside out and were well aware that we probably had half an eye on Wembley. They were determined to leave their mark on us, one way or another. Early in the game, Harry Beverley kicked Trevor Skerrett in the head at a scrum and we all thought: 'Oh, fucking hell, here we go'. It was a scrappy, bad-tempered match which we ended up losing. We never got into our stride and the defeat meant the title was no longer in our own hands.

However we did beat St Helens a few days later, so the title was still in the balance as we approached the final weekend of the season. We were level on points with Leigh but they had a game in hand. We had to play Widnes while Leigh faced Hull KR and the bottom club, Whitehaven. We had to play Widnes while Leigh faced Hull KR and the bottom club, Whitehaven.

There were over eighteen-thousand fans at the Boulevard for our game with Widnes, but most of them were paying at least as much attention to the game at Hilton Park, hoping that Rovers could beat Leigh and help us win the title. Although Widnes were out of the running for the title, they were determined not to give us a psychological edge a week before we met them again at Wembley. It was close for a while but, eventually, we won comfortably which meant the focus shifted to what was going on at Leigh. Their game had kicked off a little later than ours so we were able to follow the last quarter on a radio in the dressing room. Leigh were winning but not by many and the atmosphere was tense. A Rovers comeback would more or less win us the league title and we could go back out onto the pitch to celebrate. Meanwhile, most of the fans had also stayed in the ground to listen to the same commentary through the PA system. What a very peculiar end to the league season - Hull FC players and fans all cheering for a Hull KR victory!

Sadly, though, it wasn't to be. Rovers lost and, three days later, Leigh beat Whitehaven to win the title.

I was very disappointed not to win the league in 1982 because I really believed that we were the best team in the competition. It was the sheer number of games that we had to play towards the end of the season which caused us to slip up in the run-in. Forty-five games were played that season but, because of the bad weather in December, twenty-nine of those were played after Christmas and fourteen of them during March and April. In many ways, we were victims of our own success having reached two major cup finals. It was simply too many games even for a squad of our quality and size.

We didn't dwell on the disappointment for long, mind you. Just six days after realising that our victory over Widnes was in vain, we faced them again - in the 1982 Challenge Cup final. Our season was far from over and, for me, the next few weeks would catapult me to the top of rugby league.

From Hull to Hell and Back

*****

I absolutely loved the build up to big games and I still do. In 1982, the routines were all new to me and I was swept away with the excitement of it all. We met up at the Boulevard on the Wednesday beforehand to travel down to London. This was also the day when we collected our cup final suits. I could never believe how much gear we were given each time we went to Wembley.

In 1982, our official outfit consisted of grey trousers and a blue blazer, but we were given loads of other things to wear as well, most of it burgundy; burgundy trainers, burgundy corduroy pants, sweater and polo shirts. Arthur would choose the outfits and we were quite happy to wear what we were given as it was usually decent quality stuff. But it was difficult to remember when we were expected to wear each outfit. Arthur would tell us we should wear the slacks and pullover to travel down in, then change to the burgundy for our pre-match tour of the stadium and then wear our suits on the day of the game. It was a minefield but between us we managed to figure it out and usually ended up wearing more or less the right clothes.

Hundreds of fans came down to the Boulevard to see us off that Wednesday, which put us in great spirits for the journey to London. We stayed at the Runnymede Hotel in Windsor as I recall. The club took these preparations very seriously and Arthur and some of the directors had been down to stay at the hotel beforehand to check that it had everything we needed. By Friday, the first team party had been joined by the directors, the rest of the squad and the players' wives and girlfriends, who stayed in their own hotel prior to the game. The colts players came down on the Saturday morning; we left no-one behind.

The day before the game, we went to the stadium for our walkabout. Some of the team had been before but for many, like me, it was our first visit. As pleased as I was to be able to walk around the place, I have to admit to being a bit disappointed. When it was empty, the place just looked run-down and it seemed smaller than I had expected it to be. The dressing rooms were massive, though, with a couple of large baths in each and lots of room to get ready for the game but, again, everything looked old and scruffy.

Despite having played in almost every game that season, my place in the cup final wasn't guaranteed. Hull had plenty of back-row forwards and, in the weeks building up, I was convinced that Arthur would pick Sammy Lloyd ahead of me and that I would be on the bench. I prepared myself for that outcome but, when Arthur read out the team and I heard Sammy's name instead of my own, I was still gutted. I had started the majority of the games that season so, of course, I wasn't happy but I dealt with it. Before I joined Hull, I had never experienced being dropped. I was usually the first player on the team sheet for any side, whether at Ainthorpe, Hull Boys or England Boys. Not being picked was a thing I had to get used to once I turned professional but it wasn't easy and, at first, I would find myself hoping that the player chosen in my place might pick up an injury or that the coach might change his mind. I suppose I always felt a little bit insecure. The following season, Arthur signed a new second-row forward called Dave Busfield and I remember going to Arthur and asking him what I had done wrong that meant he felt the need to sign someone else. Arthur just laughed. He said it was all about strength in depth and that I hadn't done anything wrong.

*****

From Hull to Hell and Back

After the team meeting on Friday night, we went off for a beer to settle our nerves. We had a couple of pints before heading back to our rooms to try to get a good night's sleep. Arthur would choose who everyone shared rooms with and he liked to mix things up. He was very keen that everyone got along with one another and he would try to put a younger player with an older player; or a quiet bloke with a more extrovert character. In those early days, I occasionally roomed with Dave Topliss because we were both quite different and also because I could learn a lot from his experience of preparing for big games.

We trained in the morning and then prepared to head to Wembley. I will never forget the sight of Wembley Way as we passed the thousands of Hull fans making their way to the ground. We were just like them; fans going to a cup final, full of expectation and a bit of trepidation. Until suddenly we weren't fans any longer and we pulled away from them, headed under the stands and parked up in the space allocated for the team coaches. The Wembley tunnel was exactly that; a tunnel that ran from the back of the stadium straight under the stand and onto the track surrounding the pitch. As our bus pulled up it, we could see out into the bowl of the stadium, the sunlight on the pitch and the terracing at the opposite end. There were still two hours until kick-off, so there would have been few fans in the ground, but we could see enough to get us just that little bit more excited about what was to come.

With more time to prepare than normal, I had time to take another look around and get used to the place. I went for another walk on the pitch and watched the fans start to come into the ground. I read some of the banners and tried to spot some familiar faces. I think I might have watched a part of the schoolboys' game too, before heading back inside to get changed for what was going to be the biggest game of my life.

Sitting on the bench during that match was the most nerve-jangling time of my career. To keep us loose, Arthur would tell the substitutes to get up and run along the line, sit down, get up again, go for another run. It was murder. When I finally got on the field there were only about twenty minutes left and I felt way off the pace. The pitch was much spongier than I expected it to be. We had never been given the opportunity to train or even walk on it in studded boots, so it came as quite a shock to find myself running around on what felt like a deep shag pile carpet. Consequently, my legs felt like jelly and I seemed to take ages to find the rhythm. We were 14-6 down when I got on and the game looked beyond us. Widnes probably felt they had it won as well; we had tried everything and hadn't been able to break through. Then, suddenly, Knocker made half a gap and crashed over for a try. Sammy converted and we were right back in it at 14-11. The try gave us a huge lift and it helped to settle me down as well.

I immediately felt more comfortable and was able to take the ball up more confidently along with making an impact in defence. But we were still behind going into the last five minutes. Eventually, though, we found ourselves in good position, camped on their line, and when the ball came to me I spotted a chance to get a step on one of their defenders. As I stepped to the left, the Widnes centre Keiron O'Loughlin missed me completely and I was in the clear. Instinctively, I headed to my right taking me away from the defence that was clustered under the posts. Dane O'Hara had drifted in off his wing looking for the ball and, as three cover defenders closed in on me, I just managed to pop the ball out in time for him to plunge for the line. He managed to touch the ball down just as the winger came in to tackle him. It was a try. I had managed to stay on my feet and stumbled over the line myself. My instinct, for some reason, was to pick Dane up off the ground while our team-mates went mental around us. I was still clinging onto Dane as everyone caught up with us; Kemble, Wileman, Stone, Topliss, so I received the congratulations just as much as Dane did, which was fantastic. As a substitute you just hope that you can make an impact when you get your chance and I had certainly done that.

The try was scored midway between the posts and the touchline. The score was 14-14 with just a couple of minutes left. It was a kickable conversion for someone of Sammy's ability, but the touch judges pointed their flags downwards and waved it away. To this day, Sammy still insists that his conversion went between the posts, but he kicked it so high that the touch judges couldn't be sure and they decided it hadn't gone through. And so the game ended in the first draw in a Challenge Cup final for nearly thirty years.

Because we had come from behind, we were more pleased with the result than Widnes but there was still a feeling of anti-climax and none of the players knew what to do. We all stood around on the pitch looking at each other. We knew that the winning team would be expected to go up to the Royal Box to receive the Cup, and they would be followed by the losers. But what if the game was drawn? We had no idea what to do. An official ushered both teams toward the steps and we all went up to shake hands with whoever happened to be the guest that year. Everyone walked past the Cup without touching it. It wasn't until we got back into the dressing room that people started telling us that there was going to be a replay a couple of weeks later.

After the game, we went up to the long bar between the twin towers where the players would normally go for some food and a couple of beers. We left the ground an hour or so later and went to a party at our hotel. All the players had got together to buy Arthur a huge cigar, intended to celebrate what we hoped would be our victory. We decided to present it to him anyway and he said he would save it and smoke it after we won the replay. It was the strangest atmosphere; a bit deflating since you hype yourself up to win and probably prepare yourself for how you'll feel if you lose, but no-one really contemplates a draw in a rugby league cup final.

Hull city council had also laid on a civic reception for when we came back on the Sunday afternoon. It was going to happen regardless of whether we won, lost or - as it turns out - drew. We had time to stop off in Northampton for food and a few beers which inevitably turned into a bit of a session. It was a long way back from Northampton so we got some bottles to take back on the bus. Sammy Lloyd and Ronnie Wileman bought themselves a bottle of vodka and supped the lot by the time we got back to Hull. Ronnie was absolutely steaming drunk as we got off the bus, so much so that he was incapable of walking to the edge of the balcony to wave to the fans. Someone had to hold him up and lift his arm for him.

We were all physically and mentally exhausted by the end of the weekend, yet we still had to pick ourselves up for a Premiership play-off against St Helens the next Wednesday. It's incredible that - in the week after the drama at Wembley - we won the game quite easily and then beat Warrington the following Sunday to set up yet another game against Widnes in the Premiership Trophy final, just four days before the Cup final replay.

Although Widnes beat us at Headingley, I played well again, scored our try and kicked two goals. It was a strange game for me. Although it was a cup final in its own right, it felt more like a trial game since I knew that I was probably playing for a place in the team for the replay. After missing out at Wembley, I was determined to make sure that I was in the starting thirteen. I had played out of my skin in all three Premiership games and was hopeful that my form would make it very difficult for Arthur not to pick me ahead of Sammy Lloyd.

We went into camp in Harrogate on the Monday after the game and I was itching to find out if I would be in the team. Arthur named his side the following day and, as he read through the names, I was desperate to hear mine. There were quite a few changes to the team that had played at Wembley and it took ages for Arthur to get through the team sheet. Dane O'Hara was dropped for disciplinary reasons and Arthur brought in 38-year-old Clive Sullivan on the wing. Arthur also decided to be more adventurous and decided to leave out the defensively-sound Kevin Harkin and bring in the more creative Tony Dean at scrum-half. Ronnie Wileman had picked up an injury and so 37-year-old Tony Duke came in at hooker. Finally, he got to the back-row forwards and I heard my name. I was in the thirteen. The rest was a blur. I wasn't listening. I was just overwhelmed at the thought that I was going to be starting such a big game.

I was obviously very pleased and proud that I'd forced my way into the team for the replay and was probably a bit over-excited and enthusiastic the night before the game. After our usual eve-of-game meeting had finished around nine o'clock, Arthur told us all to go off and have a couple of beers. As ever, I was quite happy to go along with whatever everybody else chose to do, so we all headed off to the pub just around the corner from our Harrogate hotel. We got the beers in and started to enjoy ourselves. Someone suggested we have another drink. And then another. Some of the lads opted in, some didn't. I did and before I knew it had probably sunk four pints. I wasn't pissed but I knew that I'd had a drink and, when I woke up the next morning, I didn't feel quite right. I remember getting out of bed and thinking to myself: 'fucking hell, what have I done?' On the biggest day of my career, I'd woken up with a hangover! It wasn't a huge hangover, but I had woken up feeling crap and it made me even more nervous about the game ahead.

The way it turned out, I needn't have worried. Once I'd got some food inside me and drank plenty of water, I felt fine. Besides, once the adrenalin kicked in, I don't think anything would have distracted me from the game.

Evening games are usually the worst ones to prepare for since there is so much time to occupy before kick-off. In this instance, I was pleased to have more time. We trained in the morning and tried to relax in the afternoon. By the time we reached Elland Road in Leeds, the venue for the replay, we were uncharacteristically tense. There always used to be a bottle of sherry that the players could swig on to give themselves a kick and help to settle the butterflies. Nobody ever really used to drink from it until that night, when we couldn't get it out of the hands of Mick Crane. Craney had worked himself up into such a nervous state that he kept swigging on it. If nothing else, watching Craney bouncing around the dressing room, face flushed with sherry, telling everyone else to calm down, at least distracted us from our own nerves.

The nerves can't have been a bad thing as we took the game to Widnes straight from the start. With Deany at scrum-half, we played a different game from the one we'd played at Wembley. Dave Topliss led from the front and had a stunning game that night scoring two tries and picking up the man of the match award. His second try was an audacious run-around move that he and Gary Kemble had practised for ages in training. It was copied by every team in the league the following year, but it never captured the element of surprise that it did in that replay and was never as effective again.

Widnes were a team full of champions, though, and they kept coming back at us. Even though we looked the most likely winners, it was still only thirteen points to nine, with about five minutes to go, when the chance fell to me to win the game.

When I look back at that unbelievable night, it amazes me how easily everything seemed to come my way. Whenever you set out on a career in professional sport, you know that there will be bad times as well as good but, in my first two years, there weren't any bad times at all. Unlike most young players, I never really had to learn how to deal with disappointment. Each month seemed to bring about another amazing high. Yet there was much, much more still to come.

3

Testing Times

The best team performance I was ever a part of came at Castleford, relatively late in my career. I will tell you about that in due course, but my best individual performance came just months after helping Hull to win the Challenge Cup and led to my promotion to the Great Britain Test team, earlier than I could ever have dreamed of. And once I became a part of the international team, I was something of a fixture for the next three years.

Leeds came to the Boulevard in October 1982, unbeaten and top of the table. We weren't far behind them but they were definitely favourites when we faced each other in a midweek league game. Evening fixtures at the Boulevard were always a bit special. Under floodlights, the atmosphere from the terraces just seemed that bit more intense and intimidating to the opposition. I liked playing at night and I felt in great form going into the game. But I had no idea just how good I would feel once the game kicked off.

It was one of those nights when everything I did came off

and I knew that nobody could do anything to stop me. The whole team played well, to be fair, but I was more than happy with my own performance, to say the least. We won easily, 35-5, and I had a hand in most of the tries. I scored three myself and kicked all seven conversions. It was one of those performances that come along only once or twice in an entire career. I was so confident in myself towards the end of the game that I completed my hat-trick by chipping the ball over the defence from halfway and beating the full-back for pace before regathering and scoring under the posts. Steve Evans thought that the kick-through was intended for him and was a bit shocked when I outpaced and almost pushed him out of the way to get my hands on the ball.

Leeds scored their only try in the last few minutes. They hadn't played badly. We were awesome.

My signing-on fee at Hull included a bonus if I played for Great Britain. I never gave it much thought at the time; I couldn't imagine it would happen. It was a dream to play for Hull and I looked no further than that, but the speed of my achievements meant that - by 1982 - almost anything seemed possible. Even so, nobody was prepared for what was about to happen to international rugby league and I had no idea that I would play a prominent role in one of the most significant Australian tours ever.

*****

With the Australians already in the country, there was lots of talk about who would be selected to face them. I hadn't been chosen in the forty-man training squad named at the start of the season and, although that didn't surprise me, it gave me a bit of extra determination to play myself into the frame. After the Leeds game I knew that there was no more I could have done to force my way into the squad, particularly since the GB coach at the time was the ex-Hull FC player, Johnny Whiteley, who had seen the match in question.

On the day of the team announcement, I was painting the offices of Glenrose Fish Merchants on Hull Docks. When I saw Arthur's car pull up outside, I assumed he was coming to check up on me. I did not expect him to come in and say that I had been selected to play for my country. Arthur took me to a workers' café around the corner to get me a cup of coffee and I used the phone there to ring Janet and my mam and dad. It was all a bit weird. Everyone was congratulating me but the enormity of my achievement hadn't yet sunk in. I can't remember whether Arthur made me go back to work or not but, by the time I got home, the phone was ringing off the hook with enquiries from the media.

For the next few days, I didn't do much beside talk to the press. At just turned nineteen, I was one of the youngest players to be selected for GB for years and they all wanted to know how I felt about it. It was the first time I had found myself in the spotlight in that way. I didn't particularly mind but found it difficult to say anything interesting. I just went with the flow. Quite soon, I began to take great satisfaction and pride in what I'd achieved, especially as I hadn't been in the original forty-man squad. I felt like I had earned the right to be there even more than if I had been in it from the outset. It became a common experience. I never felt like I was guaranteed a place in the British team and always had to work hard to earn and justify my place.

The bottom line for the First Test was that I had just over a fortnight to prepare for my full international debut which, to make the occasion even sweeter, would be played in front of my own fans at Boothferry Park in Hull. By the time I was selected, however, it was already becoming obvious that we were in for one hell of a game.

Previous Test series had been fairly close and, although

From Hull to Hell and Back

Australia had won four on the bounce, they had all finished 2-1, so nobody expected the 1982 visit to be any different. Prior to the tour, I knew very little about the Australian game. There was no Sky TV in those days and there weren't many opportunities to watch games from Australia. Reports and coverage were available in some of the rugby league newspapers and magazines, but I had been more concerned with my own career at Hull to take any notice of what was going on at the other side of the world.

Nevertheless, the early tour games were given some TV coverage and so, by the time I joined up with the rest of the squad, I was expecting to find that we would be doing lots of analysis of our opponents. It was wishful thinking. The management wasn't much better informed than I was and there didn't seem to have been much homework done on our opponents at all. Other than the first game, which I went to watch myself at Hull KR, I didn't see any tour games - live or on video - prior to the First Test.

I later heard that some of the coaching staff who watched the Aussies play that first game at Craven Park (which the tourists won easily) had then bragged that we would beat them comfortably. I was new to the squad and didn't know whether this kind of confidence was normal, although I did have a suspicion that it wouldn't be as easy as they thought.

The GB squad met up on the Wednesday prior to the Test and went into camp in Cleethorpes. I was the youngest by a long way. Because I was also making my debut in Hull, I was in great demand from the press, which at least stopped me thinking too much about the size of the occasion. There's a photograph somewhere of Steve Nash spooning trifle into my mouth as if feeding an infant, illustrating the point that I was the 'baby' of the team. While Australia had backed the youngsters in their squad and gave debuts to Wayne Pearce, Peter Sterling and Mal Meninga, the British selectors had played it safe, sticking with players of experience. Five of the blokes selected were over the age of thirty, including guys like Les Dyl, Jeff Grayshon and Nash.

I roomed with Knocker, who'd played for Britain several times before. He was very relaxed and confident, and this calmness helped me to relax and settle into things. Once we had checked into the hotel, we met up in the bar where Johnny Whiteley bought us all a drink before we sat down for our meal. Even though I'd played against them for Hull, I was still in awe of my new team-mates and probably a bit quieter than normal. I didn't really know what to expect of them but I soon realised that they were all up for a good time. While we were having our first meal together, Les Dyl started a food fight and then we all ended up getting drunk in the Winter Gardens nightclub in Cleethorpes.

I already had some experience of what it was like to be in an international camp after touring Papua New Guinea and Australia with Great Britain Colts the summer before. But the sense of occasion now was greater than anything I'd ever known. Media interest was intense. It seemed like everyone I met was totally obsessed with the game.

Unless you have personally experienced it, it is difficult to explain how it feels for a player on the morning of a big game. From the moment you get out of bed, the excitement and tension begins to build. The drill, though, was mostly the same. We'd meet over breakfast, attend a team meeting at which the coaches ran through the game plan one more time, board the coach and then head for the ground.

As our bus travelled over the Humber Bridge, I could already see the floodlights of Boothferry Park and had a good idea of what would be going on around the stadium. As we got closer, the streets were packed with supporters wearing shirts of every colour, including quite a few fans in the green and gold of Australia. As the fans recognised our team bus, they began to wave and cheer us on. The atmosphere was electric and the tension on the bus went up a notch or two.

Even though the Aussies had won their first six tour games easily, we had no idea that they would be such tough opponents in the First Test. I didn't feel particularly nervous; I soon felt comfortable in the environment and loved every minute. Arthur Bunting had given me one piece of advice before I went into the GB camp: 'Hit them before they hit you, son'. It was good advice and I remembered it once I got on the field. I already had a bit of a reputation as someone who would try to rough up and irritate the opposition to put them off their game. I admit that I threw some cheap shots now and again. But my opponents could always be certain that if I smacked them, I wouldn't complain if they hit me back; I would just smack them again. It meant that I had a pretty poor disciplinary record, particularly in my first few years, and I also hold the unenviable record of being the first Hull player ever to be sent to the sin-bin. Nevertheless, the reputation meant that nobody ever took a liberty with me and none of my team-mates or coaches ever complained at my style, so it must have had some benefit to the teams I played for. I doubt the Aussies knew much about me before the First Test, but they soon did. I managed to get a few big hits in and kicked a couple of penalty goals before I injured my knee and had to come off after about half an hour.

At half-time we were still well in the game, trailing just 10-4. I was in the dressing room getting treatment when the second half started. By the time I came back out to watch the rest of the match from the bench, I still had the impression we were in the game until someone told me we were losing by thirty-odd points to four. The way they dominated the second half was a rude awakening for the GB camp and the British media as well. It was obvious that this wasn't just another touring team.

*****

While the Kangaroos kept on winning throughout October and November, so did Hull FC. We were top of the league as we prepared to take on the tourists in the game which some people believed would be the toughest club match of the tour; the so-called 'Fourth Test Match'.

The game was set to be played on the Tuesday prior to the Second Test at Wigan. I was still in the British squad but, because of the injury, was only travelling reserve. Although I was unlikely to play, I was still officially on international duty and so wasn't allowed to play for Hull in midweek. I felt we had a great chance of beating them and knew it would be an amazing night at the Boulevard. I was desperate to play but the only way that could happen was if I was stood down from international duty. I joined the GB camp at the start of the week and went to see the team doctor so he could check on my knee. I probably exaggerated a little when I told him I was in agony and could barely run on it. He gave it a check, while I winced and complained. As soon as he agreed that I wasn't fit and could leave the GB camp, I promptly told Arthur Bunting that my knee had made a miraculous recovery and declared myself fit to play for Hull the following day against the Aussies.

The tourists had tended to pick fringe players in most of their midweek games but the match against Hull was the exception. The Aussies had won all eleven games so far and didn't want to risk their perfect record. They named a full-strength team because they really thought they might lose otherwise. I was confident that Hull FC was a stronger team than Great Britain and I knew that the best chance I had of beating the Australians on that tour, was not in a red, white and blue shirt, but in a black and white one.

From Hull to Hell and Back

I don't think we set out to kick the shit out of them, but that is exactly what happened once we took the field. Mick Crane, in particular, thoroughly enjoyed getting stuck into the tourists, and I wasn't far behind him. Many people said it was the toughest game the tourists played on tour and it was hard to argue. They beat us 13-7 but, years later, people still talk about the disallowed Dane O'Hara try that could have won us the game. In the end, it took one of the best tries of the entire tour - Mal Meninga and Eric Grothe combining up the left wing - to finish us off. We were gutted that we had missed our chance to go down in history as the only team to beat the Invincibles. For the Australians, most of their Test team had to prepare themselves to play the Second Test just five days later.

The Great Britain management had been shocked by what had happened in the First Test in Hull and responded by making nine changes. It never made much difference and the Australians won easily, 27-6, to take the series.

The Third Test was the last game of the tour and, by that stage, I don't think the selectors had a clue what to do. The team they picked bore no resemblance to those for the first two games. There were one or two older players brought back into the team like Hull's David Topliss, alongside a few debutants such as Brian Noble. Having fully recovered from injury, I was back in the side and determined to play the full eighty minutes this time. But it wasn't to be.

Although we managed to score our only try of the series, the Australians dominated yet again. They were in control from the first whistle and, once they knew they were going to finish the tour unbeaten, some of their players couldn't resist winding us up, taking the piss and giving us verbals. The atmosphere was tense and ready to blow up and, as Max Krilich went over for their third try, I tripped over someone's leg and fell on top of him. Krilich thought that I had flopped on him deliberately and so he jumped up and hit me. I was pissed off with all the grief they had given us so I hit him back. Soon, everyone was diving in and I managed to land some good shots on Krilich before we were pulled apart. The French referee had lost control of the game by that point and decided to send us both off, although the incident was no worse than much of what had gone before. As I headed for the changing room, Ray Price came onto the pitch with the sand for the conversion attempt. Price wasn't even playing in the game but he started to give me some verbals as well. I gave him some back and it almost came to blows again.

So my first full international series ended prematurely. But while we hadn't been nearly as competitive as we had hoped, I took a lot of personal satisfaction from it. I had been pitched in with opponents like Les Boyd and Craig Young and had not been found wanting in any way.

Of course, collectively, the series was a big disappointment and its effect was felt throughout the game. As a group of players, we felt we had prepared well and we definitely took the games seriously. The Australians, meanwhile, were flesh and blood like us, but their level of fitness surprised everyone. It wasn't just their strength but the speed at which they played that we were unable to match, especially as we started to tire. Off the field, they knew how to enjoy themselves, at least as much as we did. But, they had something else that we couldn't match. We didn't know what it was and British rugby league has been searching for it ever since.

The difference between sporting sides is often mental and down to attitude. That was certainly the case with the 1982 Kangaroos. There can be no other explanation for why that particular group of players was so special. For them, it wasn't just a regular sports tour, it was an opportunity to become a part of history and every one of the blokes in that squad must look back on the '82 tour with an unbelievable sense of pride and achievement.

Whenever we bumped into any of their players during the tour, they didn't seem to be doing anything that we weren't. But, once they took the field, there was an intensity to their play that took everyone by surprise. It was relentless for eighty minutes and, although there were times when the British team, and some club teams, managed to hold them at bay, it was very rare for any side on that tour to dominate any part of a game.

The 1982 Kangaroos were an international rugby league landmark and I am proud to have been involved. But I soon grew frustrated at how we British invariably responded to defeat. It was ironic that the series which launched my international career should also lead to a change in outlook that meant that I was to struggle for my international place ever afterward. When the series ended, the common view was that the only way to compete with the Australians was to copy the way they played. From then on, the British style of play began to change and it became more and more difficult for players like me to make the team.

What's worse, the strategy didn't work. Every time it seemed as if we had caught the Australians up, they just got better. We are not much nearer reaching their standard now, after nearly thirty years of trying. Those efforts to constantly catch up with the Australians stifled what was good in the English game, which had been all about skill and guile and craft.

I couldn't help comparing how we did things at Hull FC and I was surprised that Arthur Bunting wasn't involved in some way with the GB set-up. Johnny Whiteley certainly brought in plenty of support. Prior to the First Test at Boothferry Park, three or four different coaches spoke to the team in the dressing room; Roger Millward had a role and I think Malcolm Reilly was involved in some capacity or other. It was odd that there was no place for Arthur, who was probably the most successful coach in the country at the time.

On reflection, I think the whole Great Britain set-up had been a bit of a disappointment to me. Perhaps that explains why I wasn't always on my best behaviour when on international duty.

*****

In early 1983, Great Britain played two games against France and I was chosen as travelling reserve for the first game in Carcassonne. Previous trips to France had been spoiled by poor refereeing by local officials, so they brought a New Zealander called Don Wilson over instead. To be honest, he was even worse and had no idea what he was doing. The game was a farce but we still won and, afterwards, everyone headed back to the hotel for a few beers, expecting to be told that we had an early flight back in the morning. We were surprised to find out that we weren't due to fly back to England until the following evening.

When I came down for breakfast on Sunday morning, everyone was in a leisurely, unhurried mood. I came down early and sat with Arthur Brooks, who covered rugby league for *The Daily Mirror*. When he suggested we have a drink, I assumed he meant a coffee and was surprised when he came back from the bar with two pints. We were soon joined by Len Casey and Mike Smith and, within the hour, we were on our way into Carcassonne town centre for a few more.

We were outside a café bar in the centre of town when someone noticed that Don Wilson was sitting nearby. With a few beers in me, I started to give him a bit of abuse. I was well into my beer and totally out of order but there was no quieting me down. 'You didn't know what the fuck you were doing, did you?' I said to him. Casey, Smithy and the others thought it was hilarious, but then they were as pissed as me. A couple of hours later, we were all quite drunk as we headed back to the hotel to get ready for our return flight. I was still steaming when we boarded our flight home and I made the mistake of sitting behind the team manager, Dick Gemmell. I was loud and swearing quite a bit. Dick turned around and told me to stop swearing and behave myself but that was like a red rag to a bull.

'What's up with you, Dick? You know I swear all the time, I'm from fucking Hull, aren't I?' I settled down for a bit as the crew got the plane ready for take-off but, once the stewardesses started to give the pre-flight safety briefing, I was off again. As soon as they had finished, I jumped out of my seat and started waving my safety card at them in appreciation. Dick had had enough and turned round to tell me to shut up again. It didn't make much difference. I just ignored him and kept babbling on, effing and blinding. I wasn't the only one but I was certainly the loudest. Eventually, I fell asleep and the rest of the flight passed without incident. We landed at Heathrow and boarded the coach taking us north. Dick never spoke to me throughout the entire journey. Even when we arrived back in Hull and he drove me home, he still wouldn't speak to me.

A week later, the team was announced to play the return game in Hull. It was usual at that time for the selectors to release the team to the press who would then phone the players to inform them and invite comment. I got a phone call from Paul Harrison of *The Sun*.

'Hello, Lee, how are you?'

'I'm fine, Paul mate, how are you?'

'Fine. Do you want the good news or the bad news, Lee?'

'Don't mind, Paul.'

'Well the good news is that the selectors have announced the same starting thirteen.'

'Okay. And the bad news?'

'You're dropped. You're not even travelling reserve, Lee. Dick said it's a disciplinary measure. Care to comment?'

Dick Gemmell never did speak to me about it. He never had the nerve to give players bad news himself and would always do it through the press. He was an odd character, Dick; I think he ended up driving a taxi in Hull.

I had only been involved in the GB set-up a few times and there is no doubt that being dropped was a setback but I didn't dwell on it for too long. There wasn't much I could do about the reputation I had already earned for myself as a hard drinking, rough and tumble type of bloke. No matter what I did in the rest of my career, that reputation was to stick with me and prove very hard to shake off.

*****

Fortunately, I was playing well enough to make it difficult for the British selectors to leave me out no matter how badly I behaved. By the end of the following season, I was chosen to travel to Australia, New Zealand and Papua New Guinea.

After the last series, the general view was that the previous generation of players had had their day. It was time for some younger players to step up and so a new bunch of players were selected for the first time. As well as myself, Garry Schofield and Wayne Proctor were also chosen from Hull, while Ellery Hanley, Andy Gregory, Andy Goodway and Joe Lydon were selected for their first tours.

Since it was my first full international tour, I was really excited about the whole thing. But to be honest, it was a disaster from start to finish and reminded me very much of the first time I'd toured Australia and Papua New Guinea.

From Hull to Hell and Back

The 1982 Great Britain Colts tour already mentioned had been an amazing experience - a mad, crazy adventure from the start. We'd been due to fly from Heathrow, via Oman, but the flight was delayed so we had to kick our heels at the airport for a few hours. As we hung around the terminal, someone from the airline noticed the GB logos all over our luggage and assumed we were the senior Great Britain team rather than the Colts. Before we knew it, we were shown into one of the airport's executive lounges while we waited for our flight. Of course, we all thought that was brilliant and it didn't take us long to notice that the bar was open. Although it was early in the morning, the bar was free, we were in holiday mode and so we well and truly tucked in. I have no idea how long it was before our flight was called but we made full use of the facilities. I couldn't drink very much back then and so I was steaming drunk and had to be wheeled through security on a luggage trolley. Somehow, I managed to get through customs and onto the plane. I went straight to sleep as soon as I fell into my seat and didn't wake up until we stopped to refuel in Muscat.

The GB Colts spent a week and a half in Papua New Guinea, en route to Australia. PNG is an amazing country; huge parts of the rainforest have never been explored and, as our plane approached Port Moresby, it seemed almost impossible that we could land on the tiny runway in the middle of the jungle. Most of the lads on the tour had never been outside Europe and some of the party had never been farther away from home than Workington, so it was an incredible experience for a bunch of seventeen and eighteen-year-old lads.

The Great Britain BARLA team was also touring at the same time and we would often cross paths with the older players from the amateur game. Harry Jepson was our tour manager and he kept reminding us that, even though we were younger, we were the professional team and that we should behave accordingly at all times. Whenever we attended an official event, he insisted that we wear the official tour gear that we'd been provided with; trousers, shirts, ties and thick woollen jumpers. It was over 90 degrees in the shade and the humidity was close to 100 per cent and it would have been much more appropriate for us to travel around in vests, shorts and flip-flops, but Harry insisted we dressed up all the time so that he could claim that we looked smart and professional. But we were never in any doubt that we were the poor relations of the two. The BARLA team flew everywhere while we travelled up and down the country by bus. To be fair to Harry, he had been made lots of promises about how we would be looked after and many of them weren't kept, which meant that he had a tough job to keep us all in decent shape while we were out there.

After a game in Goroka, we were headed for a town on the east coast of PNG, called Lae, where we were due to play the Test Match. It's only a two-hundred mile journey but we are not talking Hull to London. There are no motorways in PNG and it took us fourteen hours.

The journey was a nightmare. We were worried as soon as the bus turned up and we spotted the driver chewing on beetlenut, the substance that everyone in PNG chews, which makes them high as kites half the time. To make matters worse, the minibus broke down halfway through and, as we got out to stretch our legs, a tribe of natives came wandering out of the jungle. We didn't know if they were friendly or not and so we were quite apprehensive when we saw them carrying spears! Luckily, Andy Sykes had taken his shirt off and the locals were fascinated by the tattoos all over his body. We told Andy to keep his shirt off while the driver fixed the bus, so that the natives would be diverted from whatever else they might have decided to do. We were soon on our way but poor Andy had third degree burns from standing in the sun without his shirt for a couple of hours. We were too young to know much about touring but, even at that age, it struck me as daft that we had to prepare for our games in that way. The way we were treated probably affected our behaviour as well and we gave Harry a real runaround.

In Mount Hagen, we stayed in a motel where the hosts organised a party for us. There was a pig roast, lots of free beer and some local girls who had been brought in to dance. Not in the Spearmint Rhino sense; it was much more decent than that, although we all found it hilarious and a bit embarrassing to watch the little lasses dancing around, supposedly for our entertainment.

There was a general election in PNG at the time and a curfew was in place to maintain control. At nine o'clock our party had to come to an end and we were all supposed to go back to our rooms. But it takes more than a curfew to keep a bunch of randy, boozed-up teenagers down and we were soon messing around in the courtyard outside, chatting to local girls and generally pissing about. When Harry heard the noise, he came bursting out of his room to see what was going on while we all scattered back to our rooms to hide. Tony Marchant chose to hide in the swimming pool, while I dashed back to my room and jumped into bed, fully clothed. When Harry came in, he saw me sitting upright in bed. 'Sorry, Lee,' he said. 'I didn't mean to wake you up. I'm just trying to find the buggers who were making all that noise outside. Get back to sleep, Lee. There's a good lad.'

*****

After the PNG leg of the tour, the GB Colts party flew on to Australia. It was the first time that any of us had been to Oz and we were due to play in some of the best known stadiums in the world. Our very first game was played at Lang Park in Brisbane, the curtain-raiser to a game between Queensland and New Zealand. We played Queensland under-18s and my first experience of playing against an Aussie team was everything I expected. The intensity never let up. It was non-stop; every tackle was full-on and very tough. I enjoyed it and felt quite comfortable at that level but unfortunately it was the only game I played in Australia. In the first half, on my way down to pick up a loose ball, I took a kick in the face. After a bit of treatment, I came round and managed to continue but, in the second half, another big collision gave me a dead leg. I couldn't run on it at all and had to come off. I was gutted not to be able to continue and the injury was so bad that I had to sit out the rest of the tour. There were so many great experiences to be had, but I had to watch them from the touchline.

The next game was played at the Sydney Cricket Ground. It was the curtain-raiser to the State of Origin game between New South Wales and Queensland and my place had been taken by Alan Platt from Oldham. Platty was keen to get stuck in but he overstepped the mark when he was sent off for kicking one of our opponents as he lay on the ground. I don't know if it was deliberate or whether he was retaliating for something, but kicking an opponent isn't something that anyone likes to see and the Aussie crowd didn't like it one bit. Within minutes of Platty being sent off, the crowd showed their anger at the rest of the touring party and started throwing empty bottles and other stuff down at us. The mood was hostile to say the least and we were glad to get away from the ground and back to our hotel.

While Harry Jepson had been keen to have us behave professionally at all times, someone had decided it would be a good idea for us to stay in a hotel in the Kings Cross district of Sydney, which is renowned as the seedy end of town. Of course, it was great for us to have bars, clubs and entertainment on our doorstep but it exposed us to one or two temptations that could have been avoided if we'd stayed down by the beach somewhere. Nevertheless, we loved it at the time and, after the game, Tracy Lazenby, Tony Marchant and myself went out for a couple of beers in the 'Cross'. On the way back to the hotel, we stopped to get a kebab and while we were stood waiting for our food, we noticed that a group of Aussie lads had recognised us, probably on account of the thick woolly tour jumpers we were wearing!

'You're them Pommy bastards, aren't you?' they said. 'You dirty bastards. Think it's fucking tough to kick a bloke in the head do you?' They were a bit drunk and dead keen to set about us, but I sized the situation up quite quickly and told them: 'Hang on a minute. There's five of you and only three of us. Let me go get two of our mates and then we'll sort it out fair and square.'

They agreed to a more evenly-matched scrap and stood waiting outside the kebab shop while I went back to the hotel and started knocking on doors to round up a posse. By the time I got back to the kebab shop, I had half the team with me and we kicked ten bells of shit out of them.

Realising they had taken on more than they could handle, the Aussies ran off to lick their wounds. As they rounded the corner out of view, they bumped into Tony Marchant's dad Alan, who was coming back to the hotel in his team blazer, and they gave him a bit of a roughing up. When Alan got back to the hotel, he told us what had happened, so we all went out again to give them another kicking. By now, the police had arrived, Harry had been summoned and he wanted to know what was going on. I was never afraid to put my hand up if something was my responsibility and so I told him that it had all been my fault.

It took some sharp talking by Harry to smooth it all over with the police and calm the whole situation down.

The tour ended with a game against the Australian Schoolboys. They had been dominant in their age group for years but, even with players injured, we only lost 11-5, a respectable result in the circumstances. But on the whole, we hadn't been particularly successful and that was due, partly, to how badly organised the tour had been. At the time, I assumed that it was Harry Jepson's fault because he was the manager, but I later discovered that the poor planning and logistics were mainly the fault of the RFL. Nevertheless, by the time I came to join the senior tour down under in 1984, I was more than prepared for the chaos that followed.

*****

British rugby league tours were always quite amateurish. In 1979, for example, one player took his fiancée to Australia so they could get married in between fixtures. It wasn't much better by 1984. There were no rules whatsoever; no curfews, no dress code, nothing. It didn't take long for the players to start behaving as players always do in such circumstances: badly.

The organisation was ridiculous and the itinerary didn't help. We started the tour in tropical Darwin, when we ought to have started in the south where it would have been much cooler. The club sides weren't interested in playing us so, between Tests, we played representative and county sides in front of crowds of three or four-thousand supporters, in places like Tamworth, Rockhampton and Wagga Wagga.

For most of these players, it might be the only chance they would get to play against Great Britain and they were determined to get stuck in. One team in Queensland fielded forwards so big and frightening that Garry Schofield, while playing centre, spent most of the game outside his winger in order to keep away from them. We won most of the warm-up games but the standard of play wasn't high enough to prepare us well for the Tests.

By the time we reached Sydney to begin the build up to the First Test, things seemed to have picked up when we found we were staying at the Sheraton Hotel. It was a real swanky place and we who had never been on a Lions tour before were impressed by the luxury. Nevertheless, nobody had really thought things through. Having booked us into one of the most expensive hotels in the city, we had been given a pauper's allowance to live on. Each player had the equivalent of around £125 per week to take care of day-to-day living expenses and we had to pay for our own meals from that. I had already arranged to have fifty quid a week sent home to Janet which left me with about a tenner a day; nowhere near enough to buy a couple of meals at the Sheraton. The only meal included at the hotel was breakfast. But because we used to train early each morning none of us dared eat anything for breakfast, so the only meal we didn't have to pay for, we couldn't even eat.

In truth, the Sheraton couldn't have been a worse choice for a touring sports team. It was a city centre hotel with none of the leisure facilities we needed and we had to train on a public park in the middle of Sydney. After that, we would head back to the hotel for a shower and then most of the players would go down to the New South Wales Leagues Club where we could at least afford something to eat.

After afternoon training, some of the lads would go back there again for a couple of cheap pints. Since Dick and Frank had imposed no curfews, many of the players would stay in there all night. This was at the start of the tour and discipline just got worse.

The locals in the Leagues Club couldn't believe that the

Great Britain touring squad was basically using their club as a soup kitchen. I'm not fussy, I don't mind eating or drinking anywhere, but I was shocked at how badly we were being looked after when we were expected to represent our country. Perhaps I was spoilt. Whenever Hull FC had a big game, we would stay somewhere smart like Mottram Hall Hotel in Cheshire, which had brilliant training facilities and where all of our meals were included. Mottram Hall was very popular with sports teams and we would often rub shoulders with the top footballers of the day from Liverpool, Manchester United and Nottingham Forest.

If we weren't at the Leagues Club, some of us would go over the road to the Tattersalls Club. Tattersalls is a well known club in Sydney. It's quite traditional and even had a dress code; all the gentlemen had to wear a tie before they were allowed in. What they didn't say, though, was what you had to wear *with* your tie, so we would turn up wearing a T-shirt and shorts, with a tie on top.

While we were there, the club was hosting a big snooker tournament and we spent quite a bit of time having a drink with the likes of Eddie Charlton and Bill Werbeniuk. I soon discovered that being on tour with an international sports team certainly opened doors. While we were in Sydney, we found out that Manchester United were on a pre-season tour of the country and were playing at the Sydney Cricket Ground. Someone managed to blag us some tickets and a group of us went along to watch the game, which was where I came to meet Joe Bugner. Joe was in the process of staging one of his many comebacks at the time, but he also knew a fair bit about rugby league. As I stood in a sponsors' bar at the SCG watching Manchester United while having a couple of drinks with Joe Bugner, I ought to have reflected on how quickly and dramatically my life had changed, but I don't think I gave it a moment's thought.

From Hull to Hell and Back

Over the next few years, I had the opportunity to meet a number of people I never thought I would meet. People like Sir Michael Parkinson were often around big rugby league games, but the greatest pleasure always came from meeting other sportsmen from other sports. While I was at Leeds, the players were invited to lots of sponsors' functions and I got to know several football players quite well. David Batty was a big fan of rugby league and the late Billy Bremner was very knowledgeable about the game as well. Both would often come over and have a chat. As club captain in my second year at Leeds, I was often required to go to lots of sporting events and that's how I came to meet Geoffrey Boycott. We didn't have what you would call a conversation; as I walked past him, he called out: 'You've put some weight on, young Crooks.' I didn't know what to say and hoped that a witty reply would come immediately to mind, but it didn't. To be honest, he could have called me a fat bastard and I would still have been pleased that he knew who I was.

*****

Back to the tour and the introduction of so many new faces into the squad made life very difficult for our coach Frank Myler, whose memory was awful at the best of times. Frank could never remember anyone's name and had to write everything down on the back of his cigarette packet.

At the team meeting the day before the First Test in Sydney, all the players assembled around Frank, waiting to hear him pick his team. Out came his cigarette packet and he started to read from it. 'At full-back, Mick Burke. On the wings, I've gone for Ellery and Dessie Drummond. Keith Mumby and Garry Schofield will play in the centres. Des Foy at stand-off. At scrum-half, I've gone for.... err... ..ummm,' Frank paused, scratched his head, stared at Neil

Holding sat in front of him and asked: '...what's your name, son?'

It's a story I try to tell if I do any after-dinner speaking but, to be honest, I don't tell it very well and it's nowhere near as funny as when Frank first said it. After picking me and Andy Goodway in the front row, John Joyner nudged hooker Kevin Beardmore and said to him: 'There's no way you're going to be playing, Kevin. There isn't enough room for your name on the back of that cigarette packet.' Kevin had been playing brilliantly but never got near the Tests. Not because of the length of his surname; as tour captain, Brian Noble was guaranteed the number nine shirt.

There are certain stadiums in the world that are iconic and I've been lucky enough to play in several. Undoubtedly, Wembley is one and the Sydney Cricket Ground is another. The place has incredible atmosphere and comes with its own unique set of conditions. Getting changed in the members' stand and walking out of the pavilion is peculiar as it's an environment designed for cricketers but it's still special. The pitch is very unusual too. When you play at a new ground you try to find your bearings from where the grandstands are. They help you to locate the touchlines and generally feel comfortable. At the SCG it's totally different because the playing area is oval. In some areas the stands are on top of you. In others, it feels like you're miles away. The middle of the pitch is also the cricket square, so it's as hard as concrete.

The First Test was fiery right from the start. In the very first scrum of the game, Dave Brown and myself had a pop at each other and the whole scrum erupted in a brawl which saw us both get a formal warning from the referee. It never stopped either of us and the scuffling continued throughout. In the second half, I was sent to the sin-bin after a ruck with Greg Dowling and, before that, I had also been drawn into a fight with Ray Price. I still felt a bit of animosity toward

Price after our confrontation on the pitch in the Third Test in 1982. I didn't need much of an invitation to renew his acquaintance, but I made the mistake of giving him a whack in the wrong place and at the wrong time, when I was surrounded by his team-mates and when there wasn't a red, white and blue jersey in sight. I got a bit of a battering on that occasion. All my shoulder pads ended up being ripped out and the brawl made it onto a rugby league video called *Bad Boys*.

We were in the game until well into the second-half but, once they had it won, they scored a couple of late tries which really pissed our lads off. David Hobbs, in particular, must have seen the red mist because it was totally out of character for him to elbow-smash Greg Conescu in the last minute. Conescu lost a couple of teeth and had to be carried from the pitch while Hobbsy was probably lucky to get a three-match ban. The incident was shown on TV constantly, whipping up the atmosphere even more for the next Test.

That Second Test was in Brisbane but I have no reason to remember it. I injured my shoulder early on and had to come off. We lost that one as well and I never played again on the Australian leg of the tour.

One of the things that people always seem to remember about the early part of my career is the way in which I took on the Australians. It's true that my games against them were eventful; after the game in Brisbane, my record against them was; played four, lost four, substituted with injury twice, sin-binned once and sent off once. By then, I had a reputation as someone who never took a backward step. I had brawled with Les Boyd, Ray Price, Greg Dowling, Dave Brown and many more besides. Although I don't regret any of it, with the benefit of hindsight I think I got carried away with the aggressive side of my game. By 1984, there was more to me than a wild firebrand. I should have been more focussed on playing rugby than trying to do battle. My aggressive approach played into their hands and I missed an opportunity to build my reputation for the right reasons. It wouldn't have made any difference to the outcome of the series, but I think I could have made more of a personal impact on the team if I had been less aggressive.

By the time we were beaten in the final Test, most of us were glad to leave Australia. It was a really disappointing tour because we'd been no more competitive than we had in 1982. That said, we never stood a chance. The players tried to take it all seriously, trained exceptionally hard twice a day and gave it our very best in every game, but the overall level of preparation lacked the professionalism that had already become a part of the Australian game.

As one of the youngest players on my first tour, I went along with whatever everyone else was doing and most of the others were out drinking a lot of the time. After a while I began to feel disappointed. This was the peak of my career and even though I was enjoying myself it all seemed a bit amateurish. We weren't doing ourselves justice and the players never had much idea of what we were expected to do from one day to the next. Most of my recollections of the tour involved what we got up to off the field, mainly in the Kings Cross area of Sydney.

'The Cross' is a colourful place to go drinking. I must be quite naïve because I could never figure out which were the gay bars and which weren't. Garry Schofield and I were in a place called The Bourbon and Beef one night when one of our team-mates got more than he bargained for. He spotted a good looking blonde girl leaning against the bar. Schoey and I looked on in admiration as he stood up, ambled over and bought her a drink. We were even more impressed when they began chatting and cuddling up. He was getting on very well with her for half an hour or so before one of the barmen came over to tell us that our mate's new friend was not all she looked. She was - in fact - a fella. The barman suggested we go and have a word with him before he got too carried away. We gave the idea some thought before deciding it would be far more interesting if we left him to find out for himself.

Our mate carried on chatting and smooching for another half-hour or so, all the while getting more intimate. Until suddenly we heard a scream. A glass hit the floor and our team-mate reared up and headbutted the poor 'girl' before heading straight out of the door. Meanwhile, Schoey and I were rolling around on the floor in hysterics.

*****

We flew out of Brisbane the day after the Third Test and headed for New Zealand. It had been a difficult few weeks and we were relieved to be moving somewhere new. I was sat near the back of the plane and a few of us decided to have a drink.

After we'd had a couple of beers, Frank Myler came down to the back of the plane and asked: "What do you think you're doing, lads? We're having a training session when we get there!" Throughout the tour, we had never been given an itinerary or a training schedule or anything of that kind so we never had any idea what we were meant to be doing from one day to the next. Nobody had told us that we would be training and we were a bit pissed off to be told while we were in the air. Anyway, Frank was the boss and so we stopped drinking and tried to get some sleep. Half an hour later, Frank came down the plane again with a large glass of whisky in his hand, and said: 'Tell you what, lads, let's not train when we get there. We'll have a few beers instead and start afresh in the morning.' Seriously, nobody had a clue what they were doing.

Once we arrived in New Zealand, I had my own plans; I'd arranged to meet Gary Kemble. When we reached our hotel, there was a message waiting to let me know where Gary had been playing that day. As soon as I had checked in, I jumped in a taxi over to the ground to meet up with Gary. As I walked through the door, I realised the place was full of New Zealand Maoris and the entire bar fell silent as they all looked around to see who had just walked into their local. Suddenly, Gary spotted me and came marching over to the door with the biggest bottle of beer I'd ever seen. 'Crooksy, Crooksy,' he shouted. 'Get yourself over here for a beer!'

We had more than a few beers in there and we were soon joined by Dane O'Hara and James Leuluai. Later, I took them back to the White Heron, the hotel where the British team was staying. By the time we got there, all the British lads were pissed as well. It was quite a raucous night and next morning Dick Gemmell came down to breakfast to inform us that the manager of the hotel wasn't happy at our behaviour and had asked us to leave. 'But, it's not all bad,' said Dick. 'I've managed to get us booked into The Sheraton instead.'

*****

I'd been looking forward to playing against the Kiwis and was really keen to recover from the shoulder injury I'd picked up in Brisbane. I did lots of rehab and trained hard but every time I put any pressure on my shoulder, I knew that it just wasn't right. I kept telling the GB physio, Ronnie Barrett, that it wasn't getting any stronger.

Ronnie was a bit old-school. He would give you some treatment and then a couple of Anadin for the pain. He couldn't figure out why I wasn't fit to play and, between them, Ronnie and Frank probably came to the conclusion that I wasn't as badly injured as I was making out. That's how Brian Noble came to give me and John Joyner a bollocking for not taking the tour seriously.

We'd only been in New Zealand for a couple of days or so and neither JJ nor me had played for a few weeks. Because we weren't playing or training much, we had plenty of time on our hands and so we decided to have a few pints together now and again. We weren't the worst behaved by any means but we were probably the loudest, or at least I was. Anyway, Frank got the impression that we were taking the piss a bit but didn't want to confront us himself so he sent his captain to sort it out. I think Nobby was a bit embarrassed but he did what was asked of him, coming down the bus one day to tell us that Frank felt we weren't taking the tour seriously and that, if we didn't shape up, we'd be going home early.

I was quite shocked because I didn't think we had done anything that most of the other players weren't doing, but JJ was furious. He had toured a couple of times before and had a very good record of representing his country. He confronted Brian in the hotel shortly afterwards and told him what he thought of the tour and how other people had been behaving. It was quite obvious that Frank was a bit frustrated at how things had turned out and had decided to make an example of a couple of players; the two of us.

I decided not to let it bother me since the entire tour was becoming a farce. Frank decided to cancel training one day just because it was raining. I also felt under pressure to play even though I knew that my shoulder wasn't strong enough. Eventually, I told Frank that I would have a painkilling injection and give it a go in one of the warm-up games. Just as I had feared, in my first tackle of the game against the New Zealand Maori, my shoulder went and I had to come off. I had no chance of making the next game and so my tour was basically over.

Once I realised that I wasn't going to be playing, I quickly got fed up and was pleased to be told I could leave early and travel back to England. I wasn't the only one to end the tour early either. It started to unravel towards the end as the team suffered a number of injuries and I flew back with Harry Pinner, Garry Schofield and Ray Ashton. I was just glad to be going home, but it was a long and miserable journey. Ray had saved up all his money while he'd been away and, even though Harry, Schoey and myself were skint, he wouldn't even buy us a cup of coffee at the airport. To cheer myself up on the long flight I decided I was going to have a go at breaking the record for the most cans of free beer consumed on a flight from Australia. I had heard that the record was thirty-eight, by the Australian cricketer Rodney Marsh. The flight was scheduled to take over twenty hours and I could think of nothing else to do but get drunk and so I thought that I might as well try. But it wasn't to be. The Air New Zealand cabin crew weren't amused when I told them what I planned to do and refused to serve me.

*****

Over the next couple of years, I played some of the best rugby of my career for my club, so when the New Zealand team toured Britain in 1985 I was confident that I had done enough to be involved.

There was a new coach in place by then, Maurice Bamford, and I was pleased when he selected me to play in the First Test at Headingley. Most of the Kiwi team were playing their club rugby in England at that time, including Gary Prohm at Hull KR and, of course, Kemble, Leuluai, Ah Kuoi and O'Hara, my Hull team-mates. It was a great game which we only lost by a couple of points.

When the team for the Second Test was announced, I

wasn't in it. That was the first time I had been left out of the national team, other than through injury, and it was a really frustrating experience. Neither Maurice nor any of the staff explained why I wasn't included. How could you possibly go about improving and playing your way into the team if you didn't know what it was they wanted you to improve? When Maurice then picked the 36-year old Jeff Grayshon instead, my peculiar relationship with the Great Britain team took another twist.

In twelve years of Test rugby I never felt like I belonged. I was always on the fringes, battling to justify my presence there and I always felt like an outsider. As much as I got on well with all the lads and the coaches and staff, I never felt secure and knew that one bad performance or one daft comment could cause me to be left out again.

*****

What was even more frustrating was that, with Jeff in the team and Garry Schofield on top form, the British lads won easily. It was all set up for the third deciding game at Elland Road, Leeds. Maurice's decision was vindicated but I still didn't know why I had been dropped. Even more oddly, despite squaring the series, Maurice then recalled me for the Third Test, albeit on the bench.

Although I was pleased to be back, I still felt that Andy Goodway was wearing my shirt. I found myself watching everything he did, hoping he would make a mistake so that Maurice would take him off. In fact, Andy did start the game badly and made a couple of errors before he was flattened by one of the Kiwis' many high tackles. With twenty-five minutes gone, I got my chance.

As soon as I was on the field, I adjusted quickly to the pace. There are some games where you seem to have time on your side, you take the right options and everything comes off. I didn't play a perfect game by any means, but I did manage to find a few gaps, lay off a few decent passes and put in some good kicks. By half-time I felt very happy with my performance and confident we could press on and win, even though we trailed six-nil at the break.

It was a real battle of a game. We were awarded twenty penalties in total and many of them were for foul play. We never managed to create many try-scoring chances so we opted to take the points however we could. From two penalty kicks, I narrowed the deficit to 6-4. With about fifteen minutes left, an all-mighty brawl erupted on the touchline in front of the dug-out. Hull KR's Dave Watkinson was in the middle of the ruck and, at one point, just about every player on the field was involved, including some who'd jumped from the dug-out to join in. I even saw a photograph later of a policeman trying to pull the players apart. Of course, I dived in to help my mates and that was quite funny because, as I was getting stuck into a couple of Kiwi forwards, I felt something thrashing away on my back. I turned to see my Hull FC team-mate, Dane O'Hara, trying to join in. He was hanging off my shoulders, while frantically trying to swing punches at the side of my head. I tried to shrug him off. 'What do you think you're doing?' I growled at him, politely. By this stage of the tour, the Kiwis were mixing it with anyone and everyone and, determined not to be intimidated, even the pretty boys like Dane wanted to join in.

When it settled down, both sides were given a real bollocking by the referee and a player from each side was sent to the sin-bin. Tempers calmed down but the penalties kept on coming and, with just a minute left, Gary Prohm was penalised for another foul. We were trailing 6-4 and the penalty had been given about thirty yards out and a couple of yards in from the touchline, in front of the main stand. I didn't need anyone to tell me what I had to do.

At that stage in my career, I'd developed a habit where I visualised scenarios that might occur in a game. I would lay in my bed the night before bringing it all to life in my head, trying to imagine the angles I might run in order to make a break or how I would go through my kicking routine. This was long before clubs brought in psychologists to prepare players mentally. I didn't know if anybody else did that and nobody told me to, it was just something I did. Once I made the decision to go for goal, I just went into a routine that was as familiar to me as walking down the street.

*****

I walk over to the mark, it looks a fair way out. I've got the ball in my hands, wiping off the mud. The sandboy comes on with the bucket. I get down on one knee, inches from the touchline, take a big handful of sand and start to make my little mound. Everyone uses sand nowadays, but I was the first to do it in this country. Concentrate now, Crooksy. Tee the ball up nice and steady. I start to get a feeling of déjà vu. It feels like I've been here before. I've gone through the whole thing so many times now it feels like second nature. I don't feel anxious at all. This is what I do.

The ball is sat up nicely and I lean it slightly forward. I check the seam; make sure it's lined up. Point it straight at the near post. I'm a right-footed kicker and if it heads for the near post, the arc of the kick will take it through the middle. That's it. It's lined up. Perfect. Stand up, step back. Take another look at it. No, it doesn't look right. Step forward again, down on one knee, straightening her up just a little bit more, take off another tiny piece of mud and turf. Stand up and take another look. Yes, that's better. I can't hear the crowd now. They've gone very quiet. I've shut it out. Get the feet right now; right foot directly behind the ball, left foot just to the side. Six paces back, two to the side.

I'm not thinking about anything other than my routine. I take a deep breath. In my mind, I can see myself running up to the ball. I can feel the contact with the bottom third. I'm staring at the posts, not looking at anything else. The crowd to the right, a few people down the touchline in front of me, twenty-odd players in front and behind, every one of them watching me.

I take another look at the ball, then a look at the posts and then back to the ball. Nothing else; posts, ball. I wipe the end of my right boot on the back of my left sock and take another look at the posts. Another deep breath. Lift my shoulder pads up. Crowd quiet. They know this will tie the series or we lose, but not me. Not in this moment. I briefly imagine the noise if this goes over and then forget it. Once I take the first step there's no going back. Like going off the end of a diving board. No going back. Another beat, deep breath. Crowd silent. Step up.

I strike the ball clean and true. I know it's good as soon as it leaves my boot. It just feels right. I watch the ball for a moment, long enough to see it heading toward the near post. One glance and I turn away. I'm the first person in the ground to know that it is going over, so I turn towards my team-mates and back to my mark for the restart. I glance at the dug-out and they are going mental. All except Maurice Bamford who is clutching his head. He's jumped out of his seat and smashed his head on the roof, the daft bugger.

A fraction of a second later comes the roar. It begins just behind where I have taken the kick and spreads like a Mexican wave.

*****

While I was taking the kick at goal, the stadium announcer named me as the GB man of the match. I hadn't heard a thing.

*****

Although there was still time for that restart there was no time for either side to build an attack. And when the hooter sounded we celebrated as though we had won. After being hammered by the Aussies for a good few years, we were just relieved to hold our own against the New Zealanders.

The penalty goal that made it 6-6 is how many remember my Great Britain career. If that's the case, I have no problem. It certainly gave me the greatest satisfaction and meant that, for a year or so at least, my selection was reasonably secure.

I retained my place for the games against France in early 1986, but the biggest prize came later that season when the Aussies were over again. I was desperate to be in the squad.

After successive whitewashes, the GB management invested a lot of effort and money into preparing for the '86 series. A number of training camps were held and they even brought in specialist coaches. Joe Lydon and myself spent a fair bit of time with a specialist American Football kicker who had played in the NFL. We were shown how to get more height on the ball, which would help us make more of our attacking kicking game. That proved very useful and showed that the management was taking preparation more seriously than in the past.

Maurice Bamford was still coach and he put in place a rigid game plan. He drilled us on exactly what to do in each tackle. We all knew what was expected but I felt that took away some of our freedom. I believe it is important for players to respond to what goes on out on the pitch; to try something different if an opponent makes a mistake or shows signs of tiredness. We were now beginning to move from the core strengths of our own game towards copying the way the Australians played. That disappointed me. We had no autonomy. Nevertheless, we did feel much better prepared.

The First Test at Old Trafford attracted the biggest crowd ever seen for a Test Match in Britain and there was a terrific atmosphere. But, just like '82, it turned out that we were totally unprepared for the blitz to come. We were 16-0 down at half-time and it could have been worse. I don't think we put a foot wrong, but we had no answer to the power and pace of the Aussies.

In the second half, though, I kicked a penalty to make it 16-2 and then put Schoey over for a try. The Aussies began to get nervous. And their nerves got worse when Joe Lydon went the length of the field shortly afterwards. Game on. Unfortunately, I couldn't convert either score, but we were back in the game, 16-10.

There was now a spring in our step and we were playing some of the best rugby I had ever seen from a Great Britain side. But we were unable to press on and in the last twenty minutes they ran away with it. Although Australia went on to win 38-16, our last try gave me some satisfaction. Schoey and I worked a move that led to him scoring; we used to do it at Hull when Peter Sterling played with us. We called it the 'Parramatta' after the club where Sterlo learned it. Sterlo couldn't believe we had managed to pull it off against him but it was all in vain.

In the dressing room afterwards, Maurice told us he was pleased with how we had played and promised there would be no changes for the Second Test. I immediately thought that a mistake. Although, we had played well in patches, there were lots of things we could improve on. A number of people hadn't been in the side for one reason or another and to rule out the likes of Andy Gregory with an emotional decision straight after the game wasn't smart.

Sure enough, two weeks later, more or less the same team turned up at Elland Road and were never in it. We were 12-0 down at half-time and 34 points behind before Schoey scored our only try three minutes from the end. The hoped-for improvement hadn't happened. We were blown away and the difference between the two teams was at least as great as it had been four years earlier. By now, some pundits were starting to say that this touring team was even better than the 1982 'Invincibles'. There was no doubt we were much better, but it seemed the Australians had moved up into an altogether different league.

What impressed me most about the 1986 tourists was that they still had the drive and desire to improve. After 1982, it was hard to imagine how they could have done that, but they had managed to find a way. On reflection, it's easy to see what was driving them on. They knew that if they didn't go through the tour unbeaten, like the 1982 team had, they would be considered failures back home; that's how ruthless Australian sports fans are. The fact they matched that record while playing literally breathtaking rugby does make them the better of the two teams in my eyes.

With the series dead, there *were* a few changes for the Third Test but it made no difference. We lost again.

Being beaten by the Australians in 1986 was way more demoralising than either of the two other series I played in. In 1982 we hadn't prepared well and were caught out by how quickly the Australian game had progressed. We were more competitive in 1984, but the tour was poorly organised and the players were never given much chance.

Ahead of the '86 series, our preparation was much better and we were really confident we had closed the gap. But we never imagined that the Aussies could become even better.

It was like chasing the wind. Every time we caught them up, they got further away.

My best individual performance came in 1982 and earned me my very first Great Britain cap, but in all honesty I rarely reached those heights for my country. I was too interested in knocking my opponents around and missed an opportunity of showing them what I could do when I was arguably at my best.

Nevertheless, I still look back on those Test Series of the 1980s with great fondness. They were iconic tours that will linger long in the memory of anyone who played in or observed them closely. I am just very, very proud to have taken part. Even if the Aussie bastards did beat us every time!

4

Captain Crooks

By 1983 my initial signing-on payments had been paid and it was time to negotiate my first full contract. Before I went in to see the chairman I got the only bit of financial advice I ever received at Hull; Knocker Norton suggested I ask for twenty-five thousand pounds a year.

It was an unimaginable amount of money. I was still only a teenager and the average wage in Hull was a fraction of that. I said there was no way I could ask for so much but Knocker insisted that was what I was worth. 'You're the biggest young star in the game,' he told me, with absolute certainty. 'That's what you ought to ask for.' Eventually, I managed to summon up enough bottle to go in, where the negotiations went something like this:

'How much do you want, Lee?'

'Well, er, I was thinking about fifteen, Mr Chairman, sir.'

'Fifteen thousand?'

'Yes.'

'Fifteen thousand pounds?'

'Er. Yes.'

I looked at my shoes and fidgeted while the chairman sucked in his breath like a dodgy mechanic.

'We can give you ten.'

'Okay. Thanks.'

*****

It was typical of me to ask for less than I deserved and not surprising that I should come away with even less than I asked for. That's the way things stayed. I never liked asking for money and I never used an agent to do it for me. As a result I was underpaid for most of my professional career and ended up more or less skint at the end of it.

*****

It would have been nice to have money in the bank when I retired but that's just not the way it turned out. There's not a lot of point worrying about it. I've never been particularly bothered about material gain and if other players managed to negotiate more than me, good luck to them. If I wasn't prepared to try and do the same I have no right to say it was unfair. When I look back, there are lots of occasions when I could have held out for more. I was still only on ten grand a year when Leeds made me the world-record signing and the pay rise was nothing to write home about either.

On reflection, it may have been a mistake not to have an agent but it didn't feel like it at the time. When I started at Hull, nobody used an agent; players did their negotiations themselves. I don't recall anyone being unhappy with the arrangement. Only in retirement have I had a manager to help me out.

Arguments over contracts were rare but disagreements

with the club over win bonuses seemed to go on forever. We reached lots of cup finals and it was only fair that the players shared in the money but negotiations were always shambolic. There were times when we would still be arguing over money the day before. Dave Topliss was club captain and would be first to discuss player bonuses with the board. Dave was a lovely guy who would put forward our demands reasonably and calmly. He tended to ask for much more than we would expect to settle for, perhaps three grand for a cup final win. Roy Waudby, the chairman, would then explain that the club faced lots of expenses and could only afford to pay something like five hundred per man. Toppo would then ask for time to consult with his team-mates and speak to the rest of us.

Once we heard the club's first offer, we would usually send Knocker to handle things from then on. Knocker would be more direct and tell Roy there was no way we were going to play for such a pittance. They had better come up with more money or else they'd be playing the cup final with a reserve team.

Of course, we always reached agreement. Both sides knew the score and we were well aware that, ultimately, the club had us by the balls. There was no way we would ever seriously refuse to play, but the arguments went on. We hit pay dirt for the 1982 cup final, though. We were on £1,200 to win and £500 to draw. Because we ended up doing both, we earned both bonuses! The club didn't mind. Those games earned them a fortune.

Back then, of course, everything was different. Although we spent lots of time helping out with sponsors and going to various club events, I don't think anyone got paid any extra. Our rewards were usually a bit of free gear or a night out, there were never any endorsement or appearance fees.

But, if I was ever undersold by Hull FC then it didn't really feel like it. The club helped me out in other ways, such as finding me a job. After a couple of years working for Arthur Bunting, we reached the conclusion I wasn't very committed to being a painter and decorator. After a while they managed to find me a vacancy in the lottery office.

At first, all I had to do was go around the pubs and clubs of Hull and persuade them to sell club lottery tickets. It was easy work; I could enjoy a laugh with the fans, have the odd pint and more or less choose my hours. It was right up my street, until the club decided they wanted me to start cold-calling for new business by going door-to-door around people's houses. I didn't fancy that, especially when it was suggested I start by knocking on doors on Preston Road - right in the middle of East Hull! Friendly banter is one thing. There was no way I was going to start knocking on the doors of hardcore Hull KR fans. I was liable to get lynched. I told the lottery manager he needed to find someone else and that was the end of another job.

*****

I was earning enough to get by on. I could afford to pay the mortgage and one of the club sponsors provided me with a car (I hadn't passed my test, but nobody seemed bothered). There was enough money for Janet and me to enjoy ourselves and I suppose that was all we needed.

Truth be told, there were times during those years where I was enjoying myself so much I would have played for nothing. It was an especially good time to be involved with Hull FC. The club was on the up and up with new stars arriving every year, and we were magnificently supported by the most passionate fans in the game. On top of that, Hull KR were also enjoying a lot of success. For a few years in the 1980s, there was nowhere better to be for anyone passionate about rugby league than the city of Hull.

From Hull to Hell and Back

There have been a lot of reunions organised recently to raise money for the Roy Waudby Foundation. Each time the call has gone out, everyone involved in the Hull FC team of that era has dropped what they are doing and headed to Hull to attend. The likes of Peter Sterling, Gary Kemble and James Leuluai have flown in from the other side of the world rather than miss a celebration.

The reason why that era is so fondly remembered isn't because we won so many trophies. If we are honest, we didn't win half as many as we ought to have. Instead, we all remember the incredible team spirit and the unbelievable support that the fans gave us.

The catalyst off the field was Keith Tindall's testimonial season. Keith's benefit events tended to fall on Tuesday and Thursday nights, which was great because that's when we used to go out anyway. They were also a great opportunity for new signings to get to know their team-mates. Soon they were part of the furniture; Arthur seemed able to identify exactly the right type to fit in. The mixture was important. There were older players as well as younger ones like me; star names like Knocker, Steve Evans and Dave Topliss, and players signed from the lower leagues such as Kevin Harkin, Tony Dean and Terry Day. The core of the team was made up of Yorkshiremen and Welshmen, but when the Kiwis arrived we were all fascinated by their background as well.

Although we enjoyed each other's success all the time, there was a special pleasure when local blokes did well. By 1982, I was about the only local who played on a regular basis. But there were lots of Hull-born players on the fringes of the first team ready to take their chance if it came along. The '82 Cup final was a good example. Both Clive Sullivan and Tony Duke played in the replay and won medals they might not have expected to get.

Clive, of course, was already well-decorated, but Tony

Above: My first victory at Hull KR's Craven Park, Ainthorpe Junior School win under-11s Schools Cup. I'm holding the trophy and wearing the muddiest shirt.

Above: Covered in mud again, this time in a Hull Boys shirt with under-13s team-mate David Carr.

Left: Me, mum and brother Richard on holiday in France, 1978.

Right: On holiday in France again. Quite the tourist! 1978.

Left: Dad, Richard and me, France 1978

Above: A civic reception for the four Hull boys chosen to represent England Schools in 1978. I'm on the left with the classic 1970s perm. Shaun Patrick, *fourth from left*, went on to play for Hull FC.

Above: I also made the Sydney Smith cricket team, pictured front row third from left, but I couldn't bat or bowl...

Above: ...and I could run a bit too! Here I am finishing the school's 800m race, 1978.

Above: It was back to Craven Park to make my debut for the England Schools team in 1979. I'm on the back row, third from right.

Above: The magnificent seven: Alan Bell, Steve Larard, Andy Taylor, Ian Patrick, me, Peter Flanagan and Wayne Proctor. We were all chosen to tour France with England Schoolboys in 1980.

Above: A few weeks after coming back from France, I signed for Hull. Here I am shaking hands with Hull coach, Arthur Bunting, while my proud dad looks on.

Below: Half of Hull went to Wembley in 1980 for the all-Hull Challenge Cup final. Me and my future brother-in-law, Andy Taylor are asleep on the backseat of our bus heading home. Note the black and white dyed hair.

Above: Getting engaged to Janet Taylor, 1980. I hardly ever took off my England Schools jumper!

Below: The all-conquering Hull Colts team of 1981, with the Colts Cup

Above: 'Knocker' Norton was my hero. Imagine how proud I was when he presented me with the Young Player of the Year award (and I'm still wearing my England Schools jumper!)

Left: Pictured with my brother, Richard, on my wedding day, July 1981.

Above: Celebration time in the Hull dressing room after we've beaten Hull KR at Headingley in the John Player Trophy final, 1982. From left - Trevor Skerrett, Dane O'Hara, Chris Harrison, Terry Day, Paul Prendiville, Kevin Harkin, Tony Dean, 'Knocker', me, Ronnie Wileman, Charlie Stone, Keith Tindall, Mick Crane, George Robinson and Gary Kemble.

Above: More John Player celebrations with the toughest prop forwards in the game - Trevor Skerrett and Charlie Stone, 1982.

Above: Me scoring the winning try in the Challenge Cup final replay, Elland Road, 1982.

Left: ...and being congratulated by the legendary Clive Sullivan.

Duke had been at Hull through the worst of times, so we were all pleased for him when he got his chance. George Robinson was another invaluable member of the squad who never grumbled when he didn't get in the side. When he did get his chance he never let the club down.

Tony Dean and Ronnie Wileman were the jokers in the pack. They were a double act, constantly bouncing off each other. Tony was a typical scrum-half; cheeky, chirpy and always up to something. Ronnie was great company and a very decent down-to-earth bloke. Everyone was stunned when Ronnie died in late 2009. It was such a sad loss, but I'll always remember what a great laugh he was.

'Taffy' Prendiville was always good for a laugh too, and he became one of my best mates. Mind you, I still blame him for the time when Arthur Bunting dropped me for turning up to training drunk. We usually trained on Tuesday and Thursday nights but would often meet up on other nights as well if, for instance, we had a midweek match. One time, Arthur called a team meeting for a Monday night, when we could expect to watch a video and discuss the forthcoming game. At least I thought that was the arrangement.

The Boulevard was usually deserted on a Monday afternoon but I was often there, doing painting work for Arthur or helping out around the ground. On this occasion, I bumped into Knocker and Gary Kemble. It was suggested we go for a beer to kill an hour or so before the get-together. We headed for my local pub and, on the way, crossed paths with Taffy, who was doing some building work for one of my neighbours. He put down his tools and decided to join us. After a couple of pints, my neighbour came in to find out where his builder had got to. When he found Taffy having a pint with Knocker, Gary and me, he needed little persuasion to join us. So we ordered another round.

Before long, the neighbour's wife came in looking for her

husband. Finding him propping up the bar with four of the Hull FC team, she decided to join us as well. And so it went on, until three o'clock when the pub shut. At that point, we were invited back to the neighbour's house to crack open some cans. It crossed my mind that we had to be back at the Boulevard later, but we convinced each other it was only a team meeting. It wouldn't matter if we had a couple of pints, so we went back for one or two more.

When we arrived, Taffy proudly showed us the garden wall he had built earlier. Later, as we were leaving the house, I tripped over the front door step and fell straight through it. I was covered in dust and cement. There were bricks and mortar everywhere. Taffy did his nut while I laid on the floor pissing myself.

At half-seven, Knocker, Gary, Taffy and I rolled up at the Boulevard, expecting nothing more strenuous than some time in the sauna and a meeting. Unbeknown to us, though, while we'd been drinking and knocking down walls, Arthur had decided we were going to have a full-on training session and the four of us shit ourselves. We knew we would suffer.

Saying nothing, we began to lumber our way through training, heavy with beer and feeling a bit pissed off that Arthur had changed his mind. We probably would have got away with it had it not been for Taffy running around the training ground, pissed as a newt and acting like a lunatic. Anyone could see that he'd been drinking and, after a while, Arthur asked me if I'd been with him. I said that I had and Gary and Knocker also put their hands up. That left Arthur with no choice but to discipline the four of us. He dropped the lot of us from the first team and gave us a week in the reserves.

Normally, the 'A' team attracted just a few hundred dedicated fans, but when it was announced that Crooks, Norton, Prendiville and Kemble would be playing against

Rovers 'A' of all teams, over three thousand turned up. We took plenty of stick from the opposition and their fans who thought it was all quite funny. It wasn't the last time I did something like that, but it was the only time I did it to Arthur. I still felt we had been unlucky. I hadn't set out to get drunk before training, but I didn't argue. No one did. We took our punishment and got on with it.

*****

Charlie Stone was another character; the perfect example of the head-down, sixty-tackles-per-game prop that existed in England during the 1970s. He toured Australia with Great Britain in 1979 and I would love to know what he made of that, since he was a real homebird and creature of habit. One season, Arthur rearranged a training session to a Monday night and when he told the players Charlie's face turned to thunder. Actually, it already looked like thunder, but the colour drained from it and Arthur realised his prop forward wasn't happy.

'What's up, Charlie?' he asked.

'Can't train Mondays, Arthur,' said Charlie.

'Why not?'

'*Coronation Street*'s on.'

Arthur would do anything to help his players and he had a soft spot for Charlie as they both came from Featherstone. I think he even offered to bring his black and white portable in so Charlie could watch it.

Mick Crane is not widely known in rugby league but he is a legend in Hull. He played for both clubs during the 1970s and was often compared to George Best for the way he approached the game. Mick could do things on the pitch that defied belief, but he was so unpredictable his coaches never really knew what to do with him until he returned to

From Hull to Hell and Back

Hull for a second spell in 1981. Arthur got some great performances out of Mick that year and he even earned a Great Britain cap against the 1982 Kangaroos. But, off the field, Craney was hilarious. He would have us in stitches while giving Arthur headaches. I remember one occasion when Mick found himself with nobody to look after his kids, so he decided to bring them to training. While Mick was huffing and puffing through some drills on the Boulevard pitch, his kids were running up and down the speedway track and causing havoc for the groundstaff. We'd be in the middle of a routine and suddenly Mick would yell out: 'Get down from that floodlight, you little sod!'

You never knew what was going to happen next with Mick. There is a story that he could often be seen stubbing his half-time cigarette out on the edge of the pitch as he took to the field. I never saw that but it is true that he would light up before and after training. Arthur always passed comment and urged him to stop, but Mick would reply: "Arthur, me mam tried to get me to stop smoking for years and she couldn't do it. So you've got no chance.'

Welshman Graham Walters was already at the club when I signed. Gay-Gay as we called him for no obvious reason, since he was a real ladies man, had a tendency to spin tall stories. At best, he would exaggerate. Usually, he just made things up. He once told us how he had been pulled over by the police while driving too fast around Hull and how he had managed to get away without charge.

'How did you manage that, Graham?' someone asked.

'I told him I was in an emergency,' said Gay-Gay, in a broad Welsh accent.

'What emergency?' we said.

'I told them I'd had a call from a barman who said that Lee Crooks was in his pub fighting and he needed someone to come over right away and sort it out.' Not a word of it true.

One or two of his stories turned out to be genuine, but we just didn't believe him. Graham always used to tell us that he was known as 'The Royal Centre' back home and that he was well known for carrying men down the mountains of Carmarthenshire on his back. We never believed a word, until the night he was chosen to play for Wales against England at Craven Park. Half the population of Carmarthen came up to watch their local boy. As his mates poured into the bar they asked: 'Where's The Royal Centre? He's carried many men down the mountains of Carmarthenshire!' Turns out Gay-Gay had actually been a rescue volunteer.

Paul Woods played for Wales alongside Walters and was quite simply the hardest player I ever shared a rugby pitch with. He wasn't particularly big but he was a lunatic who would tear your head off if you got on his wrong side. Fortunately I never did, but lots of opponents saw the worst of Woodsy. He was sent off more times than I can remember.

Paul was a very good friend of Knocker's and once you earned his friendship he was unbelievably loyal. He had left Hull FC by the start of the 1981 season but he still had great affection for Knocker. We played Oldham in the John Player Trophy semi-final that year and, during the game, Knocker was the victim of a late, high tackle. The game was shown live on *Grandstand* and Woodsy watched it at home on his telly. Next weekend, Paul was playing against Oldham for his new club, Cardiff. As soon as he got the chance, Woodsy cleaned the culprit out, breaking his jaw. As the poor guy lay on the floor in agony, Paul stood over him and explained: 'That's for smacking my fucking mate!' Sadly, Paul died in 2007, aged just 57.

There isn't much I can say about Tim Wilby that is fit for print. Tim came from a fairly middle class background, which stood him apart from the rest of us, but he was a nice guy and really quite a character. He returned to Hull FC as chairman in the late 1990s, when he loved to mix with the supporters at the Boulevard. One day, Tim was chatting to some fans in the bar when a supporter started to have a go at him, bringing up the rumour he was gay. Whatever else you say about Tim, he certainly wasn't effeminate, that's for sure. He jumped up and thumped the bloke, then stood over him and said: 'There you go, fella. You've just been flattened by a poof!'

*****

No matter what your background, you were welcomed with open arms at Hull and expected to muck in. As a young bloke growing up in such an environment, I couldn't believe my luck. Not only was I being paid to do something I loved, I was working with my best friends and, in Knocker's case, one of my heroes. I have never told him, but I once carved his name into my desk at school. Knocker was head and shoulders the biggest personality in the team. I learned a lot from him and tried to emulate him, both on and off the field. Nobody could truly keep up with Knocker but I gave it a good shot for many years.

I loved every minute I spent with my team-mates. It didn't matter what we were doing; travelling to matches, training, having a beer, I enjoyed it all. Going out with those blokes was always a pleasure and, inevitably, we developed a bit of an entourage. We were as close as it got to celebrities in Hull in the early 1980s, so it shouldn't come as much of a surprise to learn that we also had our share of groupies. There were plenty of opportunities for mischief since we stayed overnight in hotels on a fairly regular basis, but some blokes didn't need such luxuries. The car park of the Norland pub in Hessle saw plenty of action, I can tell you.

The Hull fans have always been fantastic and the

support they gave us back then was incredible. They never missed an opportunity to talk to the players about rugby over a beer. There were always lots of supporters around whenever we went out for a drink together and we always enjoyed their company.

One of the first things Arthur Bunting did when he took over as coach was to persuade the directors not to travel on the team bus. After that, it was basically up to Arthur what we did after a game and we usually found a pub chosen by Knocker on the basis of whether it served up a decent pint of hand-pulled bitter.

We would often stop off at a hotel in Rothwell which had a disco every Sunday night. It was usually full of rugby fans and we had lots of good nights in there. Once, Mick Crane got bored of the DJ and unplugged his speakers so that James Leuluai could play his guitar and lead a singalong instead. We sang old drinking songs and Maori anthems but eventually they all merged into a medley of tunes that we would murder. One or two blokes could sing a bit, such as the Welshmen, Walters and Prendiville. Most of us couldn't.

The following year, Arthur brought in a fitness conditioner called Ken who none of us really liked very much, since it was his job to flog us in training. Ken was into country and western and liked to dress up as a cowboy on nights out. He was really keen to get on with us, so when Knocker invited him to our end-of-season celebration he accepted straight away. Unfortunately, Knocker told Ken it was a fancy dress night and suggested he should wear his cowboy outfit. When Ken turned up in denims, boots, checked shirt and neckerchief, he was horrified to see us all dressed in black tie and suits. He was livid. He had even put on a holster and pistol.

*****

We were having the time of our lives and, for four years between 1981 and 1985, were the best team in the country by far. Yet I'm afraid we didn't win as much as we should have. We never lost a semi-final but we lost far too many finals. Most famous of all was the 1983 Challenge Cup final against Featherstone.

As Cup holders and having won the Championship a fortnight earlier, we went into it as overwhelming favourites. Everybody talked of a mismatch between the millionaires from Hull and the smalltown boys from the pit village and by the time we checked into our hotel in Windsor three days before the game we were supremely confident that we would win. And why shouldn't we be? With only Featherstone to beat, the double was inevitable. We even started betting with each other on which of us would win the Lance Todd Trophy. In hindsight, it's clear our mental approach wasn't right. We were ripe for an upset.

At Wembley the year before, we'd gone for a few beers together in the week before the game but, before the Featherstone match, we pushed the boat out a bit too much. Don't get me wrong, I never thought there was anything wrong with our preparation at the time; I enjoyed myself as much as anyone.

You only had to look at our suits to see we were headed for a fall. We did our pre-match walkabout wearing lime green suits, white shoes and yellow ties. That look was naff, even in the 1980s. In 1982, I had been shitting myself when I stepped out onto the pitch. In 1983, I was wandering around dressed like an ice cream waving a big sponge hand at our fans in the crowd.

Our actual preparation that week was no different from the year before. Arthur wouldn't have let us slack off in training even if we had wanted to, so we prepared hard on the training pitch and went about our business in the normal way. The difference was mental: we underestimated our opponents. That's a very dangerous thing to do in the week before a cup final.

*****

Once the game kicked off, Featherstone came at us with an intensity we hadn't expected and it knocked us off our game plan. They were well organised, hard working and very, very motivated. They must have taken one look at us in our green suits and thought: 'look at those arrogant bastards'. We played right into their hands. Before we knew it, they were all over us and the referee probably got a bit carried away as well, sensing he might be involved in a huge upset. The odd decision began to go their way.

In seventeen years as a player, there are two occasions when I can remember being on the wrong end of a shock result. One was while playing for Castleford when we were overwhelming favourites to beat Rochdale in the Regal Trophy. The other was our Wembley defeat by Featherstone. The circumstances were just about identical.

For a player, it's a peculiar experience. As soon as you realise things aren't going to plan, you convince yourself there is still plenty of time to turn the game around and that you'll run away with it in the second half. Once the second half starts and you're still struggling to put the opposition away, you tell yourself 'we can get them in the last twenty minutes', or the last ten minutes or the last five. Before you know it, there are only a few minutes left. You and your team-mates start to panic. You force things, take the wrong options and then you've blown it.

At Wembley in 1983, we had plenty of opportunities to win the game early on but we never took them. By the final quarter we were only slightly ahead when we should have been forty points clear. We were nervous; they had their tails up. By the time David Hobbs strolled through Keith Bridges' tackle to level the scores, all hopes of a record win had gone. We just hoped we could scramble home any way we could.

While we tried to find our rhythm, Featherstone were awarded a controversial penalty when Charlie Stone was judged to have head-butted Peter Smith. Steve Quinn kicked the goal and we found ourselves behind for the first time. There's a debate about whether Charlie nutted Peter or whether it was the other way round, but it shouldn't have mattered. We should have been out of sight by then. Once they took the lead we couldn't get the ball off them. Even when we managed to get some possession, they would force an error or we were penalised for some offence or other.

At Wembley, you are a long way from the bench and the supporters. It is very hard to judge how long there is to go. Nevertheless, in those final few minutes we knew we were in trouble and started to panic. Everyone sensed that a major shock was about to happen but we seemed to be powerless to have any impact on what was going on. The hooter went and we'd lost 14-12.

It was the biggest shock that Wembley had seen for years and I was devastated; the lowest point of my short career. I was inconsolable, in floods of tears right there on the pitch. James Leuluai saw me and couldn't quite believe how upset I was. I sobbed all the way through the lap of honour and couldn't wait to get off the field. We all knew we had let ourselves down badly. We had spent all year demoralising every team in the league and then we had lost in the Cup final to a team that had almost been relegated. There was no way to explain it.

There was always a civic reception at Hull Guildhall whenever we came back from Wembley. Unfortunately, we never won on any of our visits, so they tended to fall a bit flat. The reception after the 1983 final was the worst of all. All of our achievements that season - winning the League, the Yorkshire Cup and almost beating the Australian tourists - counted for nothing. We were embarrassed and hurting very badly. Mick Crane always tried to find a funny angle to every situation and did his best to cheer everyone up. While we were on the balcony, Mick grabbed the Lord Mayor's hat, put it on his head and announced that he was cutting taxes on beer and fags. It raised a laugh but, to be honest, we all just wanted to go home.

*****

When the shock of our defeat wore off, there were lots of excuses flying around. Dubious refereeing decisions, such as the incident where Featherstone's Terry Hudson kicked our scrum-half, Kevin Harkin, in the head at an early scrum, which went unpunished. The late penalty against Charlie, which could have easily gone the other way. But, if we were honest with ourselves, we should have won the game easily. This could have been the year that we won the double and laid to rest the jinx that the club have never won at Wembley.

We should have known the game was a potential banana skin but our approach typified our mentality. We would have called it confidence but, in reality, it had turned to arrogance and it wasn't just the players to blame. A number of decisions were made that year which summed up the attitude at the club. For example, we had so many players and so much strength in depth that the directors even considered entering our 'A' team into the Second Division and calling them 'Hull White Star' - Hull FC's original name when it was formed in 1865.

We also felt that we were more than a match for the best club teams down under and, rather than give the players the

summer off, the club had organised an end-of-season tour of
New Zealand and Australia. I think the objective was to give
us a chance to learn from some of the best but it was an ill-
fated trip. By the time the squad reached Australia, it had
been decimated by injuries and Arthur was forced to call on
a bunch of reserve grade players to make up a team. Even
our physio, Ray Norrie, was on the bench in the last game. I
can't comment much on how the tour degenerated into farce
because I wasn't on it. When the prospects were discussed
earlier in the season, the general view amongst the players
was that it was basically an end-of-season jolly to the other
side of the world. When Janet realised that, there was no
way she was going to let me go.

To be fair to Janet, our lives had changed very quickly.
Even though I was still only nineteen, I had a wife and child,
and there was another on the way. Over the previous two
years, I had spent large parts of the year away from home
playing for Hull and Great Britain. I had also spent the last
summer in Papua New Guinea and Australia, and Janet was
understandably not best pleased at the thought of me going
away again for another couple of weeks. And so, while some
of my team-mates flew off to let their hair down and enjoy
playing some games together, I stayed home to mull over
my disappointment at the way the season had ended.

*****

After losing against Featherstone, the wind was knocked out
of our sails massively. Nobody talked much about it but I
definitely felt we were underachieving. Nevertheless, there
was a lot of determination to put things right.

We were determined to get back to Wembley to make
amends as soon as possible, but the following campaign was
a disappointment by our high standards. Despite signing

the Australian scrum-half Peter Sterling for a brief spell in mid-season, all we managed to win was the Yorkshire Cup and we were toppled as Champions by Hull KR, which was very hard to take.

By the start of 1984-5, I think everyone at the club felt that it ought to be our year. Peter Sterling returned for the full season, as did another international, Fred Ah Kuoi. With Kemble, Leuluai and O'Hara still in the side, Knocker at his peak and Schoey and myself now established internationals, the team was perfectly balanced. With so much experienceto choose from, I was surprised when Arthur asked me to be captain.

At the time, there weren't many people who agreed with Arthur's choice. I still had a lot to learn about how to conduct myself off the field and there were several occasions when I landed myself in trouble and needed to be bailed out.

*****

We had been going for a drink together after training for a few years and, once we began training in Hessle, just west of Hull, we began to use a pub called Top House. I wouldn't say we were all big drinkers, but everyone went along to enjoy each other's company and have a few laughs. Within a few weeks of starting to use the pub, word got out and a number of fans began to join us. It wasn't long before we had an entourage and one group of female supporters, in particular, became known as 'Pam's Posse'.

Pam Thurstan is still a huge Hull fan and, back then, she and a group of friends used to follow us around. Wherever we went, those girls seemed to be there, much to the irritation of Janet and the other wives, who could often be heard wondering: 'How the hell did those women get in here?' Having a group of women around was great, of course, and it also helped us get into one or two places that otherwise wouldn't have admitted a large group of single blokes. One club in Batley wouldn't let the team in, so Pam and her mates started going in with the players, one by one, pretending to be a couple. Once inside, the girls would slip out of the fire escape and go back around the front, ready to twin up with someone else.

One of the group, Sue, was a WPC for Humberside police, which came in very handy indeed. Everyone down at the station knew that Sue was good mates with most of the Hull FC players and if one of the boys ever got into a scrape, they'd pass the case onto her. Sue would do her best to smooth it all over and keep the story out of the public eye.

Sue helped me out once or twice too. I'd been out for a drink in Hull one night with Carl Sanderson and a couple of his mates and we ended up at a pub, The Yorkshireman. We were a bit pissed and I was being a bit boisterous and flirty with one of the barmaids. I thought she was taking it in good spirits and I got a bit carried away. When I put my hand up her skirt, she understandably took offence and I was told to leave. I insisted on finishing my drink and gave them a bit of abuse as I left. I was being daft and should have just walked away, but I suppose my pride had been injured and I acted immaturely. I couldn't resist one last gesture and as, I banged on the window of the door, my fist went through it. Apart from being a bit shocked, my reaction was to start laughing but, as soon as the window broke, one of Carl's mates tore off down the street and disappeared into the nearby bus station.

'What the fuck's got into him?' I asked Carl.

'He only got out of prison last week and he's on probation,' he said.

We decided we had better get out of there as well and so we headed for home. The inevitable call came in to police HQ from the landlady of The Yorkshireman and Sue was asked if she wanted to deal with it. So she rang me up and asked if it was true. 'I can't lie to you, Sue,' I said. I never saw the point of lying if I'd done something wrong. In any case, Sue had already been down there and sorted it all out. I just had to go back to the pub, apologise to the staff and pay £25 to get the window fixed.

Contrary to what people might think, we weren't out drinking every night and you have to remember that some players would usually drive back to West Yorkshire after they'd had just a couple of pints. Nevertheless, there were times when we went a bit mental and obviously that didn't always keep me in good favour with Janet. I remember coming home late one night to find she had locked me out and I couldn't wake her up to let me in. It was freezing and I was tired. As I walked down our terrace, I noticed a set of ladders propped up in a neighbour's front garden. I also noticed our bedroom window was ajar. As an occasional painter and decorator, I was more than comfortable up a ladder so figured it would be easy to climb up and let myself in through the window.

Being worse for wear meant that it wasn't easy to handle a set of ladders. There was plenty of clattering around and by the time I scrambled to the top Janet was wide awake and standing at the open window to greet me. I thought I might be able to charm her into letting me in but she was still pissed off with me and pushed the ladder away from the window, meaning I went arse over tit back into the front garden. I felt like I was in a *Tom and Jerry* cartoon.

I was living on Perth Street West at that time but, a little later, I stayed out late again, this time in Castleford and Pam of Pam's Posse drove me back to Hull. I was drunk and soon fell asleep in the back of the car, not waking up until she switched the engine off. 'What we doing here, Pam?' I said, 'I don't live here any more. I've moved.'

From Hull to Hell and Back

There were times when even I couldn't remember where I lived. After we'd moved to Graham Avenue, I came home late one night and, by mistake, walked up the next door neighbour's path rather than my own. We hadn't lived there long so I didn't realise it wasn't my own house even when I went through the front door, walked into the lounge and sat on the sofa. It was only when I tried to find the remote control that my neighbour took objection and asked what the hell I was doing sitting in his front room.

Even though I was married with a daughter, I was still only young and I found it very hard to say 'no' to all of the temptations that came my way. Few people realise just how well-known the Hull FC team was and every time I walked into a pub there was no end of people who wanted to talk to me and buy me a drink. There were many occasions when I would set out with the intention of not getting drunk, but I found that I didn't have much willpower. I was twenty years old and everyone in Hull wanted to buy me a beer. How could I say no?

*****

Arthur was well aware of the scrapes I was getting into but he gambled that the extra responsibility of captaincy would do me good. David Topliss would still be club captain but it was me who led the team out on match days and I suspect that Arthur also liked the idea of having a local bloke doing that. I never hid my passion for Hull FC and I was forever going on about how much the club meant to me. Being made captain was a huge honour and, when I think about how the next three years panned out, 1984-85 was definitely the peak of my Hull career.

To be honest, the job was made fairly easy by the fact that I was captaining a team which didn't need much leading.

On paper, we had the best side in the country but our league form was patchy and we saved our best performances for cup competitions. We played seventeen cup games and reached three finals, two against Hull Kingston Rovers.

Whenever we played Rovers, we felt that we weren't just competing to be the best team in the city, but the best in the country. Rovers had their own share of international players such as Gary Prohm, Mark Broadhurst, Gavin Miller and Gordon Smith; there wasn't much to choose between us all year. First spoils of the season, though - the Yorkshire Cup - went our way. We were trailing 12-0 at half time but stormed back in the second half, inspired by Knocker and two tries from Gary Kemble, to win easily.

It was one of those seasons with many big games and it wasn't long before we also qualified for the John Player Trophy final where, again, we would play Rovers. I recall the quarter-final at Dewsbury all too well. Halfway through the first half, I went to make a tackle on a Dewsbury forward and caught an elbow in the face. I went down as though I'd been shot and it felt like all the air had been sucked out of my head. I struggled to breathe at first and had to be carried off for the first time ever.

The next day, I was taken to hospital back in Hull to discover that I had a depressed fracture of the cheekbone. To fix it, they had to make a cut in the side of my face and use a metal rod to flick the cheekbone back into place. It sounded like something I might do to knock a dent out of the side of my car. To be honest it wasn't as painful as it sounds. I was sent home and told to rest over the Christmas break.

I was out for around four weeks, the longest injury I had suffered until that point. Being injured over Christmas and New Year isn't necessarily a bad thing for a sportsman, but I wasn't able to take much advantage of the free time as I had to be very careful what I ate and didn't feel much like getting drunk.

The break healed well, though, and physio Ray Norrie was confident I would make the final. Sports medicine wasn't very advanced in 1985 and a couple of days before the game Ray 'tested' my cheekbone by laying me down on the treatment table, kneeling over me, placing a folded towel on my cheekbone and pressing down hard to see if the bone could support his weight. I asked him how I would know if it hadn't healed. 'You'll know, mate,' he said. 'You'll know.'

Luckily, my cheekbone was up to the task and I was passed fit to play. The weather in Hull had been awful all week and on the morning of the game the Boothferry Park pitch was covered in two inches of snow. Underneath the white stuff though, the pitch wasn't too hard and the referee decided that the game could go ahead, providing the lines on the pitch could be cleared so that the players knew where the try line was. Peter Sterling thought it was all completely hilarious. He'd probably never seen snow before and he had certainly never played on it. He was bouncing around the changing room, saying how crazy it was that we were playing on snow. When he was thrown the orange ball we would be using, he thought it was a wind-up.

'I can't believe you blokes have orange footy balls. You must play on snow all the time,' he said.

Just as in the Yorkshire Cup final, Rovers led 12-0 at half-time but this time we were unable to come back and that is exactly how the game ended. It was disappointing and reminded us just how good Rovers were at grinding out results when it mattered. As with all derby defeats, it hurt. Once again, we had lost out to them in a major final but the disappointment spurred us on to an unbeaten run of eight matches, which also included the first few rounds of the Challenge Cup. I think we all felt that we needed to win the

Cup in 1985 to lay to rest the disappointment of our last visit in 1983.

The quarter-final against Widnes was shown live on BBC TV on a Saturday afternoon, but that never seemed to affect the number of Hull fans who would turn up to watch us. There was a huge crowd at the Boulevard to watch a tight game finish six-all. The following Wednesday, we went to their place for the replay. Very few teams went to Naughton Park and won and Widnes were hot favourites, but we still had plenty of character about us. We were terrific that night; there must have been around five thousand Hull fans there and they cheered us on to a great performance.

Early on, the Widnes forwards decided Sterlo would pose the biggest threat and they tried to take him out of the game any way they could. After one particularly high tackle, Sterlo took a bad cut to the head and spent the rest of the match wearing a headband stained with blood. But he and Knocker were brilliant and we won 19-12. I was so proud to captain the team, particularly when we played like that, and I began to get very excited at the prospect of leading us out at Wembley. We were now only eighty minutes away.

*****

We were certainly good to watch and the two semi-finals against Castleford were massive occasions.

The first looked to be slipping away from us until Sterlo scored a great, late try out wide and I kicked the conversion to level the scores at ten points each. That's how it ended and an already congested fixture list was made worse by us having to meet Cas again four days later for the replay. Most people probably won't realise that we played another game in between those two Cup ties! In making three Cup finals that season, we'd had lots of games postponed earlier in the year which led to a massive fixture backlog. It's hard to imagine how we did it but we played ten games in seventeen days during April. The only way Arthur could fulfil the fixtures was to use practically every bloke on the books so, two days after the semi-final, a reserve team went up to Barrow and drew 12-12.

A couple of days after that, the first team travelled over to Leeds again to have a second try at settling things with Castleford. Another two days later we were due to play Hull KR at home in the Good Friday derby but our chances of winning the league had gone and we were totally focused on the Cup. In any case, games against Cas in those days were just like derbies for many of our lads who, like Arthur, came from either Castleford or Featherstone. They were usually hot-blooded affairs and the semi-final replay of 1985 was no different.

The match was already close to bubbling over when Ian Orum flattened Gary Kemble with a high tackle. All the Hull lads piled in and the game erupted. Gary was stretchered off with concussion but the ref did no more than give Orum a warning. We were all furious and even Arthur Bunting came storming onto the pitch to have a go at the referee. Arthur was sent off for, I think, the first time in his career. When Cas next had the ball, our tackling was so fierce they could barely get over the advantage line. The Orum incident had really fired us all up and the crowd, most of them from Hull, was right behind us as well.

Amidst all the battling, I was having quite an impact, setting up three tries in the first half and landing three goals, one of them from the touchline. As the game settled down, Sterlo and me started to become more and more dominant. If they were going to win, Cas had to come up with a way of stopping us. There was no doubt in anyone's minds that when Malcolm Reilly came on as substitute he would try to stop Sterlo, by fair means or foul. At the first opportunity, he pounced on Sterlo at a scrum and roughed him up, which resulted in another brawl.

The game erupted again just before half-time. We were given a penalty near halfway and I stepped up to take the restart. We were just happy to run the clock down and get into the dressing room for a break but, for some reason, as soon I tapped the ball, I decided to roll over at the feet of the Cas defender and conceded an involuntary tackle. It was a stupid thing to do and, straight away, I knew I had dropped a clanger. Cas were awarded a penalty and, with the hooter about to go, Malcolm Reilly decided to hoist a bomb. Peter Sterling caught the ball behind our posts and, in doing so, took another big shot from Malcolm. Sterlo took exception and all the Hull lads piled in for a twenty-six-man brawl. I found myself in front of Reilly and, for a few moments, we were throwing punches at each other. It didn't bother me in the slightest that Malcolm was one of the most feared and well respected players in the game; he had clouted one of my mates who I felt obliged to back up. I had gone toe-to-toe with some of the biggest, toughest forwards in the world by that stage and I wasn't going to back away from Malcolm Reilly. While it was all going on I could just see, out of the corner of my eye, Garry Schofield getting battered by a pair of Cas players. He was pinned against the wall behind the tryline at Headingley, so a few of their fans joined in.

As we were walking off at half-time, my blood was still up and I couldn't resist giving Malcolm some abuse. He wasn't used to being treated so disrespectfully and was so angry he could barely contain himself. I don't know why but Malcolm never came out for the second half and we went on to win. Just before the end, I heard the announcement that I had been chosen as the man of the match and I was chuffed to bits. I knew it would be one of those games I would always remember and to be chosen as the best player on the pitch meant a hell of a lot. And, of course, it now started to sink in; I would be leading this team out at Wembley.

As both sets of players mingled in the Headingley bar afterwards, Castleford's John Joyner pulled me to one side. 'Keep out of Malcolm's way, Lee', he said. 'He's not right happy about what you said to him at half-time'. I was a less mature bloke in those days and I just saw that as a challenge. To my mind, if I avoided him it would look as though I was afraid. Before I knew it I was heading in the direction of Malcolm Reilly. Once I reached him, I didn't say much, just stuck my hand out and thanked him for a good game. I don't know what he thought of me and my downright cheek, but he just shook my hand and that was the end of that.

People always comment on my age when they talk about how I behaved back then, but I never gave it a moment's thought. It never mattered to me that I was seventeen when I got married, or nineteen when I first played for Britain, or twenty-one when I captained Hull and had a fight with Malcolm Reilly. It didn't faze me. But while I was physically mature, I guess I still had a bit to learn, especially when I went looking for confrontations with people like Malcolm. He deserved a bit more respect than I gave him that day and it was to his credit that he recognised my behaviour as just a bit of immaturity. That's probably why he didn't smack me in the mouth. That, and the fact that I'd have hit him back.

*****

The 1985 Challenge Cup final is remembered for many reasons. There were ten overseas players (a record), ten tries (a record) and the game is widely acknowledged as being the best final ever. Few people remember that, at twenty-one years of age, I was the youngest ever player to captain a Cup final team and hardly anybody but me remembers how it was my fault that we didn't win.

Captaining a team at Wembley is a big deal for anyone. I don't think I had much more to do in the build-up but I remember feeling a bit of apprehension at the prospect of having to introduce the team to the visiting dignitaries before kick-off. It would have been quite embarrassing if I hadn't been able to remember the names of my team-mates. As captain, I fully intended to lead by example. I wanted to play a blinder and help us win the Cup but it didn't turn out that way. I spent too long worrying about other people and what they were doing rather than concentrating on my own game and, as a result, didn't make the impact I had hoped for. Sterlo and Knocker played brilliantly and almost won us the game but I was disappointed with my own performance. I was also on goal-kicking duty and missed four kicks. If I had kicked three, we'd have won. I didn't, we lost, and instead of being the only Hull captain ever to lift the Cup at Wembley, I sat on the pitch in tears while the Wigan players celebrated. I was still very emotional when I spoke to the press and can remember telling them that, one day, I would return to Wembley and win the Cup for Hull FC.

They say losing a semi-final is the biggest disappointment you can face but I don't agree. Blaming myself for my team losing a cup final is one of the hardest things I have ever had to deal with. It was the first time in my career that I had felt such a level of responsibility and it certainly knocked a bit of the swagger out of me for a while. Some people said that I had too much responsibility, but I didn't think so. I felt equipped to handle the pressure but just didn't do it on the day. Other players might hold their hands up and say they were as much to blame for the defeat as I was, but that doesn't make it any easier for me to deal with.

From Hull to Hell and Back

*****

Nothing was ever quite the same again after 1985. Within a few years, Wigan were back at Wembley and went on to dominate the sport for years. For Hull, that was about as good as it got. Within a couple of years, the money ran out and half the players were moved on, including myself.

At Hull FC, we had always thought of ourselves as the most professional club in the country and we thoroughly enjoyed our time as the best team in the game. But for whatever reason we never quite fulfilled our potential. We thought we were dominant when we made it to a couple of Cup finals a year, but Wigan would soon show everybody what dominance really meant.

When I look back on the period between the Cup finals of 1982 and 1985, I think we sold ourselves short and that seems to sum up that period of my career. I never fulfilled my earning potential because I was never all that bothered about money, and my team never saw their full potential because we just weren't ruthless enough when it came to the biggest games of all.

Whenever we lost one of those big games, we told ourselves that we'd go back again and put it right next time. After 1985, we never got the chance.

5

Wests Life

After the Challenge Cup final, most of the team went on the piss. There were lots of end-of-season functions to attend. On the morning after one of those, Janet and I set off, me still in my club suit, on our first journey to Australia together.

Thirty-six hours later, via a stopover in Japan, we arrived in Sydney and were met by Rick Wade, chief executive of Western Suburbs - my new club.

*****

I'd been smitten with Australia the first time I went there, in 1982 with the GB Colts. I was impressed by the lifestyle, the climate and I loved how rugby league is such a popular sport, especially in Sydney. More than anything, I had great respect for the Aussie people; they were straightforward, honest and optimistic. I had been very proud they rated me as a player whenever I played against the Kangaroos and I was very keen to lock horns with them again.

From Hull to Hell and Back

The approach to play in Australia came originally via Paul Harrison, rugby league writer for *The Sun*. He'd heard that Wests were looking for a back row forward and he suggested my name. After a couple of years playing for my country, I was reasonably well known in Australia and with the ban on international transfers lifted a number of clubs had begun to sign up English players for short spells. When the offer came my way, I felt it would be a great experience for me, Janet and the kids, and accepted straight away.

Steve Norton had spent some time playing for Manly in the 1970s and knew a bit about the game down under. He advised me that if I ever had the chance to play in Australia, I should sign for one of the top sides. 'Pick a club with plenty of money, big crowds and a decent team', he said. I usually listened to what Knocker had to say and welcomed his advice, so I'm not sure how I came to sign for Western Suburbs, who had finished bottom the previous season with average crowds of less than four thousand a week.

But the more I found out about Wests, the more I liked the idea of playing for them. The fact that they had struggled the previous season actually appealed to me. I felt I might be able to make more of an impact at a club like that and, after all, they were the only club that had actually offered me a deal so I didn't have a lot of choice in the matter.

I never really thought much about how playing in Australia might develop my own game. If I had, I might have had second thoughts and opted to join a better side, but I was happy with my choice and, for once, forthright in telling Janet that I had agreed to play in Australia and that I wanted her and the kids to come out there with me.

After he met us at the airport, Rick took us straight over to the training ground for me to meet my new team-mates. He had also arranged for the press to be there to take some photos of the new signing. It was seven in the morning and

I was still stinking from the thirty-six hour flight, not to mention the beer I'd drunk on the journey. So I'm not sure their initial impression of me was very good. They also probably thought it odd that I had turned up in Australia wearing a Hull FC club suit.

Ken Gentle was my new coach and after introductions were made he asked if I was ready to play the next day against South Sydney. I wasn't sure I was ready to step straight off the plane and into first grade so I played in the under-23 competition instead, as a curtain-raiser to the main event. I played half a match and my only memory is that the young blokes from Souths tried to kick ten bells of shit out of me. I knew it was going to be tough so I kept getting stuck into them and had a decent enough game. I also managed to kick a couple of goals from the touchline which really pissed them off. Wests won the senior fixture and man of the match was a second-rower called Craig Clarke. As he accepted his award, Craig's first words were something like: 'I hope Lee Crooks isn't holding his breath waiting to take my position in the side'. I knew that the Aussies were very competitive but that sentiment didn't make me feel entirely welcome. I didn't mind a bit of banter but, judging by the way they had been playing, they needed all the help they could get. The win was their second of the season and they were next to bottom after round ten. I hadn't really done my homework, but it didn't take me long to realise that it wasn't going to be a walk in the park.

*****

The following week, Janet and I began to settle into our new life in Australia. After the first training session, all the boys went over to a pub, the Lidcombe Hotel. The owner was a club sponsor and when the players rolled in he had cold beers ready and a pile of thick steaks on the barbecue. It was just as I had imagined and a great welcome.

Another bloke who helped me settle in was a guy called Herbie Smailes, one of the club's strappers, originally from Featherstone. Soon after we arrived, Herbie took me out for the day. After picking up some training gear in the morning, we called at a pub belonging to one of his mates. I was keen to get to know as many people as possible and quite happy to have a few beers. Needless to say, a few pints turned into a major drinking session. We stayed out all day and I didn't get home until around half-ten that night, steaming drunk.

Training was at seven the next morning - a Saturday - and I wasn't in great shape when I turned up. I was due to make my debut the very next day and was shitting myself that I would be in trouble before I'd even played a first team game. But as soon as I pulled into the club car park I realised I needn't have worried. Most of my team-mates were stumbling out of their cars, at least as hungover as I was. Some had slept in their cars by the look of it. The fact that I wasn't the only one to turn up with a hangover made me feel more at ease.

As training got underway, it was obvious the majority of lads had been out drinking the night before. As we packed down, the stench of stale beer was overwhelming. Anyway, we trained hard and I was determined not to show any weakness. Wests had spent a lot of money bringing me over and I didn't want to let anyone down the next day at Penrith.

Craig Clarke had nothing much to worry about; I was picked to play alongside him against the Panthers. I scored a try, we won the game, 18-9, and it was just as well that my debut had gone so well because when Ken Gentle found out that Herbie had taken me on the piss he gave him a right bollocking. Rick Wade, on the other hand, reckoned I could go out every Friday if it would guarantee performances like that. As pleased as I was with the outcome, I didn't intend to make it a regular feature of my time in Oz.

After the game, I was surprised to find the dressing room so full of people. There were media, sponsors and even some fans. It was totally different from what happened in England; everyone was cracking open the beers and having a great old time. Suddenly, I heard a familiar accent. 'Now then, Lee. How you doing, mate?' It was a Hull FC fan who, it turned out, had emigrated to Australia the year before. I still don't know why he was in the Wests changing room, but he was very friendly and invited Janet and me out to his house in Penrith the following week for a barbecue. At the time, it was great to be meeting so many friendly people and, when we got there, his house was full of other ex-pats, most of them from Hull. It was great to hear so many familiar accents and to be made to feel so at home.

Rick couldn't have been more welcoming either and he was always making sure that I was settling in well. Shortly after the game in Penrith, he took me out for a night in Kings Cross. We spent some time bar-hopping and finished the night off at a Chinese restaurant. He was very generous and had spent so much money that, when it came time to settle the bill, he didn't have enough left and nor did I. He didn't know what to do, so I told him exactly what I was going to do and promptly bolted for the door. Halfway down the street I turned around expecting to be chased by an angry Chinese waiter, only to find Rick right behind me. He wasn't your typical chief executive.

It wasn't all highlights. The accommodation originally arranged for us was a real dive and the club had obviously tried to cut corners by trying to get us into a place that belonged to someone there. It was damp, dingy and nothing like what we had been promised. I told Rick it wasn't good enough. He admitted it wasn't in great condition but said: 'I thought you might be able to brighten it up a bit yourself, Lee, with you being a painter.' Not only was he trying to get me to live in his granny's old house, he expected me to decorate the place as well.

There was no way I was going to let Janet and the kids stay there, but it took a few days to find us somewhere else. My early performances didn't harm the negotiations and I managed to get us moved to a much bigger apartment for the rest of our stay. Wests weren't a wealthy club but they did their best to look after us.

The decision to go to Australia had never been about money. In Hull, I earned ten grand a year plus winning pay. The short contract at Wests only added another five grand to that. There were obviously lots of times when I would be out playing, training and socialising with my new team-mates and Janet would be left alone. But we found plenty of time to explore Sydney and other parts of the country and we enjoyed every bit of it. Garry Schofield is one of my best mates and he was playing for Balmain at the same time. Our families only lived half an hour from each other, so Janet and I spent lots of time with Garry and his girlfriend, Adele. Although we trained four times a week, we still had lots of time on our hands and also got to know many of our team-mates very well. They would invite us over for barbecues and Garry and I also spent time ten-pin bowling and even playing golf, although I am one of the worst golfers I know, so I didn't spend as much time on the course as Garry.

Arthur Bunting and his wife, Margaret, also came out during that spell and both Garry and I were keen to have them stay with us. Arthur dealt with it very diplomatically by spending a week with each family. It was great to have familiar faces around and I think Arthur enjoyed it even more. He was as proud of us as we were of each other.

After just a few days I realised that, even though Wests

weren't the best team in the country, there was still much that I could learn. I was very keen to find out anything I could about the Australian game. I realised that aspects of the Australian competition were much tougher than in England. Physically, the players were generally fitter and stronger, largely because of a tougher training regime than we had at Hull which, in itself, was pretty advanced. The Aussie clubs made more use of weight training, boxing and conditioning in general. It took me a few weeks to catch up with the fitness of my team-mates, but considering I had played forty-odd games in the previous nine months I never felt I lacked fitness or stamina.

*****

While down under, I tried to work out why the Australian game was so much stronger than the English one but if I had an easy answer then I would be running the RFL. It really comes down to the fact that there is so much competition out there; competition for the teams and competition for places. That's because so many young men are playing the game in a quality environment.

Whatever sport they're playing, kids learn how to play instinctively if they are given the freedom to do so. That requires good facilities and lots of opportunities of the kind I had when I played on the fields behind our house. There is no doubt that children today have far less freedom than I had thirty years ago.

When I was a kid, there never seemed to be much concern over where we were; we'd be on a field playing sport until it got too dark and we had to come in. There were plenty more open fields than there are now and a lot less fear about what might happen to us. Nobody was bothered if we played with bigger kids, even if that meant we got hurt now and then. It was all part of growing up; sometimes you got hurt, so you learned to avoid the things that hurt you.

I don't think the Australians have the same constraints we have; they have an outdoor lifestyle and I soon noticed how much open space there was where young people could play sport. There were pitches and parks all over the Sydney area as well as sports centres and gyms. The climate was better and society seemed to be less fearful of what might happen to young people if they were given some freedom. Consequently, there were so many young people playing rugby league that they had to be pretty special to succeed, which drives up standards across the board. Even though amateur rugby was quite healthy in Hull, it didn't seem as prominent as it was in Sydney. Over the years, I suspect the gulf in terms of the number of people playing has widened.

*****

I actually enjoyed playing against the Aussies week in, week out because they didn't know how to cope with my style of play. They played straight up and down with not too much skill, especially amongst the forwards. I could do things with the ball they didn't expect. As a result, I could make other blokes in the team look really good and, of course, that made my team-mates value my contribution even more. Early on, I noticed that our stand-off, Trevor Cogger, had a bit of pace so I told him that whenever I made half a break, he should follow me; he wouldn't always get the ball but, when he did, he'd be through a gap. It worked a treat and I made Trevor look like Garry Schofield that season. In return, because he was always on the end of my passes, he made me look pretty good as well.

My personal success meant that I was more than happy at Wests. I felt appreciated by everybody at the club. Even the fact that they played in black and white, just like Hull FC, was important to me, in a daft way. Nevertheless, I was aware that there might be other offers on the table if I decided to return in 1986. From Schoey, I became aware that Balmain were interested in signing me and had to admit that the prospect of playing for a better team was appealing.

Rick Wade was very keen to keep me, though, and he kept trying to get me to re-sign for weeks before we were due to go home. After the last game of the season he took me out for a farewell drink and asked me what it would cost to get me to sign for another year. By the end of the night, I drunkenly told him that if he doubled my wages, I'd sign for Wests again. The next morning, he was round at our house with a contract ready for my signature. I signed it and that's how I came to spend my second year at Western Suburbs.

But it wasn't the same at Wests in 1986. On the face of it, it ought to have been an even better year for me. The club had shown some ambition and signed up more English players, bringing over Des Drummond and John Henderson from Leigh and Deryck Fox from Featherstone, but the team didn't improve much. Dessie didn't play many games and I think Foxy struggled a bit at that level.

In 1986, the team only won eight games all season - six of them in the fifteen matches I played in - and finished next to bottom for the second year running. The crowds were up but I just didn't enjoy it as much. The novelty of playing and living in Australia had worn off and, away from rugby, my relationship with Janet was breaking down.

When I was offered the chance to go to Australia again the following year, I opted finally to join up with Garry at Balmain Tigers. The Tigers had made the play-offs in 1986 and their success was partly due to the tries that Schoey had scored. Garry and I played very well together for club and country and I looked forward to us teaming up again.

From Hull to Hell and Back

*****

The week before we were due to fly home, we began to tie up loose ends. After my final training session, we all went out for a beer. I was enjoying a final drink with the blokes who had been my team-mates for two years and we decided to go on elsewhere. I'd run out of cash so I nipped back to my car to grab my wallet but, by the time I reached it, I had changed my mind and decided to go home instead. Stupidly, I decided to drive.

I'd had half a dozen beers but the roads were quiet and I felt perfectly okay for a mile or two until I felt something wrong with one of the wheels. I assumed I had a flat tyre and pulled over to take a closer look. It was then that I noticed the police patrol car that had pulled over behind me. I decided to stay in the car while the two officers got out of theirs and walked towards me. As I wound down my window I must have leaned against the door because, when one of them opened it, I practically fell out of the car. There was no point trying to claim that I was sober and I prepared myself for the worst.

The older cop recognised me straight away and told me he was a Balmain fan. He could see that I was trying to co-operate and said that he would do what he could to try and get me out of the mess I'd found myself in. His younger colleague had other ideas, though, and once he realised I was a professional footy player, he started to think he could make a bit of a name for himself.

They took me back to the police station and locked me up for a couple of hours while they decided what to do. Eventually, once I had sobered up, they took me back to my car, helped me change the wheel and let me go. But I had still been charged and, because I was due to fly home a couple of days later, I think they rushed through my appearance at the magistrates court. I had to appear the very next day.

I had no time to prepare any sort of defence so I just decided to turn up and take whatever was coming. Everyone I spoke to said that I would get away with a warning, so I wasn't too concerned when I turned up at court. But when the judge began by saying that the maximum penalty for driving under the influence was seven years hard labour, I broke into a cold sweat at the thought they might decide to make an example of me and that I might actually get locked up. Once my representative explained that I wasn't driving erratically and told them I had no previous convictions for drink-driving, I managed to escape with a $700 fine and an eighteen-month ban. The fine was about a week's wages so it wasn't the end of the world, and the driving ban only applied to Australian roads. I felt I had got away quite lightly, especially after the judge's opening comments.

I was still an arrogant bastard, though. As relieved as I was to walk away from court with a fine and a ban, I still jumped in my car and drove home.

6

Marching on Together?

In 1990, after two-and-a-bit years at Headingley, Leeds sold me to Castleford for exactly the same fee they had paid to get me there. To many, it looked as if Leeds were cutting their losses on someone who hadn't lived up to the expectations of being the world's most expensive player. Others thought I'd be relieved to put my Leeds nightmare behind me and start afresh elsewhere.

To be honest, that's not the way it was at all. I had found some form and happiness at Leeds during 1989 and didn't actually want to leave. Rather than being desperate to get rid of me, there were lots of people at Leeds trying to persuade me to stay only days before I left. There was nothing inevitable about it. I could have quite easily played out my career for them - if I hadn't been so badly let down by the club directors.

One thing guaranteed to put my back up is when people in authority don't honour their commitments and act with integrity. In my view, the board at Leeds made a pledge that they didn't honour. Once they had done that, there was no going back. I had to leave.

*****

After signing in June 1987, Leeds allowed me to fly back out to Australia to finish my stint at Balmain. It wasn't a great decision as I spent most of the next six weeks getting drunk with Benny Elias and torturing myself over the decision I had made earlier that year to leave my wife and kids.

Eventually, I flew back to England, with a bad back and half-a-stone overweight. Just before I met up with my new team-mates for the first time, I spoke to Knocker. He knew me better than almost anyone and was aware of how I upset I was, but he knew I was in danger of blowing a great opportunity if I wasn't careful. He told me to look at the positives; Leeds was a big club with lots of potential, they had recruited well and had money to burn. Hull FC was a club in decline while Leeds were on the up.

By the time I arrived at Headingley for pre-season training, there was definitely a positive atmosphere. The new chairman, Bernard Coulby, brought Maurice Bamford back as coach and they were putting together a decent squad. As well as me, they had also signed Ray Ashton and Alan Rathbone, as well as splashing a load of cash on a bunch of Australians. Andrew Ettingshausen came back for a second spell and was joined by Marty Gurr, Dave Morris, Peter Tunks, Peter Jackson and Cliff Lyons. It should have been an exciting time but I didn't want to be there. As much as I tried to get used to the idea of being a Leeds player, it was very hard to focus on my game.

I soon realised that playing in Leeds was going to be quite different to playing in Hull. Leeds is a much bigger and more cosmopolitan city and the rugby league club reflected that. There was evidence of wealth everywhere you looked, especially the directors' car park which was always full of gleaming BMWs and Mercedes. In contrast to Hull, money didn't seem to be a problem.

However, although the club felt bigger and richer, the team spirit wasn't as good as it had been at Hull. Blokes like Carl Gibson and Dave Heron had been there for years but the majority of the squad were new and the challenge for Maurice was to try to mould a group of strangers into a team. It was never going to be easy, particularly when so many of them were on short-term contracts. Most of the Aussies were doing exactly what I'd done in the previous three summers; making some extra cash during their off-season by playing on the other side of the world. Everyone got on well and there was a good team spirit of sorts, but it was the wrong kind of spirit at times and Maurice was never really able to channel our enthusiasm and experience into the kind of attitude that we needed to win games regularly. Nevertheless, there was no in-fighting and we always played as a team. Not very well at times, it has to be said, but there was a positive atmosphere and the players got on fine.

Although everyone knew how I felt about signing for the club, there was only ever a bit of banter in my direction and some of the blokes such as Heron, Gibson and David Creaser were really supportive. There was a lot expected of me due to the transfer fee and it was helpful to know that they understood the pressure I felt.

What happened at Leeds at that time is proof that money doesn't buy success. Although Maurice had spent a lot on signing and paying players, I don't think he really knew what to do with us once we arrived. He had no systems or processes in place at all. For one thing, he had a million pounds worth of playing talent, but nowhere decent to train.

We used to train on a small field behind the stand which,

for a club of Leeds' ambition, was a joke. Maurice still had some kind of hold over many of the players though; he had a reputation as a hard-man but I hadn't seen anything that impressed me very much. Obviously, he had something to offer as a coach and had been successful in the past, but I think he was the wrong man for that particular job. It required someone who understood elite players and could get more out of them.

My first game for Leeds was against Leigh. Although I managed to score a try, I gave away an interception and had a poor match. The next few weeks weren't much better and I had an absolute nightmare in my first game against Hull. The Leeds fans were quite patient and gave me time to settle in but I knew what they were thinking. Even so, they got very excited when they discovered that Leeds also wanted to sign Garry Schofield. We had been a lethal partnership for Hull and for Great Britain and they no doubt hoped that form would be reproduced at Headingley.

For me, the signing of Schoey gave a flicker of hope that I could make a quick return to the Boulevard. The way I saw it was that if Hull needed money they should have sold Schofield and not me! My hopes were raised when Len Casey called and told me he was hoping to arrange a swap that would take me back to Hull. It was important, he said, that I didn't play for Leeds in their next game just in case I got injured. It was great news for me and I was so desperate to do whatever it took to get back to Hull that I went to see Maurice Bamford and told him I couldn't play. I didn't even bother to come up with an excuse. I just said that I didn't want to play for Leeds any longer because I was going back to Hull.

It soon turned out that Hull weren't looking for a swap at all. They wanted to sell Schofield as well and bank the cash. I had to go back to Maurice, grovel and ask for another chance. I was so desperate to get back to Hull. I just felt that, if I could sort out my career, then everything in my private life would be sorted as well. I didn't realise that the problem was the other way around.

*****

Schoey signed for Leeds in October 1987. By then, the new players had settled in and were thoroughly enjoying themselves. The social life of the players in that first year was ridiculous, to be honest. We had a high profile around the city, particularly with so many Australians in the team, and there were a number of places where you could always expect to bump into a Leeds player. There were two nightclubs in the city centre called TC's and Mister Craig's that we used on a regular basis. We would walk straight up to the door without queuing and get in for nothing, which would really piss everybody off.

Maurice was well aware that most of the team enjoyed a beer but he never seemed very concerned about it. The only rule in force was that you never drank on the night before a game which, by and large, most players observed.

Nevertheless, there was a party culture in place and the players could do more or less whatever they wanted. Peter Tunks had been brought over at great expense; he was a good forward but had his own way of doing things. Once he had got the measure of Maurice, he told him he wouldn't be able to train. It put too much strain on his body, he told the coaching staff, and he would need to rest between games. Amazingly, he got away with it all year, which more or less set the standard for everyone else.

Despite my busy social life, I was in decent shape and playing quite well by the time we played Wigan in the John Player Trophy semi-final in December. I had played in dozens of semi-finals with Hull and it was great to be involved in a big game again, but I ought to have known that 1987 was just not my year. Midway through the first half, Henderson Gill came running into midfield with the ball, stepping this way and that, showing off his footwork. I decided that if he came anywhere near me, I was going to put him on his arse. Unfortunately, as I swung my right arm to give him a whack, he ducked underneath me and I went right over the top of him, landing on my elbow.

As soon as I hit the floor, my right shoulder exploded in the most excruciating pain I had ever known. The collision pushed my arm upwards and forced my shoulder out of its socket. Dislocations are always painful but this one was particularly bad, as it dislocated through the back of the socket which is rare and the most painful. The Leeds physio was an old-school type who treated every kind of injury with a wet sponge, so it was no help at all to see him rushing towards me. I knew it was a serious injury but he decided to shove his wet sponge down my shorts and onto my bollocks. If I'd been able to move I would have twatted him.

My game was over but I had to wait around for what seemed like hours before I was taken to Bolton Infirmary. Once I got there, I was rushed straight into A&E, but no matter what they tried the doctors just couldn't put my shoulder back in and I was howling at them to give me some painkillers. After a couple of hours, they decided to give me a general anaesthetic. Apparently, it was only when the drugs started to take effect and I went under that my arm relaxed enough for them to put it right. The doctor wrapped it in a sling and, a couple of hours later, one of the Leeds directors picked me up from the hospital and took me back to Leeds.

Without me, the lads had beaten Wigan to earn a place in the final. It was a big day for the club since they hadn't reached a major final for over ten years. The rest of the team had headed back to Headingley and, by the time I got there, the celebrations were in full swing. I sat down with a pint and tried to join in but I couldn't face it. I was gutted to miss out on the party; I hadn't had much to celebrate for most of the year and couldn't believe that my luck had turned sour again.

I sulked and felt sorry for myself for a couple of days and, once I was up to it, went out and got pissed, partly to celebrate belatedly but mostly to bemoan my bad luck. By the time we returned to training the following week, the physio was already talking about the injury ending my season. I couldn't believe it - how bad could my luck get? The injury also looked like costing me a place on the 1988 Great Britain tour down under.

My mood darkened even more when I wasn't on the team bus to Wigan for the final against St Helens. I wasn't the only one who didn't travel with the first team squad, but I took it as a snub and can't even remember if I went to the game or not.

*****

Leeds weren't getting much value out of their world record signing, but I was determined to get myself fit enough to return before the end of the campaign. I wasn't given much motivation from Maurice Bamford, though, who just assumed I wouldn't play again.

Recovering from a serious injury is as much a mental challenge as it is physical. It's a very lonely experience and quite daunting to face the prospect of so much time out of action. I couldn't play for the best part of five months and faced week after week of rehabilitation in order to rebuild the strength in my shoulder. In their wisdom, Leeds decided to send me to the National Sports Centre at Lilleshall for rehab, but it was a complete waste of time. I was booked in to stay from Monday to Friday but decided to go out in Cas on the Monday afternoon instead, so didn't get to Lilleshall until Tuesday afternoon. I spent a couple of days in the gym and having a drink with the England footballer, Peter Reid, who was doing rehab there at the same time. I didn't do anything that I couldn't have done back in Leeds and, besides, it was going to take ten weeks for my shoulder to get back to strength again so I have no idea what they hoped I would achieved in four days at Lilleshall. It was pointless. I checked out a day early and went home.

Fortunately, there was one man who went out of his way to help and reassure me that I could still return in time for the tour. Even though I was injured, Malcolm Reilly, the GB coach, included me in one of his train-on squads where he said that he would also pick me for the tour, providing I was fit. Not only that, Malcolm also took a close interest in my day-to-day recovery.

Malcolm still lived in Castleford and spent a lot of time around the club. He knew that I was finding it tough being out of the game for so long and asked me to train with him. I was really touched that he took the time to help me out, especially after our earlier scrap when I had treated him so disrespectfully. It was a mark of the man that he was prepared to forget all of that. He obviously wanted to get me fit for the tour and find the mental strength that I needed to fight my way back to the top.

The target Malcolm set for me was that I should get through at least one game before the end of the season. That was all the incentive I needed and I managed to fight my way back into the Leeds team for the last game at Castleford. I got through it okay and it was a relief to be fit again and to be looking forward to going on tour.

But it had been another disappointing season for Leeds despite the money they spent. Maurice had struggled to get good performances out of the team. I never had a problem with him but I wasn't particularly motivated by him either. He was quite an old-fashioned coach and lacked the man-management qualities needed to get the team to gel.

On the other hand, Maurice had the misfortune of being the bloke who had to get me back to the sort of form that had persuaded Leeds to spend £150,000 on me in the first place. He never really stood much of a chance.

*****

In the summer of 1988, I set off again with Great Britain but was never really fit and didn't play in any of the Tests. Between run outs against county games, I had time to reflect on where my career had got to.

The year 1987 had been the worst of my life and my first season with Leeds a disaster. My last two seasons at Hull hadn't been covered in glory either, so I approached the start of 1988-89 desperately in need of a good season. I was still only twenty-four years old but many were already starting to write me off. That was understandable. All the evidence pointed to a player in rapid decline but I was determined not to let that happen. I had two kids and was settling into a new relationship with Karen. The only way I could provide us with a decent lifestyle was to get my rugby league career back on track.

I've never expected to be the highest-paid player but I've never liked being taken for a ride either. I was on fifteen grand a year when I signed for Leeds but I had been tied into a ten-year contract which was a blatant restraint of trade. It gave me no room for future negotiations and was just plainly wrong.

For the start of the season, Maurice Bamford had been

moved out and replaced by the GB coach, Malcolm Reilly. I was delighted at the prospect of playing for Malcolm at club level. I had spoken to him about my contract situation and he promised to try to help me sort it out, but we both knew I wasn't in a strong position to negotiate. He sat me down and we discussed the kind of relationship I had with the club and what I needed to do to make the situation better. Nothing was left unsaid.

'You're a laughing stock,' he told me. 'An embarrassment to yourself and the club. But if you won't play for the club then do it for yourself and for your own self-respect. There are loads of people ready to write you off, so go and show them how good you are.'

Having given it to me with both barrels, he went on to promise that, if I gave him a good season, he would speak to the board on my behalf and do his best to sort out my contract. I was happy with that and it gave me something to work for.

By the start of the season, my shoulder had made a full recovery and I was going well. At the beginning of October, we played two games in a week against Hull. I'd hated playing against my old club the previous year. It just hadn't felt right, particularly at the Boulevard when I had to get changed in the away team's dressing room that I had last used when I was in the colts team back in 1980.

But I knew there was no room for sentimentality; I had to be more professional and that started by helping Leeds to beat Hull. We lost the first game at the Boulevard in the league but then won at home in the Yorkshire Cup. I was very happy with the way I played in both games and felt I had overcome another hurdle.

There were still rumours that Leeds might be prepared to cut their losses and allow me to rejoin Hull FC but there was never really any substance. Leeds would have wanted their money back and Hull didn't have it. Nevertheless the stories never went away and, as the teams were leaving the pitch after the second of those games, Hull's coach Brian Smith tapped me on the shoulder and said: 'You can play for my team whenever you like'. I probably didn't need to hear that. It was a bit like getting dumped by a bird you're mad about, and then just when you've started to get over her, she starts texting you again. I tried to put it out of my mind and told myself that it would never happen.

I never did re-sign for Hull but I came very close to playing for Brian Smith in the mid-1990s when I was playing for Castleford and Smith was coaching Bradford Bulls. Brian approached the Australian centre Graeme Bradley, who was my team-mate at Castleford and a good friend of mine. He told Graeme that he was interested in signing me and asked him if he thought I would consider a move to Bradford. At the time, Bradford were playing a high-impact game where the prop forwards played in short bursts. Graeme told him, quite rightly, that I probably wouldn't like to spend half the time on the bench. That didn't suit Smith and the approach went no further but, on reflection, if I had been prepared to compromise a bit, I may well have been able to prolong my career for another couple of years. And Bradford was a pretty exciting place to be in the mid-1990s as Bullmania was about to take off. But that's just one of those decisions that you have to make in sport and there is no point wondering what might have been.

*****

After just a few weeks in charge at Headingley, Malcolm had made his presence felt. When we reached the final of the Yorkshire Cup against Castleford, we were firm favourites. At the start of the season, Malcolm had made the brave decision to make me captain which was a great honour and one I took very seriously. In the build-up to the final at Elland Road, I was in great demand from the media and I felt really proud to be leading the team into the game. As captain, I began to feel some kind of connection with the club which had been lacking. Most importantly for me, thanks to the way that Malcolm related to his players, I felt wanted and valued again.

The Cup final was a big occasion for the club, but we didn't have it all our own way. Cas gave us a real battle at the start and it was very close until Garry Schofield put us in front with an interception try. That gave us all a lift and, shortly afterwards, he scored again after I had made a break through the middle. In the second half, Carl Gibson scored a couple of long-range tries and we won comfortably.

It was very strange to collect the trophy while wearing the blue and gold of Leeds rather than the black and white of Hull. Nevertheless, I was very proud to raise the club's first trophy for years. We had a great night celebrating our success, first at Elland Road and then back at Headingley. The Leeds directors certainly knew how to celebrate in style and the players and their partners were well looked after as the champagne flowed freely. It was just the start to the season that we needed and we began to feel we could put up a real challenge and win more silverware. The club had backed Malcolm to the hilt, splashing the cash to attract a whole load of new signings. We finally had the beginnings of a good team with everyone focused in the right way. The players still socialised together but we had our priorities in the right place; we were a proper team with Malcolm as the leader. The players behaved themselves, we travelled everywhere in club blazers and fell into a steady disciplined routine, which was exactly what I needed.

The second half of the season went very well and we finished third behind Wigan and Widnes, the highest position that had been achieved for years. After a tough first season, Malcolm had challenged me to show what I could do and I had done so. The Players' Player, Coach's Player and Supporters' Player of the Year awards I won were evidence of that. I was very proud with how I had turned things around and I felt much happier. All I needed now was to sort out that ten-year contract.

During the course of the season, I had been given an assurance that my good form and loyalty would lead to a renegotiation. I assumed that, once we returned to pre-season training at the start of 1989-90, I would be offered better terms, but it wasn't as simple as that.

Before the season began, Malcolm left the club suddenly and I began to worry. I was relying on Malcolm to help me sort things out with the board. The new man was David Ward and I soon paid him a visit to try and find out what was happening. After a while, David came back to see me with some bad news. He told me the board weren't prepared to take another look at my contract until they had seen another good season from me.

I was pissed off. My argument wasn't about the money. I was tied into a contract that I knew just wasn't fair. I had tried to get the club to sit down and renegotiate it properly and had been prepared to show them some loyalty for a year to get them to do so. I had done that and now they had completely gone back on what they had said. I told David how I felt; as far as I was concerned, I was finished with Leeds and I began to stay away from the club.

*****

On reflection, I was naive. I never had a firm commitment from anyone that my contract would be reviewed; it had all been quite vague and I had been too trusting. By 1989, a number of players had started to use agents to help them with negotiations. I never felt it necessary to have someone else involved but, if I had, they may well have been able to straighten things out for me much sooner.

I was away from the club for four or five weeks and, in that time, I took legal advice on the matter. The guidance I received was that my contract was a clear restraint of trade and that I would probably win if I decided to take Leeds to court. That would make me a free agent and I could leave and play for anyone who wanted me. On the other hand, if I lost I would be stuck at Leeds and would have to pay their legal fees, which could be as much as a hundred grand. I couldn't afford to take the risk. Leeds were aware of the advice I had been given and, over the next few weeks, both sides realised that it was in everyone's interest to resolve the situation amicably which would probably mean me moving. Nothing was going to happen while I stayed away, though, so moves were made to get me to go back. Reluctantly, I agreed.

Meanwhile, I was spending a fair bit of time in a pub in Castleford called The Ship. Leeds team-mate Colin Maskill and myself were on very good terms with lots of the Cas players who drank there, particularly John Joyner. It was through JJ that I first met Darryl van der Velde, Castleford's new coach. Darryl is a big, bullish character with a lot of confidence and presence. We had a few beers and he made some comment to the effect that if I played for him he wouldn't let me go out drinking on a Monday night, which was quite ironic since it was Monday night and he was out drinking with half of his own team. I reminded him that I didn't play for him, so he should mind his own business. It was a bit of banter but I think we were sounding each other out to see how we might get on if I did play for him.

Darryl was well aware of my situation at Leeds and, over

the next couple of weeks, we got to know each other a bit better. It became clear that a move to Castleford could well be my next option.

When Castleford came in with a formal offer, Leeds accepted it straight away. Leeds got their money back and I was set to become Castleford's record signing so long as I accepted personal terms. As the move was about to go public, some of the lads at Leeds tried to talk me out of it, including Schoey and even David Ward, but my mind was made up.

The offer from Cas was no better for me financially but it was only a three-year deal and it gave me some freedom to negotiate in the future. More importantly, I felt wanted by Castleford whereas Leeds had never really seemed bothered about me, or at least that's the way it felt.

I have had many years to think about why it went wrong for me at Leeds. For a long time I just blamed myself. I didn't want to go to Leeds, I took the rejection from Hull badly and I sulked for far too long and far too publicly. I felt that I let some good people down and the way I behaved hurt lots of people close to me. More than anything, I damaged myself, my career and my reputation. But I also think that the Leeds club had a lot to be responsible for as well.

The attitude of the club at that time was unbelievably arrogant. They had so much money they believed they could buy anyone they wanted. They paid transfer fees, high wages and threw bonuses around all over the place, yet they neglected to put in place the basics that any thriving club needs. They had no idea about what it actually took to make a team successful.

They made loads of big-name signings in 1987 but they never gave any thought to how they would manage all those strong and complex characters. In Maurice Bamford, they had a well-respected coach who had no idea about how the modern professional player thought and behaved. Maurice and the board thought they could throw money around and that would be that. They never considered how they might get the best out of their players and what might happen if they put them together in a city like Leeds under a decent, but ineffective, coach.

Their treatment of me was particularly ridiculous. They knew all along that I didn't want to play for them and yet they didn't do anything to support me. I'm not suggesting that they needed to mollycoddle me, but having spent so much money it was wasteful not to want to get the best out of me. Apart from the director Harry Jepson, nobody from the club ever sat me down and asked how I felt about signing for them. The attitude was that I had signed and got a pay rise; I ought to be thankful I had left Hull, a club on the slide, to join the mighty Leeds. They never considered that I didn't care about the money, nor whether Hull really were on the slide. When I look back, it is the audacity of Leeds' behaviour that shocks me most.

There was little wonder that Leeds were so unsuccessful in those years when they had such a short sighted view of man-management. It was only when Malcolm Reilly arrived that the top players really started to feel valued and began to play to their potential. Then, after just a year, the club allowed him to leave and went back to square one.

I have always accepted that the problems I had at Leeds were largely my own, but a strong club would have helped me to deal with them. It's fair to say that Leeds weren't ready for Lee Crooks, or for Tunks, Jackson, Ettingshausen, Morris, Schofield, Rathbone or Izzard. If they had taken a fraction of the money spent on signing players and used it to finance a decent infrastructure to get the best out of those players, Leeds could have dominated the game for years.

For me, there was nothing inevitable about my leaving

Leeds. When I had been challenged to show my worth I had done so but, in the end, it came down to a matter of principle. There was no way I could continue to play for a club that felt it was fair to hold me to a contract which, in theory, would last until I retired.

After my nightmare first season at Headingley, I had fought my way back from the brink. But then, just when things seemed to be looking up, I had been let down and handled it the only way I knew how. I walked away.

7

Castleford Calling

By the time I left Leeds, I was grateful to have Karen by my side. When I first met Karen, I never dreamed she would become my wife. For one thing, I was already married. For another, even if I had been a single man, I would have thought that she was way out of my league.

But, after I split with Janet, Karen and I soon became an item and as I planned to join up with Balmain in 1987, she agreed to go with me. That was far from the end of the story. The whole episode was a nightmare, especially for Karen.

I still hadn't come to terms with leaving my kids and I was shit company, to say the least. After a couple of weeks, Karen had had enough of me and flew home. It wasn't long before I was in England as well, forced to sign for Leeds.

While I was back home, I met up with Karen again and asked her to return to Australia with me. I told her that the time we had spent apart had convinced me I wanted to be with her. God knows how I persuaded her but eventually we flew back to Australia to try and work things work out. I started playing again but it wasn't long before I picked up a back injury which kept me out for a while.

I had always enjoyed the social side of the Australian game, but in 1987 I indulged far more than in previous years and became a regular fixture in the Balmain Leagues Club. After a particularly long session one night, I found myself nodding off on the steps outside, waiting for a taxi to take me home. A couple of supporters were stood near me and I could hear them talking.

'Isn't that Lee Crooks over there, on the floor?'

'Nah, mate, that guy's fucking pissed. That's not Lee Crooks.'

I opened one eye and lifted my head. 'Oh yes it fucking is,' I said, before drifting off to sleep.

When the time came to leave and go play for Leeds, I had mixed feelings. For obvious reasons, I hadn't enjoyed my latest spell in Australia but I wasn't relishing going home either. The final days were spent saying farewell to my team-mates and it was obvious what I would be remembered for. At the end-of-season Player of the Year night, I won an award for the largest bar bill at Wimpey's Well. That was a bar under the stand at the Leichhardt Oval where players could grab a beer whenever they wanted. I thought that was a great idea and tucked in whenever I was at the ground. I would also make sure I grabbed a few for anybody else I happened to be with. After a few weeks, I realised that the barman at Wimpey's kept a tab. Mine was by far the largest and I had only been in the country six weeks.

*****

Karen and I continued to fall out, make up and then fall out again. Every time we did so it was because I was wallowing in self-pity. One night Karen was home alone while I had gone out. She was pissed off that I had left her and spent most of the night on the phone to her mates in Castleford. It wasn't the only time she did that and, by the end of the year, she had managed to run up a four-thousand dollar phone bill. On top of that, we'd had four round-the-world air fares and I'd smashed up a car. I was due to earn around $30,000 for the four months I was contracted to spend with Balmain but, after all the deductions were taken into account, I went home with about two grand in my pocket.

There is no doubt I was out of control during that first season at Leeds and my relationship with Karen suffered badly. After coming back to England, I had nowhere to live at first and spent weeks living like a vagrant, dossing down in spare rooms. With Karen, our lifestyle was just as wild. I never thought about anything other than spending time with her. We slept wherever we happened to be and often stayed in hotels or guest houses so we could be on our own. Karen had a pet dog, a Bernese mountain dog called Duke. Whenever she had him with her, we wouldn't be able to stay in a hotel and would have to spend the night sleeping in my car - the three of us!

Eventually I figured it wasn't befitting of a Leeds rugby league player to be practically homeless, so I found myself a flat in Castleford. Me and Karen were still on and off though, and I'm amazed that she didn't give me the elbow. I never had any doubts about how I felt about her, but I just hadn't come to terms with the break-up of my marriage. Like most men in that situation, I underestimated how hard it would be to separate from my kids.

I guess it was only when Karen became pregnant at the start of 1989 that I really decided to make a commitment. Obviously, there was no way we could continue as we were with a baby and the imminent arrival forced us, and me in particular, to make some long overdue decisions.

With a baby due, Karen was able to get a council house quite easily, so she moved out of her flat and into the new home. Soon after, I moved in as well. It was the first time we had lived together as a proper couple and it gave me some much-needed stability, which also had an impact on my form for Leeds.

Karen went into labour in August 1989 but the delivery wasn't straightforward. She had to have a Caesarean section when they discovered the cord was wrapped around the baby's neck. For that reason I wasn't able to be there when she gave birth, but we soon had our first child, a girl we called Megan. Karen's mum, Cilla, was soon on the scene, telling Karen that our daughter looked just like her dad. Karen was in no mood to hear that. 'That's all I need,' she said. 'Another ugly bastard in the family!'

Over the next few years, with Karen and Megan to come home to each day, I began to get myself back together as my personal life settled down. I enjoyed my rugby a whole lot more and started to get back to something like my best form.

A couple of years later, Karen was pregnant again. Ben was born in June of 1993 but, again, the arrival was far from easy. For the first time, I was actually there, but I can't say I enjoyed it very much. Throughout the delivery, the nurse kept insisting that I stroke Karen's hand and forehead to comfort her. But every time I put my hand on her, she would yell: 'Get your fucking hands off me, Crooks!' The nurse insisted Karen needed reassurance but I didn't know what the hell to do and wished I'd stayed outside. Luckily, the labour didn't take too long and Ben soon arrived.

Ben's first few weeks with us were not easy though. Soon after he was born and started feeding, it became apparent he wasn't able to pass waste properly. He was rushed off to Leeds General Infirmary where he was diagnosed with Hirschsprung's Disease, a condition which prevents proper

184

digestion. He was really sick for quite a while and we both seemed to spend most of our time at the hospital hoping for him to pull through.

At times like that, you really appreciate the kindness of friends and family. We were very lucky to have so many people who were always there to look after Megan while we were at the hospital. Even one of the taxi drivers who used to take Karen and her mum to the hospital became a really good friend. Ali also had a son who had been ill and insisted on taking Karen there himself, never charging. Thankfully, as the weeks passed, Ben recovered and built up strength. Our lives started to get back to normal again.

*****

For once, my personal life was settled and at the end of the 1994 season our thoughts turned to marriage. I've never been one for making a big deal over anything and, as luck would have it, Karen decided that she didn't want much fuss either, so we settled on a fairly simple ceremony.

To be honest, if we had wanted to, we could have had a massive party and not paid a penny for it. I was still on good terms with one or two people at John Smith's brewery who had offered to pay for the whole reception, but neither of us was very comfortable with that. Even though we wanted a quiet do, I couldn't stop myself mentioning it to some of my mates at Cas. When I told Keith England, he said that he was also planning to get married that summer and suggested we had a joint-wedding. I thought it was a daft idea at first but when I told Karen she seemed to think it might be good fun and we began to make plans.

We were so determined to keep it low key that Karen even went to work on the morning of our wedding. She worked at the Rowntree's factory in Castleford and decided to do the morning shift before coming home to get herself ready.

There were only a handful of people at the ceremony: myself and Karen; Beefy and Cher; Keith's sister and her husband; and Knocker and his girlfriend, Karen. We asked everyone to meet up at our house and, after a quick pint at The Jockey, the eight of us headed off to the registry office, which was covered in scaffolding.

Karen and I went first and, despite all the noise from the builders outside, we just about managed to get through the service. I took the whole thing very seriously, but Beefy and Cher thought it was hilarious that we could barely hear each other's vows. When it was their turn the noise was even louder and Beefy struggled to make himself heard. We pissed ourselves laughing as Beefy tried to declare his eternal vows while, outside, the builders were clattering, banging, effing, blinding and wolf-whistling at the women turning up for the next wedding.

The registrar had to remind us of the solemnity of the occasion and warned us that she wouldn't carry on unless we took it more seriously. Beefy somehow managed to get through it and we were relieved to get the formalities out of the way and head back to the pub.

We had a table booked at the Bon Viveur restaurant and had deliberately taken the last sitting of the night so that we wouldn't be rushed out. The Bon Viveur is usually quite a posh French restaurant where most diners are on their best behaviour. But by the time we got there we had all had a bit to drink and were a bit louder than they had bargained for. We'd had a great day and I decided to order champagne. I don't know much about champagne except that Moët do a decent drop of the stuff, so I ordered a couple of bottles of that. The waiter tried to explain that they didn't stock Moët but that they could offer Bollinger or Verve Cliqueot instead.

I had never heard of them and thought he was trying to fob me off with some over-priced rubbish, so insisted he bring us Moët. Eventually, Karen told the waiter to bring us whatever they had and to just to tell me it was Moët. She was right. I never noticed the difference.

At closing time, we decided to head back to The Jockey for a nightcap but, just before we left, Knocker's girlfriend Karen discovered she had lost her camera. She was a bit drunk and convinced that one of the waiters had stolen it. She went crazy, calling the staff all the names under the sun until we calmed her down and persuaded her that they wouldn't have stolen her camera.

She was still in a foul mood when we turned up at The Jockey to be greeted by the landlord. 'Now then, lads and lasses, what can I get you? How's married life, Lee? Hey, Karen, you left your camera in here earlier....'

Knocker went mad at her and, after a big argument, they decided to go home. Beefy and Cher soon fell out as well and took his sister with them, leaving Karen and myself as the last couple in the pub. We finished our drinks as the landlord switched off the lights. 'Oh well,' I said. 'You wanted a quiet wedding.'

*****

Karen and I went to Zante for our honeymoon. It was a great fortnight. We were both happy and relaxed. One afternoon as we lay sunbathing by the pool, a moped pulled up nearby and someone shouted: 'Eh, Crooksy,' in a broad Oldham accent. It was Richard 'Jack' Russell, my Cas teammate. I knew he was in Zante as well but we hadn't made any plans to meet up - we were on our honeymoon, after all. It was good to see Jack, though, and Karen got on well with his wife and family, so we ended up spending quite a bit of time together. It was an enjoyable holiday, a brilliant summer and we returned to Castleford feeling very happy with life. I was approaching my thirty-first birthday and fourteenth season in the game. I knew there wouldn't be too many more and was determined to make sure I made the most of what time I had left. We also started to think about finding somewhere bigger to live.

We liked the area we lived in though and, rather than move, Karen and I talked about extending our kitchen. We went on about it for ages but never got round to doing anything until I came home from training one day to find Karen covered in brick dust having knocked the kitchen wall through. I didn't have much of a clue about building work but was pretty sure she had demolished a supporting wall. I panicked that the whole house might come down on our heads, which would have been a nightmare because it still belonged to the council.

Luckily, Cas chairman David Poulter owned a building company so I rang him up. Within ten minutes, one of his lads came to make the wall safe. Next day, two more lads came round to finish the job off properly and even plastered the walls. I didn't mind doing the painting myself. David wouldn't accept a penny for the work he had done for us; it was typical of him to look after his players that way and it was greatly appreciated.

Shortly afterwards we bought the house from the council and did it up a bit but, once I retired, we decided to move to a bigger place in Townville, on the outskirts of Castleford.

*****

The years flew by and life ticked along merrily. By the summer of 2006, I was well settled into a job at the Rugby Football League, while also finding time to do occasional commentary work for Radio Leeds. I was forty-two years old, Megan and Ben were growing up fast and the family had slipped into a nice easy routine.

We also had a lot of great friends, whom we often met up with for barbecues and dinner parties. Karen never objected when I occasionally went out with my old rugby mates like Schoey. In many ways, it was the perfect life but, deep down, I started to feel that something was wrong.

Karen and I had always had a great relationship; she was my best mate as well as my wife. We could do the romance bit, I would buy her flowers and stuff and, at times, I could be quite a Casanova. Nevertheless, we started to argue over daft things. I ought to have realised that we needed to work on our relationship a bit more, but I just brushed it off because I thought we were invincible as a couple. We each had our own things that we liked to do; I still spent time watching rugby and mixing with mates from the game, while Karen liked the outdoor life and would go camping. It wasn't something I was interested in, so she would often go with our friends instead. I tried to get there when I could but spent more and more time at RFL coaching camps.

Even when I did join her, it was obvious that it wasn't my cup of tea. Looking back, I was taking Karen for granted and I didn't realise that she was becoming unhappy.

As at the start of our relationship, I would get jealous when anyone went near Karen, a very funny and outgoing woman and quite flirtatious in her own way. As we grew closer, though, I stopped worrying. I realised that love is borne out of trust and I loved her very much. The flip side of that is that I grew complacent and just thought that Karen would never leave me. I took my foot off the pedal. It was only a matter of time before something turned things upside down.

Ironically, it happened on one of these camping trips. Someone had caught Karen's eye and made a fuss of her, something I hadn't done for a while, and that was the beginning of the end. Unbeknown to me, I was competing for her attention with someone who was doing the things I should have. He was winning her over. Once I discovered what was going on, it was too late. I had lost her.

I always believed that Karen would be with me forever, but I realised too late that you can never just assume these things. Before I retired from rugby, I promised Karen that when I stopped playing she would never have to compete for my attention again. Rugby would be relegated down my list of priorities and she would have me all to herself. But that didn't happen. I was still infatuated with rugby league and desperate to become a coach, while she grew fed up of playing second fiddle to my obsession.

I knew who the guy was and was often asked why I didn't flatten him but I was never tempted. It wouldn't have achieved anything and would have only driven a greater wedge between myself, Karen and the kids. It wasn't his fault, he was just in the right place at the right time. I had to accept that it was all down to me. Even now, five years on, I still find it difficult to believe that I could have been so stupid. But life goes on and you just have to get on with it.

8

Sidesteps and Dummies

I have always respected Malcolm Reilly. He was a tough and skilful player who, after becoming a coach, was one of the best man-managers I ever played for.

The second half of my international career coincided exactly with Malcolm's reign as Great Britain boss. I played in his first game in charge and his last game in charge. But unfortunately for me, not too many games in between.

As I have already said, I never felt like a regular in the Great Britain team. Although I earned thirteen caps before leaving Hull at the age of twenty-three, I still never thought of my place in the side as secure.

Some of that is my own fault. I didn't always behave myself on international duty. My first trip to France in 1984 led to me being dropped because of my antics on the flight home. In spite of that, I was still selected to go on tour that summer, but missed more than half the Tests through injury and again managed to upset the tour management along the way. During 1985 and 1986 I was as close as I ever came to being a regular but, by the start of 1987, my irregular form for Hull FC and my erratic lifestyle had been noted by Maurice Bamford and then by Malcolm, so my appearances tailed off.

I had done nothing much to deserve selection for the 1988 tour of PNG, Australia and New Zealand but I was picked anyway. It was frustrating to be on the fringes but it became a familiar feeling over the next four years.

*****

Although the 1988 tour was much better organised than the last one, we still flew economy class and I sat with Schoey on the outbound flight. We had three seats between us but I wasn't comfortable and persuaded him to sleep on the floor while I laid down across the seats. As if that wasn't bad enough for him, we slept top to tail. Every time the plane hit turbulence, my leg would slip off the seat and kick Garry in the head. He got a bit pissed off with that, especially when a particularly strong bit of turbulence over Asia caused me to break his glasses. As we touched down, I felt refreshed and relaxed. Garry, for some reason, seemed edgy and dishevelled.

After a few days in Australia, it was obvious that the tour was going to be more professional than 1984. Malcolm was very familiar with the places we visited and he made sure we stayed in suitable hotels. One was the Manly Pacific; a perfect place to stay while playing in and around Sydney. A bit more thought had gone into the logistics.

The players were better looked after too. We were given a decent living allowance and there were proper systems in place to help prepare us for the Test matches. Consequently, it was a more successful tour in lots of ways and, although we lost the series in Australia, the games were closer and we won the final Test in Sydney.

With no expectation of being in the Test side, the pressure was off me to an extent. I could easily have just settled down and enjoyed a free holiday. But I didn't feel comfortable in a squad where I was nothing more than a bit-part figure. I became a regular in the midweek team and although there were plenty of blokes who were more than happy to be playing for the 'reserves', I wasn't one of them. I started to wonder why I had been selected in the first place.

It wasn't until later in the tour that I discovered the real reason Malcolm selected me. It wasn't public knowledge at the time but Malcolm told me that when we returned to England he would be unveiled as new coach at Leeds. He knew I had gone through a turbulent couple of years and wanted to keep a close eye on me.

*****

In the game against Central Queensland, my shoulder went yet again and I knew that my tour was over. Without the prospect of playing in any of the Test matches, I was itching to go home. When tour manager David Howes said he had got me on standby for a flight to England, I was relieved to be leaving the tour behind.

Andy Platt was in the same position as me. After playing the first two Tests, he had picked up an injury and was also allowed to leave. Howesy wasn't keen on carrying lads who had no chance of playing so, having bought us both standby tickets, he took us to the airport.

We were due to fly with Qantas and I was determined to salvage something from the trip by having another go at that transcontinental drinking record. On my way back from New Zealand in 1984, I was denied by the miserable cabin crew and hadn't got anywhere near the total of 38 cans. By 1988, the bar had been raised even higher by Australian cricketer David Boon, who had managed to drink forty-two cans during a flight home from England. I was restless and a bit fed up when we got to the airport and, when the girl on the check-in desk asked me if I wanted a smoking or non-smoking seat, I replied: 'Drinking!'

The flight was actually full but I think the Qantas staff figured we might be more trouble if we were left to prowl around the airport for another six hours and so. After a while, they managed to find some seats and we headed for the gate. As we started to board, I saw an elderly couple complaining about being 'bumped' off their flight. I tried to pretend that I hadn't noticed and headed for my seat.

As soon as we were airborne, I told one of the crew that we wanted to have a go at beating the record. 'Just keep lining them up,' I told him. 'Don't worry, we won't be a nuisance. If we start giving you any problems, just stop serving us.'

They gave us a sheet of paper to write down how many we'd had and we got stuck into the challenge. By the time we changed planes in Singapore, we'd done about sixteen cans apiece and still felt fairly fresh. We hadn't really thought about how we would spend the time on the ground in Singapore and made the tactical error of heading straight for the bar. After a three hour lay-over and another half a dozen pints, we re-boarded feeling very confident that we could drink all night and break the record. We wanted to make sure that the new record would be acknowledged and so we made sure that each and every can was duly recorded and witnessed. That was a process which got louder and louder as the marathon went on.

We kept drinking through the night, steadying our pace. Even though we dozed off every now and then, we seemed well on course to smash the record. The cabin crew and some of our fellow passengers seemed quite amused by the whole thing but, somewhere over Europe, we fell asleep.

When I woke up to hear the captain announcing that we were starting our descent into Manchester, I checked my list and found we had stopped at thirty-eight. We were four short of the record and just half an hour from landing but the bar was shut. I woke Platty and we tried to work out if the pints we'd consumed in Singapore, when added to those we'd drunk on the plane, would add up to more than forty-two. But Platty was struggling to remember who he was, let alone anything else.

Pissed, I tried to get the attention of the steward to ask whether I could claim the pints we had drunk in Singapore. He didn't seem to think that was his responsibility and was more concerned with making sure the other passengers had returned to their seats and were fastening their seatbelts. So, reluctantly, we had to accept that we weren't going to beat the record; a tactical calamity in Singapore had ruined our bid for glory.

*****

Although my tour had ended prematurely once again, I was still pleased to have been involved and, to reassure me that I was back in favour, Malcolm picked me again for the series against France in early 1989.

As ever, I wanted to repay Malcolm for the faith he had shown and had no intention of doing anything untoward in France that could cause embarrassment to anyone. I always felt there were plenty of people just waiting to see me screw things up and was determined to give them no reason to justify the impression they had of me. I was going to be on best behaviour; a model professional.

Getting nicked by the French police, therefore, was not part of my plan.

The team won the first Test 26-10 in Wigan without me,

From Hull to Hell and Back

but it was after beating the French 30-8 in the second Test in
Avignon that the fun began. We all went out on the town for
a couple of beers to celebrate and unwind. The Great Britain
under-21s were also there, having played the curtain-raiser,
so there were over thirty British blokes, all dressed in their
red team jumpers. As we wandered around, Kevin Ward
spotted Andy Gregory through the window of a bar. Greg
was having a beer and minding his own business but Wardy
wanted to speak to him for some reason so dashed over to
knock on the window. Now, Kev is a big guy who doesn't
know his own strength and, as he rapped on the window to
get Greg's attention, it went through, shattering glass all
over the place and making a hell of a racket. I was walking
a fair way behind Wardy and only heard what happened
afterwards but someone must have called the local police.
By the time I reached the scene, there was a police van
outside the bar. I was about the only bloke who hadn't
scarpered and since I perfectly matched the description of
the bloke who had broken the window - a big Englishman in
a red jumper - I was hauled into the back and driven away.

I didn't bother to argue. There was no way I could
protest my innocence in French and I figured it would all be
sorted out at the station. As the van pulled away, I looked
around to see Tim Street sitting opposite me. Tim had been
playing for the under-21s. He asked me what I had been
doing, laughing his head off.

'Fuck all, Tim,' I said. 'I've been picked up for breaking a
window, but I didn't do it.'

Down at the police station, Tim and I were locked in a
cell while the French police tried to get someone to interpret.
After a while, our tour manager Maurice Lindsay turned up.
He was fuming.

'I'm very disappointed, Lee. I thought you had put this
kind of behaviour behind you. It's very embarrassing for the

team to have a senior player behaving in this way.' Maurice was in full flow, his voice getting more and more high pitched, until I interrupted him.

'Look, Maurice,' I told him. 'I know I've done some daft things in the past and I've always put my hands up and admitted to it but, this time, I'm telling you, I didn't do it. They just picked up the first bloke wearing a red jumper.'

If this had happened earlier in my career, I reckon I'd have copped the blame. Back then I didn't care much about what people thought of me, so I took whatever punishment came my way, rather than drop someone else in it. But this was different. I couldn't afford to have any more black marks on my reputation, so I wasn't going to take the rap for something I didn't do. Eventually, Maurice managed to get me out and we went back to the team hotel where everyone thought it highly amusing, including Kevin Ward. I told Wardy that he had to own up to breaking the window and tell Maurice that I had nothing to do with it. I don't know whether he ever did and I suspect that Maurice preferred to believe that I had done it anyway.

I got my own back on Wardy though. When we got back to Cas on the Sunday night, Malcolm and myself met up with John Joyner and Darryl van der Velde for a couple of pints. Wardy was a bit under the thumb and wanted to go straight home, but we dragged him along with us and, every time he was ready to go, got him another beer in. By the end of the night he was hammered. We knew he was going to be in big bother with his missus.

*****

The Australians were back in the country in 1990 but, to be honest, Karen had more chance of being in the team than I did. When Malcolm announced his team for the First Test of the series, it depressed me. The pack included the likes of Karl Harrison, Wardy, Paul Dixon and Roy Powell which seemed to suggest that the only way we could compete with the Australians was to copy their way of playing. That decision meant there would be fewer opportunities for ball-handlers such as me and no tolerance of players who might create one devastating break in every game, but might put the ball on the floor three or four times in doing so.

The whole team was full of 'safe' choices; players who wouldn't make many mistakes but lacked any kind of flair, such as Darryl Powell, Carl Gibson and Paul Eastwood. I was frustrated as I sat down to watch the First Test at Wembley, certain that the Aussies would just blow the British lads away.

An hour and a half later, Britain had won 19-12 and Malcolm's choices had been completely justified. It was the first time Britain had beaten Australia in the First Test of a series for twenty years. It was great to see the Aussies suffer but I had mixed feelings as I watched the game.

I was pleased for the players and for Malcolm but I wasn't comfortable with what I had seen. I hadn't liked our style of play. I still felt we could play more football but, of course, I was bound to say that, wasn't I? I kept my opinions to myself and got on with my rugby but I was pissed off and resentful that I wasn't able to contribute to the team's success and that my way of playing was no longer relevant at international level.

Even though the Aussies came back to win the series, Malcolm stuck to the view that the best way to beat them was to copy them. In the meantime, there were a lot of people who said that the job of the Great Britain coach was easy; you just picked anyone that played for Wigan. That seemed to be the view for the next couple of years and, as the 1992 tour down under grew nearer, I feared that the selection policy might cause me to miss out, even though I was playing some good rugby for Castleford.

Fortunately, I had made it difficult for Malcolm to leave me out and, in February 1992, he called me back into the squad for the two-match mini-series against France. When the call came, it was a real boost; it had been three years since I had last played for my country and it was only my third game for GB in six years. At twenty-eight, I was well aware that this was probably my last chance to establish myself in the international team and there was no way I was going to blow the chance.

It wasn't a very memorable series. We won the first game in France after a scratchy performance and won again, more comfortably, in the return match at the Boulevard. I was pleased to be back in the frame and hopeful that I might be able to earn a place on the tour to Australia and New Zealand that summer. Playing for probably the First Division's form team would do me no harm and I was so keen to do my bit for Cas that I played against St Helens the day after the Boulevard game, scoring our only try as we drew 8-8.

My good form continued right the way through to the end of the season and it certainly did no harm to my profile that Castleford made it to the Cup final that year. Just before the season ended, I got the news I had been waiting for; I was going on tour.

It felt like I had climbed a mountain. For the second time, I had come back from the brink, first at Leeds and then for Great Britain. I was beginning to make a bit of a habit of it. I didn't like the setbacks but I took a fair amount of satisfaction from my ability to bounce back from them.

I knew that taking me on tour had been a tough call for Malcolm and I was thrilled to be given another chance. Once the domestic season ended, I carried on training and got myself into the best shape I had been in for ages. It also helped that I stayed off the beer. By the time I joined up with the squad, I had barely touched a drink in weeks. As we left the UK, I was totally focused on the job in hand and there was nobody in the squad more committed and professional than I was in those first few weeks.

*****

The first leg took us to Papua New Guinea where we were treated like superstars. Rugby league is the national sport of PNG and it is an understatement to say that they love their sport; it's almost a religion. On match days, everything stops so that people can get as close to the ground as possible, even if they have no chance of actually getting in to see the game. The PNG players are national heroes and the GB players were treated in the same kind of way - until kick-off. I had a real soft spot for the place after touring with the GB Colts in 1982 and loved every minute of the time we spent there. Some of my team-mates weren't so impressed at the spartan facilities, the heat and the hostile reception from the locals, but I have never been one to appreciate creature comforts all that much and I got a buzz from being amongst passionate rugby fans. Besides, playing in Port Moresby wasn't much different to playing in a Hull derby.

At the start of the tour, I was probably some way down the prop forward pecking order and knew that I had to prove myself whenever I got a chance. I was selected to play in one of the warm-up games prior to the Test match against PNG. Playing the Islands Zone in Rabaul in front of a few thousand supporters was a long way from playing the Aussies in Sydney, but I treated every game as if it was a Test. The heat was overwhelming and the opposition incredibly tough, but I was satisfied with my performance and pleased when

Malcolm selected me to play against PNG four days later. It was a strong team and I was selected with Bradford's Karl Fairbank in what was otherwise the Wigan pack, with Phil Clarke, Denis Betts, Martin Dermott and Andy Platt alongside us. It was a tough, close game that was only won by two late tries from Martin Offiah in front of one of the noisiest and most passionate crowds I've ever seen. I was delighted to be back in a GB jersey again but still had no idea whether I had done enough to win a place for the First Test in Sydney.

The 1992 Lions tour was the first in which we played the NRL club teams rather than city and country representative sides, so the majority of games were played in decent stadiums with good facilities. We had doctors and physios and plenty of other support staff, who were just as keen to play their part as we were. It was a big deal for them, as you might imagine, to be touring Australia. In a way, they were representing their country as well. We sometimes had to rely on local masseurs and physios too though and some of them had their own ways of doing things. During an early game against Canberra, Andy Gregory picked up a hamstring injury and was treated by an Australian masseur.

While Greg was laid flat out, waiting to have his thigh treated, the masseur told him that the most effective way for him to reach the injury was from the inside. Greg was in a fair bit of pain but wanted to know exactly what that procedure would entail. He was shocked to be told that the guy would have to stick his fingers up Greg's arsehole in order to manipulate the hamstring. When Greg told us this, you can imagine the amount of stick he got. But he assured us that it was a legitimate method of treatment and that it had worked. I wasn't convinced.

*****

201

From Hull to Hell and Back

Our third game in Australia was at Illawarra. The match was played on a Monday night and, for most of the team, that meant they were unlikely to be involved in the First Test the following Friday. For that reason, I hoped I wouldn't be selected. But, it didn't come as a huge surprise when I was chosen to start in the front row. I kept the disappointment to myself but couldn't deny I was pissed off. I have always recognised that coaches have decisions to make and, when they go against me it's a judgement call, but in this instance I disagreed. I knew that Malcolm preferred the more athletic forwards in the squad and my style didn't quite fit in with his game plan. No one was publicly saying that that was the British strategy, but it was becoming clear to anyone who knew anything about the game.

Nevertheless, it was still only the start of the tour and I wasn't just going to resign myself to playing midweek games for two months. I was used to having to fight for my international place and knew that I was good enough to earn my place. I just had to dig deep and make it impossible for Malcolm to leave me out. I had been in good shape when we left England but had spent the time in PNG getting myself even fitter and I went into the game as fit and strong as I had ever been in my career.

The Illawarra fixture was played on a Bank Holiday and there was a big crowd in, despite it being shown live on TV. As I had hoped, everything went well for me and I won the man of the match award chosen by the ex-Test prop Steve Roach, who was commentating on the game for Channel 9. 'Blocker' said that he couldn't understand why I wasn't a first choice for the Test team. Even though Blocker was a mate of mine from our time together at Balmain, it was music to my ears and some of the newspapers picked up on the story as well, which did my cause no harm. I don't know whether it was my performance or the media coverage that swung it, but Malcolm ended up picking me for the First Test after all.

It was a big ask to play two games in a week, especially for a forward but I had no complaints. I was on tour to play Test rugby and it gave me an even bigger buzz to know that I was the only non-Wigan forward in the side, lining up alongside Kelvin Skerrett, Dermott, Platt, Betts and Clarke.

The First Test in Sydney was one of the toughest games I ever played in. The Australian pack - with the likes of Glenn Lazarus, Paul Sironen and Paul Harragon in it - was huge. To make our task even harder, Skerrett was injured early on and had to be replaced by yet another Wigan forward, Ian Lucas. Anyone who has seen the match will remember the tackle by Ian Roberts that took Lucas out of the game. He had no chance of coming back on and, in fact, never played for GB again. It meant we were two forwards down which put us under even more pressure. When Platty also went off injured, it meant I was the only prop at Malcolm's disposal. With no replacements available, I ended up playing for the full eighty minutes, four days after playing Illawarra. In the circumstances, we did well to stay competitive, despite losing 22-6. I ran my blood to water and practically crawled off the field at the end, feeling that I had played as well as could be expected with so little support in the pack.

*****

After a tough start to the tour, Malcolm gave his squad the weekend off, so Schoey and me decided to let our hair down. On Saturday, we went to the Sydney Football Stadium to watch our ex-Leeds team-mate Craig 'Tugger' Coleman playing for Souths. Schoey's dad, who was out following the tour, came as well. Afterwards, there was lots of beer flowing and when Tugger joined us, we moved on to the South Sydney Leagues Club which turned into another session. It was the early hours when me and Schoey got back to our hotel in Manly and the taxi driver had to wake us up when he pulled up in front of the hotel.

The midweek team kept their unbeaten run intact when they won their game against a New South Wales rep team on the Tuesday. The next match was against Parramatta and it was expected that the Test team would line up. When I was only named as substitute I began to have some doubts about how I fitted into Malcolm's plans, but I never said anything at the time. I just got on with the game, which we lost.

Two days later, the team that would fly up to Newcastle to play the midweek game was announced. Coming just three days before the Second Test, none of the Test team were expected to travel.

When I found out I was in the side I couldn't believe it and, after the team meeting, went to see Malcolm. I asked him upfront whether I would be playing in the Second Test and he told me that I wouldn't. I wanted to know what I had done wrong in the first game and Malcolm told me that I had missed too many tackles. I couldn't believe what I was hearing. I pointed out that I had played for eighty minutes and had been the only prop on the pitch at the end - didn't that count for anything? Apparently it didn't. Malcolm wasn't interested in what I had to say; his mind was made up.

I went straight to Schoey's room and told him we were going to the pub. We jumped in a cab and, within half an hour, were in a bar in The Rocks. As we downed pint after pint, I poured out to him how I felt. I couldn't have been more pissed off. Nothing I did seemed good enough when it came to the Britain team. I'd worked so hard to get into the side for the First Test and done everything that had been asked of me. I had just about carried the pack in the First Test after Skerrett and Lucas had gone off injured. I'd made some mistakes in that game but what did they expect? I'd missed too many tackles apparently. It didn't seem to matter that I had been the only front-rower on the field. I played the full eighty minutes and made forty-four tackles in that game while Skerrett, Lucas and Platt were on the bench. Missed too many tackles? For fuck's sake, four of them were on Mal Meninga in one break! Each time I missed him, I got up, chased him, missed him again, got up, missed him again. I was the only one who could get anywhere near him. I wasn't happy and I certainly let Schoey know how I felt. As far as I was concerned, I told him, Malcolm could stick his team. I wasn't interested any more.

I wasn't in the mood to do anything besides drown my sorrows and I was glad when my mate Colin Maskill arrived from England the next day. Colin was touring with a Leeds supporters' club group and had lots of duties to carry out, but I managed to get hold of him and we had another big session all day Sunday.

As the day went on, I cheered up a bit and decided to stay out with Colin. At the end of the night, rather than go back to Manly, I opted to stay at his hotel in the centre of Sydney. As we rolled into reception in the early hours of the morning, we decided to have a nightcap in the lobby bar, which was full of blokes in uniform. It turned out that the hotel was used by lots of pilots from the Indonesian airline, Garuda. I assumed that the pilots had been out on the piss all night like we had and started to give them a bit of grief. 'Eh, there's no fucking wonder your planes are always crashing, is there?' I said, 'If you lot are out getting pissed every night!'

It was only when I noticed them sipping coffee that I realised they were actually on their way out to the airport. It was about five in the morning and their day was only just starting. I sobered up a bit after that and decided I ought to head back to the team hotel. Training began at half-seven so I called a cab which rushed me down to Sydney Harbour. From there, I managed to catch one of the first commuter ferries over to Manly. By the skin of my teeth, I was showered, changed and down to training by half-seven. I'm not too sure I trained all that well, but it had been a hell of a weekend.

*****

I never played in that game at Newcastle. I feigned an injury, stayed in Sydney and watched it in a bar. I had already lost interest in what was going on and Malcolm knew it. He wasn't stupid; he'd seen how pissed off I'd been when I heard I'd been dropped, although he never said anything.

He was the boss and there was nothing I could do about it; he didn't need to explain himself. In any case, we flew down to Melbourne for the Second Test the next day and, by then, the team had been announced. Sure enough, I wasn't in it. Instead, Andy Platt moved up to the front row and Billy McGinty came into the second row. I knew why Malcolm had made that call but still disagreed with it completely. I was still pissed off when we landed in Melbourne and kept myself to myself for most of that week.

By the Friday, I had picked myself up off the floor and I turned up for duty at pitchside at the MCG to help out with the interchanges, although I really didn't want to be there. Being dropped is one of the worst things in sport and at international level, for me, it was becoming a habit.

It was an incredible match. We dominated from the beginning to end and hammered the Aussies 33 points to 10 to square the series. The victory fully justified Malcolm's decision to pick an all-Wigan pack, although he had been helped by the fact that there were no injuries and nobody had been forced to play for eighty minutes, as I had in Sydney. Whatever the reasons for the win, nobody was ever going to challenge Malcolm's team selection now and so I was frozen out once again.

There was complete joy on the British bench and after the game everyone celebrated hard, not just because of the convincing win but because it now seemed possible that we could go on to Brisbane and win the series. While my team-mates were ecstatic, I couldn't have been more depressed.

Having being dropped, it actually hurt and upset me to see the team doing so well without me and I didn't feel like celebrating with the boys at all. I know that sounds petulant and childish and it is, but I couldn't help the way I felt.

After the post-match reception at the stadium, the team headed back to the hotel where we were met by hundreds of British supporters. Everyone headed straight for the bar and I bumped into David Poulter, my chairman at Castleford. He could see how fed up I was and bought me a drink to try and cheer me up but it was no use. I finished my beer and went to bed. While my Great Britain team-mates celebrated one of the greatest of all Test victories, I struggled to sleep in my hotel room having spat my dummy out completely.

*****

It embarrasses me now when I look back on how I reacted that night. I have a very strong sense of how team-mates ought to behave and how they should support one another. But when the shit hit the fan and I found myself marginalised, I behaved really disrespectfully.

One of my strengths had become my biggest weakness. I have always had strong opinions and plenty to say for myself. When I started out, it was seen as natural leadership quality. But I was becoming increasingly outspoken when I voiced my opinion on how I thought the game should be played. Those opinions never changed and nor did my style of play. Perhaps, on reflection, they should have. If I had been able to adapt my style to the demands of the modern game, maybe I could have been more successful at international level and won more caps but I was just too stubborn to change anything.

In 1992, my views were totally out of synch with those of the coaching team and there was definitely an agenda on that tour to pick an all-Wigan pack of forwards who would play a type of rugby that I didn't believe in. But if someone had just explained that to me and told me that I wasn't in the side because my style of play wasn't what they wanted, I would have accepted it. I wouldn't have agreed, but I would have appreciated the honesty, accepted the decision, got on with the tour and supported the team. That didn't happen. I had fought my way in, playing the style of rugby I had always played, and when I was left out, the reason given was that I had missed too many tackles; a bullshit excuse. I've never liked being deceived and I felt lied to and alienated. That doesn't excuse how I behaved, but it's the way it was.

*****

After what had happened in Melbourne, I wasn't expecting to be chosen for the Third Test and it was no surprise when the exact same side was chosen to play at Brisbane in the series decider. Once again, I was selected in the midweek team instead but, at half-time against the Gold Coast, I came off with a rib injury. My knee was also playing up, so I was more or less unavailable for a couple of weeks. Excused from playing or training, I was left to amuse myself until we left for the New Zealand leg of the tour.

In the Third Test at Brisbane, normal service was resumed and the Aussies dominated, although the winning margin was only six points. Yet another series was lost, but it had been competitive and many pundits were saying that the gap between the two teams had never been narrower.

While the core of the squad reflected on a job reasonably well done, I was nowhere to be seen. I started to hang around with mates I had made from my spells in Australia and was a bit of a passenger during the second half of the tour. To be fair, even Malcolm had probably lost touch with exactly who was still there and who wasn't. Injuries had played havoc with the original thrty-two-man party; almost a third of the squad had been forced to go home early to be replaced by the likes of Steve McNamara and Paul Broadbent.

I recovered sufficiently to be chosen for the last midweek game in Christchurch. The match had to be delayed for a couple of hours when our plane was unable to land due to heavy fog, but the disruption wasn't going to get in the way of another victory. The midweek team was very proud that it managed to go unbeaten throughout and there was lots of publicity about how important they had been to the whole party. But, to be honest, I thought it was a load of bollocks. I hadn't been very impressed by the quality of the midweek opposition and couldn't get excited about playing against them, even when we were winning. There was only one team I wanted to be playing for and, having been left out of the Test side, I would have gladly headed home. It was only my loyalty to Malcolm that obliged me to see it through.

*****

It had been my third senior tour down under and each one had ended in disappointment, not just because the team had been beaten by the Aussies. By the start of the 1992-93 season, I was absolutely sick and tired of dealing with disappointment. It had been five years since Hull sold me to Leeds and, despite a couple of good years at Castleford, it seemed that I kept coming up against one setback after another.

At first, I resigned myself to having played my last game for Great Britain. Perhaps I should have retired from international rugby at that point, although most people would have chuckled and said that I didn't have any choice in the matter. But, whenever I have found myself at a low in my career, I have always taken pride in how I responded. After the disappointment of the 1992 tour went away, I decided that I wasn't finished with the GB side. A lot of sportsmen say they tried to achieve success in order to prove their critics wrong, but I didn't give a damn what any of my critics thought. To be honest, I'm not sure that I really had any 'critics'; they were just a bunch of rugby league writers who assumed I wouldn't be picked any more. I didn't feel any real urge to prove anything to anyone except myself and I would have been disappointed if the '92 tour had been my last involvement with the international set-up. Over the next two seasons, I played some of the best rugby of my career and, again, I was really proud to read the reports.

By the start of 1994, a lot of people were saying that I was the form prop in the country, but it was still a surprise when Malcolm picked me for a one-off Test match in France. After the disappointment of 1992, it was the most satisfying call-up of my career.

Alongside me in the British pack was Andy Farrell, one of the best young players in the game. He was making his second appearance for his country, aged eighteen. Eleven and a half years earlier, I had just turned nineteen when I made my debut against Australia in Hull, alongside Jeff Grayshon, who had started playing the game in the 1960s.

The game had changed beyond belief but my style hadn't changed one bit. It had been good enough to play alongside Grayshon and good enough to play alongside Farrell.

Over twelve years, I had been in and out of fashion more than shoulder pads and ra-ra skirts, but that final Test cap in 1994 gave me massive pleasure. I proved to myself - and anyone else who cared - that I had stayed an international-quality player in spite of all the shit that had happened to me or that I had brought upon myself. After earning that cap, I was satisfied and could then concentrate purely on playing for Castleford. On reflection, I really should have retired from international rugby at that point.

*****

Before I leave my international career behind, I must share my thoughts on two blokes with whom I had the privilege of playing for my country and who, to be honest, enjoyed much greater success in a British jersey than I did.

Shaun Edwards will probably go down as the most successful rugby league player of all time and he was remarkable in so many ways. I always got on okay with Shaun and we even roomed together once or twice. But when I think about how Shaun approached his sport, it helps me understand more about myself.

I always felt that Shaun must have made a decision, quite early in his career, to focus purely on achieving as much personal success as he could at the expense of everything else. To achieve that, he would have to put himself first and even sacrifice personal friendships to get where he wanted to be. Consequently, Shaun wasn't always popular amongst his fellow professionals but I think he thought that was a price worth paying. I don't blame Shaun for that at all; he has achieved everything he aimed for and continues to be successful in rugby union, but his attitude made him quite difficult for his team-mates to get along with him at times.

We go into sport for any number of reasons and I had a different set of priorities to Shaun. I get the impression that he has mellowed with age and is probably an easier bloke to get along with now. Even though I wouldn't class him as a friend, he is an intriguing character and I'm glad to have known him.

My best mate in the game has always been Garry Schofield. Schoey constantly impressed me, from the first time I saw him play as a centre, through his reinvention as a world-class stand-off to the way he managed to sustain his playing career well into his thirties. He is a great guy, a loyal friend and it's a real shame he's not still involved in the game at a higher level.

Garry is right to think that he has lots to offer but I think he feels a bit aggrieved that he's not a top coach. Like me, he has strong views on how the game should be played, but it can be very difficult to accept that other people don't share those views. Consequently, we often have to find other roles within the game where we can have an impact and just accept that we can't all be head coaches.

9

A Gottle o' Geer

By now, I hope you will have realised that when it comes to trying to 'sell' myself, I'm actually quite shy and modest. I'd rather back down than seek confrontation. Nevertheless, I have always had a very stubborn streak as well and there have been occasions over the years where I have chosen to dig my heels in.

Usually it's on a matter of principle when I have felt let down or deceived. It happened when I was a player at Leeds and it happened when I was coaching at Hull KR. It's hard to explain why I decided that enough was enough. Partly, it was just stubbornness but I was also confident that I could walk away and rebuild my career elsewhere. When I decided, on principle, to stay away from Leeds, I knew it wouldn't be long before another club came in. There were people at Leeds who let me down badly and I didn't want to play for them any longer. But, I'm not stupid. I always knew I could go somewhere else.

Fortunately, that club turned out to be Castleford and I

knew straight away that it was the right move. They weren't a big club and didn't have the stadium or the money that Leeds did, but it was a club in the best sense of the word. There was a family atmosphere and, as soon as I spent some time around the training ground, I just knew that I would be much happier. There was integrity about the place and a sense that everyone was pulling in the same direction. I was thankful to Cas for giving me another chance to rebuild my career and determined to do my best for their coach, Darryl van der Velde, and chairman David Poulter.

I went on to enjoy many successful years at Castleford, but if I thought that a change would be all that was needed to immediately improve my fortunes, I was much mistaken. The first year at Wheldon Road was no better than the worst of times at Leeds. I faced a long struggle to get myself back to where I wanted to be on and off the field.

*****

Not long after my debut I made my first return to Hull in a Castleford shirt. I'd never enjoyed playing against Hull and this was no different. I was sent off for a high tackle. The RFL was in the middle of a purge on high tackles at the time and I landed an eight-match ban. Once back, I picked up an injury and finished my first season with my new club having played only seven games and making very little impact. I was twenty-six years old, a million miles from the Great Britain team and another season had slipped by without any kind of success.

Away from the pitch, Karen and I had had our first child in 1989 and I was beginning to settle down into our normal, happy family life together. At the time, Wigan was the only club to operate a full-time squad while, at Cas, most players still held down full-time jobs. My situation was slightly different. I wasn't on a bad wage and could just about get by without working, but I was conscious that I really needed something to keep me occupied during the day.

At Leeds, I had tried, unsuccessfully, to set up my own decorating business. I hoped to be able to pick up work from club sponsors but it never really worked out. Once I moved to Castleford, I decided to advertise my services again and hoped to pick up casual work without the hassle of managing a business.

Again, it didn't really work out, but I did bits of work for a while. One year, David Poulter wanted the roof girders at Wheldon Road painting. Grant Anderson was a scaffolder so, between us, we figured that we could do the job. We agreed a price with David and set about the task. It took us ages but the job was straightforward and we could knock off and go in the gym for an hour or two after work.

Grant was forever looking for ways to wind up Steve Kirk, the groundsman. On one occasion, he asked me to help him push his scaffold over onto the pitch and pretend there had been an accident. Once it was on its side, he lay down underneath it and started moaning as if he had fallen off the top. 'Go get Steve,' he told me. I went running off, shouting: 'Steve, Steve, the scaffolding's collapsed.' As soon as Steve came around the corner and saw Grant laid under the scaffolding, he shat himself. When Grant crawled out, Steve went mental. 'Look what you've done to my fucking pitch, you daft bastard,' he shouted, oblivious to whether Grant was hurt or not.

Full time sportsmen have lots of time on their hands and when not training I had to keep busy. I spent a lot of time hanging around a second-hand car dealership in Castleford owned by a bloke called Des Kerry, a good mate of mine. Des and his dad were always in there, along with Knocker and players like John Joyner and Gary Stephens. We'd just sit around in their back office, drinking coffee, talking about rugby and gossiping about who got pissed the night before. It was all pretty boring and mundane but it kept us entertained and filled up the long hours between training sessions. Later, when Castleford went full-time, we spent more time training and on other duties such as going into schools and doing promotional stuff with sponsors. I never minded any of that.

*****

Despite signing for a new club, trouble still kept coming my way. No sooner had I signed for Castleford than I was woken early one morning by a knock on the door. It was a couple of constables from West Yorkshire Police.

'Morning, Lee. Sorry to get you up but we've come to arrest you.' After the initial shock, I invited them in and asked what I was supposed to have done.

'We've had an accusation that you've beaten up a taxi driver,' I was told.

As the story unfolded, it turned out that I had been accused of assaulting some bloke after an argument about a taxi fare. As ridiculous as it sounds, the police were taking it seriously. I was taken down to Normanton police station and locked up for most of the day until they finally got round to questioning me.

While I was stewing in the cell, Karen turned up with one of her mates to see if she could help. They knew the whole thing was a joke and weren't taking it at all seriously. They had brought along placards saying 'Free Lee Crooks' and sat all day in reception, occasionally bursting into a chorus of 'Free Nelson Mandela', but with my name instead.

The case was a shambles. The allegation was that I had refused to pay for a cab ride home. The driver complained, I had beaten him up. The bloke hadn't even been able to give a description of his attacker except that he was heavily built and had very short hair. He reported it to the police but hadn't been able to give a decent enough description. Then, sometime later, he spotted me coming out of a nightclub in Castleford. When he told one of his mates he recognised me, his pal said: 'You will do. That's Lee Crooks. He's just signed for Cas.' At which point, the taxi driver decided it was me who had beaten him up and gone back to the police.

I'd lived in Castleford for more than three years by then and was well known by most of the taxi drivers in town. I couldn't understand why the driver hadn't identified me earlier. It was also odd that I had supposedly beaten him up after being dropped at the top of my street. There's no way I would have been dropped off there. Whenever I got a taxi home it would always drop me outside my house.

While I thought the case was a joke, it was still quite a scary experience. Anyone that has ever been involved in a criminal case will know that your innocence doesn't mean you're out of trouble. I knew I needed to get myself a decent barrister. That in itself cost me a couple of grand. In the end, when it went to court, the judge threw the case out in a matter of minutes, saying there was no evidence whatsoever to put me at the scene.

After the case had been dismissed, I had no ill-feeling to the guy who made the accusation. He had been beaten up and genuinely thought I had done it. There was nothing for him to gain in accusing me; it wasn't like he was selling his story to the *News of the World*. Nevertheless, the incident reminded me of my vulnerable position in the public eye in a relatively small town. My reputation meant that I was a bit of an easy shot for anyone who wanted to cause a ruck or make a wild accusation. And it wasn't long after the court case that I came close to landing myself in bother with the police again. I had fallen out with Karen one time and was crashing down at Keith 'Beefy' England's place for a few nights. It was just before Christmas, Beefy was going out for the night round Wakefield and he asked me for a lift. Once we got to the pub, he asked me if I wanted to go in for a pint. I figured one pint wouldn't do any harm.

A few pints later, I left him in the pub and stopped off to collect an Indian take away on the way back to his house. As I approached a roundabout near Rothwell, I didn't see the ice on the road, reacted too late and lost control. The next few seconds were in slow motion. I completely shit myself as the car skidded across the road and went straight through a crash barrier on the far side. I had no idea what was going to happen next and feared the worst when it started to tip over the edge of an embankment. It was pitch black but I could see bits of tree and undergrowth in front of me. The car kept moving for another twenty or thirty feet down the hill until it finally came to a halt at the bottom.

After a few seconds I realised that, once again, I had failed to kill myself. Physically, I was perfectly okay. Nevertheless, I started to panic that if anyone called the police I might need to explain why I was in a ditch - quite possibly over the limit - and covered in chicken jalfrezi.

I jumped out of the car, clambered up the embankment and was relieved to see that there was no one else around. No witnesses. I went in search of a phone box and called Karen, who agreed to come and pick me up.

By the time I reported what had happened to the police, I knew for certain that I wasn't over the limit but that didn't stop them from coming to interview me. They had found several empty bottles of lager in the car and suspected that I had literally been drinking at the wheel. I totally forgot that Beefy had been drinking in the car and had left some bottles under his seat. Thankfully, they didn't try and nail me for drink driving.

*****

Around the same time, I made another bad judgment which could have cost me my relationship with Darryl van der Velde and led to the end of my brief career at Castleford. Instead, it prompted a conversation that finally forced me to confront problems I had ignored for far too long.

Darryl called a training session for the last Friday before Christmas. It was the day when everyone else in town was downing tools for the holiday and the pubs were heaving. I couldn't resist the temptation of joining in and went to the pub with Beefy, Grant Anderson and Shaun Irwin. After a couple of drinks, Grant and Shaun headed off for training. I had supped a few pints and was in no state to join them. I figured it was better not to go at all than turn up drunk so Beefy and I persuaded each other to stay in the pub.

It was a stupid decision. When Darryl found out where I was, he dropped me for the Hull game on Boxing Day. I never liked returning to play at the Boulevard but in this case I was desperate to play and knew that I had fucked up.

John Joyner was captain at the time. When we returned to training after Christmas, he made it clear how he felt; I had let Darryl down and it would take a pretty impressive apology to repair the damage I'd done. I went to see Darryl straight away and, as soon as I walked in his office, it was clear he was expecting me. He told me to sit down, closed the door and we started to talk.

The conversation we had that day was probably the most important of my life, let alone my career. I didn't have much choice but to listen. He was my boss and I had crossed him but, for once, I was quite happy to listen. When my turn came, I spoke calmly and honestly, maybe for the first time in my life. For most of the time, we never even talked about rugby.

Instead, we discussed my life with Karen and how I felt about having a new baby daughter. We talked about what I wanted out of my life and how I was going to go about getting it.

He was very blunt; he told me the situation could go one of two ways. I could carry on as I was and my career would go down the shitpan, or I could do something to change my lifestyle and rebuild my career and life.

I knew that I needed to do the latter but he forced me to admit it without giving excuses or being defensive. I faced up to my problems and began to accept the solutions that would sort me out. I needed to become more professional in everything I did. I needed to say no when people offered me a beer. I needed to go home after one or two pints and not stay out all night. I needed to grow up and stop trying to act like a teenager with no responsibilities.

Darryl gave me practical advice as well. He told me to buy a house in Castleford, put down some roots and start to make a proper go of things with Karen. Everything he was saying was right and, for once, I was ready to hear it. Even as he was talking, I knew I really was going to sort myself out this time. I had said it to myself before but, this time, I knew it was going to be different.

Over the coming months, I did what Darryl suggested. I trained harder than ever and cut down my drinking. Karen and I bought the council house we'd been living in and I began to make a real commitment to our relationship.

I would be lying if I said that I never behaved badly after that day, but that talk was exactly what I needed. It helped me to put right lots of things that were wrong with my life.

As the months and years went by, I gradually became a different person. I became more professional, more reliable and more disciplined. The wheels came off occasionally, but I was certainly moving in the right direction. I will always be grateful to Darryl for caring enough about me to do that.

*****

It soon became clear that Darryl was starting to put a very useful team together at Castleford. In August 1991, he made one of the most important signings of all: Tawera Nikau. 'T' was already playing in England, for Sheffield, but no one had really noticed. It was only when he pulled on a Cas jersey that everyone realised what a special player he was.

Darryl was on form that close-season and also pulled off a real coup in signing Richie Blackmore from New Zealand. Sadly for Mick Ford, hardly anyone noticed when we signed him from Oldham. It might not even have been Oldham, which proves my point I suppose.

With those three on board, though, Cas had its strongest team in years. I'd also had my best pre-season for ages and was, to all intents and purposes, like a new signing myself. My hard work since our heart-to-heart had not gone unnoticed and I was very proud when Darryl called me into his office one day, this time not for a bollocking, but to ask me to captain his team. It meant I had now captained three of the best teams in Yorkshire; Hull, Leeds and Castleford. It was a real honour and gave me a lot of encouragement to continue down the right path.

*****

Unsurprisingly, there was an air of optimism for the first game of the campaign. We were playing Wigan and I always relished the challenge of facing their pack, undoubtedly the best in the game. And there was another reason why the players were so chipper. Afterwards, we were off to Leeds for Keith England's Testimonial dinner.

The day got off to the perfect start when we beat Wigan.

From Hull to Hell and Back

All my hard work in the pre-season paid off. I felt in great shape and seem to remember that I got the man of the match award as well.

We had a beer or two straight after the game and then headed to the Dragonara Hotel in Leeds, on a double decker bus that Beefy had arranged for us. Everyone was in a great mood, celebrating the start to the season and it was a very tough audience for Steve Kindon, the ex-footballer, who was giving the after-dinner speech.

Steve was followed by a comedian-ventriloquist called Sid The Parrot; a comedian with a huge toy parrot perched on his arm. The poor bastard bombed as the roomful of boisterous rugby players heckled and jeered him. While he struggled through his act, the blokes on my table grew more and more abusive until one of them dared me to jump up on stage and steal his parrot.

I told them to shut up. We were all amused by the bloke and not in the way he had intended, but I wasn't going to make a fool of himself for everyone else's entertainment. I went to the toilet, thinking how funny it would be if someone *did* nick the bloke's parrot but also determined that it wouldn't be me. My days as the class clown were over.

The route back to my table took me directly behind the stage and, before I knew it, I had jumped up, grabbed hold of the bloke's arm and tried to drag the parrot off his shoulder. As you'd expect, he was stunned but he was a strong bugger and wasn't letting go easily. In fact he was fighting back and screaming, which I thought was a bit unnecessary. I was only having a laugh and it was only a bloody toy parrot.

Eventually, I managed to rip the thing off his shoulder, much to the enjoyment of the audience who were now on their feet yelling and shouting. As I held the parrot aloft, like I had been presented with the Challenge Cup, I noticed that the comedian was clutching his shoulder and moaning. He seemed to be in a lot of pain and I realised that he hadn't just been refusing to let go of the parrot, his arm had been all the way inside and he hadn't been *able* to let go. Unbeknown to me, I had been giving him a chicken-wing tackle.

Of course, everyone else thought it was hilarious and were out of their seats howling with laughter. I took one look at the bloke on the stage floor and knew that my joke would backfire. It suddenly didn't seem very funny and all I could think of was to get away from the place. I left straight away and went home feeling stupid and embarrassed.

I woke up next morning with a banging headache and that horrible feeling you get when you know you have done something stupid the night before. After a day off, I turned up for training on the Tuesday knowing I would have to face the music.

As I pulled into Wheldon Road, I saw an inflatable parrot pinned to the gates and figured I must be seeing things. Bloody parrots! I'm seeing them everywhere, I thought. But once I stepped onto the training ground, I realised that all of the boys were in on it. They were determined to get their money's worth out of this.

'Eh, Lee,' said one. 'Darryl isn't dropping you this week, you'll be playing on the wing.'

'Yes,' said another. 'He's putting you out to seed.'

'If he prosecutes, Crooksy, you'll be in front of the beak!'

'Leave him alone. That's a cheep shot.' And so it went on.

At the end of training, I got the dreaded call and made yet another visit to Darryl's office. After an embarrassing few moments, it was decided that I ought to write a letter of apology to the bloke, which was fair enough.

The next time I saw him he was on the telly performing at the Royal Variety Performance, so I was relieved I hadn't done his career any serious arm.

*****

After that early-season hiccup, I got on with the serious job of trying to get the best out of the team. We got off to the perfect start, making it to the Yorkshire Cup final where we beat Bradford easily, although I was disappointed to miss the game with a neck injury.

The new arrivals had taken time to settle in and our form in the first half of the season was patchy. But after Christmas everything clicked into place and we went on a twelve-match unbeaten run which saw us storm up the league.

Our winning run started with a home win over Hull and, in mid-March, we found ourselves facing them again in a Challenge Cup semi-final. In a tight game at Headingley we led 8-4 going into the last few minutes. And when Graham Steadman dropped a high ball in the last minute, it looked as if Hull's Paul Eastwood might score, but he missed the chance and we managed to hold on.

It was a strange feeling for me. If Hull had been playing any other team that day, I would have been there supporting them. Of course, I was delighted to be going to Wembley as captain of Castleford, but it gave me no pleasure at all to see the thousands of disappointed Hull followers. Some gave me stick but I was quite capable of dealing with that by now.

It had been seven years since my last appearance at Wembley and the 1985 defeat with Hull and those four missed kicks at goal still haunted me. Failure in 1985 had shaken me up and I'd promised to return and win the Cup as captain of Hull. It never happened. I went off the rails, Hull sold me to Leeds and it looked, for a long time, like I would never play at Wembley again. Now here I was preparing to go there as captain of Cas.

This would be a huge event for Castleford. Wigan had

Above: The Hull team celebrates winning the 1982 Challenge Cup final replay at Elland Road, with David Topliss held aloft. Pictured - 'Knocker' Norton, Gary Kemble, Keith Tindall, David Topliss, me, Charlie Stone, Steve Evans, Mick Crane, Tony Duke and Paul Prendiville.

Above: After winning the Championship in 1983, we celebrated with the New Zealand haka in front of the Threepenny Stand. Left to right - Paul Rose, Gary Kemble, me, Mick Crane, 'Knocker' Norton, Kevin Harkin, James Leuluai, Barry Banks, Steve Evans, Arthur Bunting and Dane O'Hara.

Left: Daughter
Emma gets a ride in
the Rugby League
Championship
trophy, 1983, as I set
off for another Cup
final appearance

Right: Defeat against
Featherstone Rovers
in 1983 was an
absolutely massive
disappointment. We
underestimated Fev
when they were
there for the taking.

Above: We played Hull KR in two cup finals during the 1984-85 season. Here, I take on the Rovers line in the Yorkshire Cup final, watched by James Leuluai, Peter Sterling and 'Knocker' Norton.

Above: We came from behind to win and I scored a try in the second half.

Left: As captain, I was hugely proud to lift the Yorkshire Cup in a black and white shirt

Above: Celebrating with my team-mates. What a line-up - Fred Ah Kuoi, James Leuluai, Wayne Proctor, Gary Divorty, Gary Kemble, me, Shaun Patrick, 'Knocker', Peter Sterling, Steve Evans, Phil Edmonds, Garry Schofield and Dane O'Hara.

Above: Hull v Castleford, Challenge Cup semi-final, 1985. I was very pleased with my two performances against Cas - I won man of the match in the replay after going toe-to-toe with the great Malcolm Reilly. Here, Gary Kemble, Shaun Patrick, Garry Schofield and 'Knocker' watch me make another run at the Cas defence.

Above: This last-minute penalty kick against the touring 1985 Kiwis squared the game and the series against a very physical New Zealand team. It was probably the highlight of my Great Britain career.

PICS: Andrew Varley

Above: Kevin Ward and Garry Schofield watch me make a break against the 1986 Kangaroos. We prepared incredibly well for the series but the Australians had got even better and it wasn't very competitive.

Left: Against Wigan, John Player Trophy semi-final at Bolton, 1987. Dislocating my shoulder was the most painful injury I ever had and capped a dreadful year.

PICS: Andrew Varley

Right: After three years out of the Great Britain squad, I was very proud when Mal Reilly picked me to play in the two-game series against France, 1992. I like this photograph because there isn't a French defender in sight...

Left: The return fixture in the 1992 Test series with France was at the Boulevard, which was a nice experience. Shaun Edwards and Graham Steadman look on as I break.

Above: Playing for Castleford against Salford in the second season of summer Super League, 1997. I thoroughly enjoyed it, but the game was soon too fast for me.

PICS: Andrew Varley

Family photo album: (Clockwise) My daughter Megan; Lee with Megan and Ben on holiday in Tenerife; Cilla (Karen's mum), Ben, Colin (cousin), Karen and Martin (son of Knocker) at a Champion Schools final; Grandad (Karen's dad, Ernie) cuddles Megan and Ben.

Family photo album: (Clockwise) Grandkids Beau, Sonny and Georgia; Ben in action v Warrington; Young Ben with Dad; Emma and Stuart at school.

totally dominated the Challenge Cup since the end of the 1980s and they'd won four on the bounce going into the 1992 final. They were also a team of full-time professionals and rugby league was certainly shifting in that direction by the early 1990s. Wigan's success showed there was a lot to be said for that but, for every other club, a team of full-time pros was a pipe dream. They just couldn't afford it.

For clubs like Castleford, the move to professionalism came gradually. At first, only a handful of players were able to commit themselves solely to their rugby and, by the middle of the 1991-92 season, there were about ten or twelve of us who were full-time. We would train together on a Wednesday and then be joined by the rest of the squad for full training sessions on Tuesday and Thursday nights. It wasn't a perfect arrangement but it gave us a bit of an edge that, hopefully, we could pass on to the part-time lads.

Once we reached the Cup final, Darryl asked all the boys if it was possible for them to go full-time for a month leading up to the big game. It wasn't easy for most of the blokes, who held down jobs they couldn't just walk away from. Nevertheless, with a bit of financial help from the directors, the club was able to do a deal with most of the players' employers to release them for four weeks and we became, for the first time, a full-time rugby league side.

Darryl also negotiated with Hicksons, our major sponsor, for us to have our lunch together in their staff canteen across the road from the ground. With all the extra training, we needed to eat 4,000 calories a day to keep our weight up, so the canteen staff were instructed to feed us plenty. The idea of eating at Hicksons was okay in principle but, in reality, the food wasn't really suitable and we ended up eating too much at lunchtime rather than small amounts regularly. I wasn't used to eating so much and put on weight.

No opportunity was missed to prepare as thoroughly as

possible, but Darryl went one step further. He wanted us to keep off the booze for a month as well. As captain, he approached me first and asked for my view. I said it was a good idea and wished him good luck in breaking the news to the lads. But Darryl had already figured that out and said he wanted me to tell them.

To be fair, in the build up to such a big game, most of the players wouldn't drink much anyway. When I told them what Darryl and I wanted to do, there was no resistance. We weren't a big drinking team in any case, although the news of us going on the wagon attracted quite a bit of publicity, which did us no harm in the build-up.

The combination of training full-time and staying away from the pub had its effect. I felt fresh and fit and I think all the players had an extra bit of hunger and desire due to the little sacrifice we had made. I suspect the pledge may have been broken by one or two lads who might have had the odd night out, but I was pleased not to be one of them. By the time of the big day, I was as fit and fresh (albeit a bit heavier) as I had been in years and fully focused on causing an upset.

*****

In contrast to the Wigan team, only a handful of our lads had played at Wembley before. It was six years since Castleford last made it to the Cup final, when they beat Hull KR. Keith England and Martin Ketteridge had both been in the team that day, as had JJ, who was now club captain but unlikely to play this time around. And then, of course, there was me. I felt a lot of responsibility as one of the senior players and knew that if we were to have any chance, I needed to play my part as well.

In spite of our best laid plans, we were never really in it. For me, it was made worse by having to sit out all but the first twenty minutes of the game after being forced off with injury. There were times when I wondered whether Andy Platt was made of granite. In tackling him, the impact on my shoulder jarred my whole body so badly that I had to go off with a groin injury. It was a nightmare. The physio told me I had no chance of returning to the field, but I refused to go back to the dressing rooms to change. Instead, I tried to run it off. But each time I tried to jog up and down the touchline, I felt shooting pains through my groin and had to agree with the physio that I couldn't return. It was always going to be hard for us to get a result against Wigan and to lose a senior player so early only made it harder. The lads never gave in but we ended up losing 28-12. Our extra preparations and sacrifices had come to nothing.

As I watched from the bench, I couldn't believe the bad luck I seemed to have at Wembley. After four appearances, apart from the drawn final of 1982 I had been on the losing side each time. And this one was probably worse, because I hadn't been able to make any kind of contribution.

Afterwards, we drowned our sorrows with a few beers in the dressing room and then went up to the Long Bar where the players mingled with sponsors and other guests. It was a part of the day I never particularly enjoyed; not because I didn't like that kind of thing, but because it was not a place for losers and, as I said, I was never a winner at Wembley. Even though the winning team would always behave magnanimously - they would leave the Cup behind and not celebrate in front of the team they had just beaten - it never felt great to socialise when you were so disappointed. I was also worried that my injury might impact on the tour of Australia I was due to go on later in the month.

Meanwhile, while I tried to drown my sorrows, Karen floated around trying to get as many people as possible into the bar. It was always a bit of a scramble to do that at

Wembley. Each player was only allowed two guest passes so I have no idea how she managed to smuggle in Knocker, his girlfriend, and Mick, our next door neighbour, and his wife. Nevertheless, it wasn't enough for Karen and she managed to get even more of our mates in. At one point, Eddie and Stevo from Sky TV showed up and even they didn't have passes to get in. Mick, my neighbour, saw Stevo struggling with one of the Wembley doormen and called over, asking him if he needed a pass.

'Yes, mate,' replied Stevo. 'Do you have one spare?'

'I do, Stevo,' said Mick. 'But you're not fucking having it!' Mick didn't like Stevo and always loved telling that story.

Somehow, the players managed to get most of their pals in. The bar was rammed and service was a nightmare. Karen found her way to the bar and started ordering drinks for everyone within sight. She didn't mind, even when she ended up standing drinks for some of the Wigan lot. They all knew Karen and were having a good laugh with her as she bought their drinks. All, that is, except Shaun Edwards. He just grabbed his pint and walked off. She had never liked him much before that, but that was the icing on the cake.

After every Wembley final, I always told myself that I would go back one day and put it right. In 1992, I told myself the same thing but, in the back of my mind, I wondered whether I would get another chance. At twenty-eight, there were a few years in me yet but there wouldn't be too many more chances to go back there and win.

We finished the season in third spot, one place higher than the previous year. We retained the Yorkshire Cup and made it to Wembley. We had come on in leaps and bounds and were now one of the top teams in the country, but ending the season with defeat at Wembley left a bitter taste. For me personally though it had been a very important year. I was enjoying my rugby again and playing with a bunch of blokes I liked and respected. I had got my lifestyle in order and, even though I still enjoyed the odd night out, it wasn't damaging my career or relationship with Karen.

*****

After the final, I needed to prove my fitness in order to take up my tour place down under, but the groin injury didn't prove serious and I was able to travel, as already described. That the tour ended badly was down to circumstances as much as anything else. But regardless of who was to blame, once I returned from Australia I had to pull myself back together and accept that another situation had blown up in my face.

It was becoming a recurring problem; whenever I had been let down by people in authority, whether it be Dick Gemmell, Roy Waudby, the board of directors at Leeds or Malcolm Reilly, I had responded by throwing a tantrum and walking away. I knew that I was a good enough player to rebuild things, but I also knew that I couldn't keep doing it. One day, people might get fed up and, also, it wasn't doing much for my own sanity.

I would never agree with Malcolm's decision to leave me out of the Test side but I had to accept that the game had changed and that my style of football was no longer the only way rugby league could be played. I had been overtaken by a different type of player and most of them were younger than me and played for Wigan. If I was going to be able to extend my career into my thirties I had to learn to behave better when things didn't go my way. As captain of one of the best teams, I also had a duty to conduct myself more professionally in public and amongst my peers. Once again, my actions had forced me to confront the fact that I needed to change my ways.

From Hull to Hell and Back

*****

I still had a year left on my contract at Cas when I came back from Australia in 1992 and, while I was away, I couldn't help but overhear how much some blokes were starting to earn from the game, particularly the full-time lads at Wigan.

I knew my existing contract of £25,000 per year was low by comparison, so when I went to see the chairman. I was hopeful he would make me a better offer. In the event, I was offered a deal which saw my wages step up in each of the next three years so that, by 1995, I would be earning more money than ever before, around fifty grand a year.

Meanwhile, Darryl van der Velde had become frustrated at Castleford. He had a vision that he could turn us into one of the biggest clubs in the game but didn't feel some of the directors shared that ambition. Mid-season, he told us he was leaving to be head coach of the new South Queensland Crushers. He stayed until the end of the season by which time John Joyner had been groomed to take over.

We finished sixth that season which was a disappointing end to Darryl's spell at the club. He had moved it forward massively and, for me personally, been an enormous figure. I was sad to see him go but was also very keen to work with John, who was someone I had a lot of respect for, as well as being a good mate. Even before the season ended, I was looking forward to the next. The summer of 1993 was the first time in years that I felt really grounded and stable. With Megan and Ben with us, life seemed idyllic. Between pre-season training sessions and spending time with the family, I also enjoyed the odd day out with mates.

I've always enjoyed a day at the cricket and, whenever England played a Test match at Headingley, Leeds Rugby Club, as landlords of the ground, would have an executive box for sponsors, directors and players to use. Occasionally, there would also be an invitation for an ex-player such as myself and I managed to blag a ticket for the Ashes series against Australia, along with some of the Leeds lads like Garry Schofield and Colin Maskill. It was one of those great summer days; the sun shone, there was a free bar and we had a great laugh enjoying each others' company while watching the cricket. I could always be trusted to find drama in any situation, though and, late in the afternoon, I accidently caused a commotion that could have made headlines around the world.

Our executive box was on the top of a four-storey block near to the players' pavilion. We spent most of our time sat on the balcony in the sunshine, only going inside to grab another beer from the fridge or nip to the toilets along the landing at the back of the box. At one point, I needed a pee. I was still laughing and joking and a bit distracted when I stepped out of our box and on to the shared landing. Not looking where I was going, I didn't notice the smart looking middle-aged chap who stepped out of the box next to ours.

We accidentally collided and because he was only a little fellow, I knocked him off his feet and almost sent him toppling over the balcony. 'Sorry mate,' I said, immediately thinking that he looked familiar, one of the Leeds' directors perhaps, or maybe someone connected to Yorkshire County Cricket Club. As soon as we made contact a bunch of burly blokes in dark suits came crashing out of the box to his defence. I was a bit taken aback but soon realised why.

'Prime Minister, Sir. Are you okay?' they asked.

In my hurry to have a piss without missing any of the action, I had almost knocked John Major out of the executive boxes and sent him tumbling forty or fifty feet to the ground. Unsurprisingly, Special Branch, MI6 or whoever they were, were understandably concerned about his wellbeing. After more apologies from me, they let me go on my way. By this time, of course, all the executive boxes had emptied to watch me being shaken down by the Prime Minister's security staff.

Needless to say, in the days afterwards, nobody talked much about the cricket, but plenty about how Lee Crooks had come close to toppling the Government.

10

The Party's Over

Professionalism has never come easy to me. Nobody in my family played professional sport and, when I started, rugby league was essentially an amateur sport played by blokes who got paid. I was ten years in the game and onto my third club and second wife before I learned how to be a true professional.

It was a tough journey but by 1993 I felt I had made it. I felt comfortable and valued at Castleford where my attitude and conduct were consistently excellent. More importantly, I was settled at home, with two kids and a partner I loved dearly. With my new-found professionalism, it's probably not surprising that the next few years were very successful for me and the 1993-94 season, in particular, was probably the most enjoyable of my whole career.

The Castleford team that year was as good as any I ever played for. When John Joyner took over from Darryl he made it clear his philosophy would be different. John first played for the club in the 1970s when the team was known as Classy Cas and he believed we had the players to recreate that style and play attractive and expansive rugby too. This suited me down to the ground; I had no time for the kind of no-risk rugby that was becoming so common.

Free to take chances and to play my natural game, I had one of the best seasons of my career. When John took over, there were already some outstanding players in the team; Tawera Nikau, Graham Steadman, Tony Smith, Grant Anderson, Singe Ellis, Mike Ford and Richie Blackmore. But signing Tony Kemp from Newcastle was JJ's masterstroke. Kempy brought extra flair and experience and, alongside Smithy in the half-backs, gave us lots of attacking options. Our side was very close to being perfectly balanced but, most importantly, there was an outstanding team ethic and I was very proud to lead them as captain.

In 1993, Wigan's domination was at its peak but we came as close as anyone to breaking their monopoly on all the game's silverware. We held our own in five epic games against them during that season.

When they came to Wheldon Road for a league game in late October, many of their players had been involved in the Test match between Great Britain and New Zealand the day before. Some were left out while a few more doubled up and played two games in two days. The Wigan players who did double up were obviously fatigued but it was a bad idea to show up tired at Wheldon Road. We hammered them 46-0. I had a decent game as well, repeatedly breaking their line to set up some of our eight tries. I also kicked seven goals and won the man of the match award.

That victory set us up for a great run of results stretching right through the winter. We also made good progress through to the Regal Trophy semi-finals where we played Bradford for the right to play Wigan in the final. Bradford were a very physical side but JJ didn't want us to change our own approach one bit. We prepared exactly as we had all season and were very confident we could beat them, although JJ had a plan in place to deal with what he believed to be their biggest threat.

Paul Newlove had developed into one of the most dangerous outside backs in the country and he was one of the few players in the Bradford team that worried us. JJ knew that Paul was the kind of player who would destroy us if he was in the right frame of mind, but he also knew that he had a questionable temperament and could lose interest if he got hurt early on. Beforehand, JJ left me in no doubt that my job was to 'sort out Newy'.

JJ's words were still in my mind when I found myself tackling Paul early in the game. What followed led some to argue that I should have been sent off, but let's just say that, when my head came into contact with his cheekbone, I wasn't desperate to move it out of the way. As JJ had predicted, Paul went down as if he had been shot. His team-mates were incensed and piled in to take their revenge. David Hobbs, their captain, appointed himself spokesman and was one of the first to challenge me.

'You've broken his fucking jaw!' he yelled.

'So you're a doctor now are you, Hobbsy?' I replied.

There was a bit of pushing and shoving as Paul rolled around clutching his face. Meanwhile, referee John Connolly wondered what the hell to do with me. John was quite pragmatic about it and said: 'If he gets up, Lee, you're okay. If he doesn't, I'm going to have to send you off.' Fortunately, Paul came round and picked himself up, but he lost interest after that and caused us no problems while I went on to win another man of the match award after one of my best performances in years. I made countless half-breaks, set up Tony Smith's try with a short kick through, kicked three conversions, including two from the touchline, dropped a goal and topped our tackle count. No wonder the opposition would have liked to have seen me sent off.

It was a major talking point afterwards and one journo said I had used my head 'without due care and attention,' which just about sums it up. Up in the directors' lounge, Bradford chairman Chris Caisley made a short speech and couldn't resist having a go. When it was my turn, I refused to rise to the bait and paid credit, instead, to Paul Newlove for not milking the situation.

I wasn't fazed by the fuss. I was happy to have played my part in getting my team to a cup final. I felt on very safe ground. The sacrifices to rebuild my career and life had been well worth it. I was leading one of the game's best teams and enjoying it even more than I'd hoped.

*****

The close-knit team spirit seemed to run through the whole town in the build up to the Regal Trophy final. Castleford is not a large place and there are times when it feels as though everyone knows everyone else. That can be claustrophobic now and then but, in the weeks ahead of the big game it created a great atmosphere as everyone fed off one another's excitement. I couldn't walk fifty yards without having half a dozen people saying hello and wishing me good luck for the big game. It made me really proud to be a part of a team that meant so much to people.

Despite our support, there was no doubt we were huge underdogs but we used that to psyche ourselves up. JJ asked us to set our own individual goals, to write them down and pin them over our dressing room peg. He had a strong belief in the players and always tried to give us the freedom to do our own thing. He knew we had the team to beat Wigan and just told us to go out and play rugby.

The atmosphere inside Headingley for the final was electric. The crowd was evenly split in terms of numbers but the Cas fans made their presence felt more. The cheering when we came out gave us a real lift.

We started well and, very early on, Richie Blackmore produced a hit on Martin Offiah that lifted him off his feet and dumped him on his backside. It shocked Martin, but I also caught sight of Shaun Edwards and saw the expression on his face. He was just as shocked and obviously hadn't expected us to come out so ferociously. I already felt we had the psychological edge and made a point of communicating it to the rest of the lads. It paid off after just seven minutes when Tawera went over for our first try. I kicked the goal and we were buzzing.

Our terrific start lifted our fans and they went mental five minutes later when Grant Anderson went over from a grubber kick into the corner. I kicked the goal from the touchline and we were twelve points up in as many minutes. We were all over them. Wigan were shocked and we were relishing every tackle and break we made. We scored again before half-time and went in leading 20-2.

It had been a flawless forty minutes of rugby. I don't think anyone missed a tackle or made an error of any kind and none of us could quite believe how well we had played. If we could repeat it in the second half, the Trophy was ours. Even so, we all knew there were bound to be spells when Wigan would be on top and had to make sure that we never lost concentration for a second.

When we ran back out we noticed Wigan sprinting to their positions; it was obvious they hadn't given up at all. They started the second period just as we had the first and soon we were under all sorts of pressure. They dominated possession and when we did get our hands on the ball we barely got out of our own half.

From Hull to Hell and Back

We knew that if our defence caved in early they would grow in confidence and we would have a real game on our hands. It was a real team effort and we dug in well to hold them out for a couple of back-to-back sets, but they controlled the ball well and kept coming back at us. We were under constant pressure on our own line for set after set for what seemed like ages, but we scrambled well and with every tackle that held them out our determination grew.

For nearly ten minutes, Wigan were camped entirely in our quarter but they just couldn't find a way to break our defence. The longer it went on, the more inevitable it seemed that they would eventually score, but we could also sense they were becoming frustrated. Eventually, the ball went to ground, one of our lads took it upfield and the pressure broke as we launched our first attack of the half. It was a significant moment; we had taken everything Wigan could throw at us and held firm. It gave us a huge boost and although we couldn't score a try on that first raid, we gained a massive advantage by scoring the first points of the half when Kempy dropped a goal to stretch our lead to nineteen points. That was the turning point. You could see their shoulders sag. They had thrown everything at us and had come up empty-handed and we had gone up the other end and extended our lead. We really started to believe we could win.

Shortly afterwards, 'Betty' Ketteridge scored his second try and that was the final straw for the Wigan lads who started to lose their rag. Kelvin Skerrett had a lunge at one of our forwards and was sent to the sinbin. It was satisfying to see them so badly beaten and losing their discipline. At 27-2 with the clock ticking down, it was almost the perfect afternoon. But there was even more to come.

It was time for the famous 'Parramatta' move from my days at Hull, where, if you remember, Peter Sterling, Garry

Schofield and I had crafted a little runaround move in the middle of the field which led to dozens of tries for Schoey. I had brought the move to Castleford but we played such an expansive style of rugby that we rarely used set plays. Nevertheless, with a couple of minutes left, we won a penalty in front of the Wigan posts and when Fordy said: 'Take two in and then it's party time!' we knew what to do.

After two drives, Rich Russell took the ball from the ruck and, instead of going forward, ran horizontally across the line, taking a defender with him. Fordy followed on his shoulder. As Rich popped him the ball, they both continued to run across the line, taking not one, but two, defenders with them and leaving a huge gap. In our wildest dreams, it was never meant to work that well. With two defenders going down a blind alley, Fordy popped a pass inside and I came charging into the space they'd all left behind. Normally, the move would have opened up a half-gap and I would put someone else away for the try but with such a gap in front of me, I wasn't passing to anyone.

There was no one in front of me and only twenty yards to the posts. With the ball in my right hand, I wasn't able to hand off Andy Platt as he came in from my right but it didn't matter; I'd angled my run in such a way that I was moving away from him and the combination of his weariness and my electrifying pace meant that I was straight through. Twenty yards began to feel like eighty but I managed to get over for our final try.

The score rounded off an almost perfect performance by everyone in the team. My conversion gave me sixteen points and equalled a record for the most number of points scored in a Regal Trophy final, although it didn't take Frano Botica long to straighten that out the following year for Wigan.

As soon as the conversion went over, the hooter sounded and the Cas players and fans went mental. As captain of the team, it would be me who would walk up the steps to collect the trophy, but it had been an incredible afternoon for everyone associated with the club. All our preparations had been in the expectation of a very tight game, perhaps won by a single passage of play. We might have imagined winning but none of us could have foreseen that we would win so comfortably and, more importantly, that we would play so well. It was, by some distance, the best team performance I was ever involved in and I would imagine most of the other lads playing for Cas that day would say the same.

The Wigan pack was totally outplayed, an achievement that wasn't lost on me since I was constantly battling to get into the Great Britain team alongside them. Collecting the trophy at Headingley was also ironic since it was a ground where I had not done particularly well when playing for Leeds, but at the time none of that mattered much. I was just delighted to be part of a group of players who had put on such an amazing display.

The lap of honour seemed to take hours. Most of my family had made the trip to watch the game, including some from my dad's side of the family from London. I spent ages with them on the side of the pitch and then, once I'd torn myself away, I still had most of the press blokes waiting to speak to me. They all wanted to ask me what it meant for the club, the town and its people. I must have been on BBC Radio Leeds for half an hour waffling on about the team spirit and the tight-knit community. I must have sounded like I was canvassing to become the town's next MP. I was the last one into the dressing room and by the time I arrived the bastards had drunk all the champagne. There was hardly any beer left either.

*****

Most players are terrible at appreciating the importance of what they've achieved and I am no different. I have very few mementoes of my playing career. Apart from my medals, I have given most things away, such as shirts, programmes and so on. When you're young and have just won a trophy, all you want to do is celebrate with your mates, you don't think about it much. But, by the time we won the 1994 Regal Trophy, I knew that they weren't going to be many more days like that, so I was determined to savour every second. I still had a good drink with the lads, of course, but I took a few minutes now and again to let it sink in and appreciate it.

Much later than expected, the team bus headed back to Castleford and, once we turned into Wheldon Road, the street was literally blocked by thousands of fans who had come out to welcome us back. It seemed like the entire town was there and it took us over an hour to wind our way through the crowd. The only way we could get into the club bar was through the fire exit round the back, there were so many people crammed into the ground. It was one hell of a night and there were some major headaches over the next few days.

We were given two civic receptions; the first at Castleford Town Hall. Then, a week or so later, Wakefield City Council threw a party for us as well, as the town of Castleford is actually in the city of Wakefield. The party was held on a Monday night and most of us had been out for a few pints in the afternoon as usual. By the time we got to the town hall, we were in great spirits.

It was one of those nights when everything seemed to be hilarious. The Mayor of Wakefield stood up to congratulate us, but he had a bit of a speech impediment and had us in stitches. Meanwhile, Kempy and Singe clambered onto the window sills around the main banqueting room, hidden behind the curtains, and began to throw food across the room at the Mayor and anyone else within range. It was a boisterous night but most of the guests humoured us and took it all in good spirits, except maybe the Mayor.

After leaving the town hall, we stayed out for a while and some of us even made it to a nightclub, where we were the main attraction. Dean Sampson stole the show, I seem to remember, laying on the dance floor pretending to be a surf board, while we took turns surfing on his back.

*****

Winning the John Player Trophy gave us a real boost and over the next six weeks we continued to play excellent rugby. Not only were we winning most weeks, we were playing the type of game that hadn't been seen at Castleford since the club's heyday in the 1960s and '70s. We scored nearly three hundred points in our next seven games and lost just one, away at St Helens.

Our achievements brought a lot of attention to the club and to me, in particular. My performances in the Regal Trophy caught the eye of journalists who suddenly wanted to talk to me about how I had resurrected my career and how I had made such an impressive comeback. The truth was that I hadn't been anywhere. I'd been playing decent rugby for a couple of years, they just hadn't noticed.

I must admit that it was flattering to read such positive coverage, though, and it was especially nice because I really felt that I had earned it. I've never really taken much notice of praise unless I felt I deserved it. I've never wanted to get a free ride or a leg-up from anyone so, in 1994, I took a lot of satisfaction from all the accolades because I had worked very hard. To get back to my best form had forced me to make sacrifices with regard to how I lived my life. It hadn't been easy but it had been well worth it. And I still had lots to look forward to, beginning with yet another big game against Wigan; this time in the Challenge Cup semi-finals, again at Headingley.

Because we had already beaten them twice that season, a lot of people were tipping us to win, but Wigan were a totally different team when it came to the Challenge Cup. When they clicked they were still far too good for anyone else. All their top players turned up and performed that day and we never really looked like winning.

The defeat took the wind out of our sails and we ended the season disappointingly, finishing fourth. Although our league form had fallen away, we still managed to beat Halifax and Bradford in the Premiership and made it to yet another final against Wigan.

We had played them four times already in the season, with the split two games apiece. Obviously, the media was billing the Premiership final as 'The Decider' but our build-up was not helped by a bust-up between Tawera and Richie Blackmore in the week before the game.

I can't remember what the argument was about but it upset 'T' to the extent that he told John Joyner he didn't want to play in the final alongside Richie. Losing one of our best players wasn't ideal preparation but we just had to get on with it. John brought Tony Morrison into the squad and we headed off for our hotel in Manchester hoping to lift ourselves for one last big performance of the season.

The night before, John called Mike Ford and myself together and told us that 'T' had changed his mind and now wanted to play. It was a dilemma for John and he wanted to know what we thought he should do. I said that if he wanted to do what was right, he should leave 'T' out of the team, but if he wanted his best team on the pitch we needed Tawera with us. At the end of the day, it was the coach's decision. John was a pragmatic man who knew we didn't have the strength in depth to be able to leave someone of Tawera's ability in the stands, so he picked him.

We got off to a dream start when Dean Sampson scored early on and I converted, but Wigan came back at us and they went in at half-time 16-8 ahead. The second half was scrappy and bad tempered and a couple of players were sent to the sinbin, the last after Dean Sampson's elbow broke Kelvin Skerrett's jaw. Skerrett, fuming, was convinced that Dean had deliberately lifted his elbow in the tackle. He left the pitch spitting blood and venom all the way down the tunnel, which was quite ironic because Kelvin wasn't averse to giving out a few high shots himself.

When Denis Betts scored late on to make it 24-8 with just five minutes left, it looked as though it was all over. I had been substituted by then and spent the final minutes watching from the touchline, disappointed but still proud of our season. It had been one of the best that Cas fans could remember and, as a team, we had enjoyed every minute. But it wasn't over just yet.

With just two minutes to go, Nathan Sykes went over for us. It was 24-12 and far too late to mount a comeback but it was still nice to score the final try of a memorable season. Steady kicked the conversion and Wigan restarted the game still looking confident that they had done enough, but incredibly we mounted an attack straight away. Wigan had taken their eye off the game and suddenly couldn't lay a hand on anyone in a gold shirt. At the end of a string of passes, Steady went over the line for yet another try and, suddenly, we were only six points behind. Sensing that there might still be time for one last, final attack, Steady banged over the conversion quickly and our lads raced back to their positions.

It was 24-20 and there was still enough time for another restart. The atmosphere had changed completely as the

Wigan players alongside me on the touchline looked nervously at the stadium clock. They knew we only needed a sniff of a chance and we could snatch the game from them in a second. But it wasn't to be. We had left it too late. The hooter sounded and our season was over.

*****

Despite the slightly disappointing end, it was still Castleford's most successful season for years. But all was not well off the pitch and there were already concerns that the club would struggle to keep the team together.

By the mid-1990s, Castleford owed a massive debt to David Poulter. David was always far-sighted and ambitious but he was in a minority on the board. After years of trying, in vain, to keep the directors working together, he decided it wasn't worth the hassle and, in 1994, decided to step down.

Under David, it had been normal practice that when a player reached the final year of his contract, the club would come in with a new offer and extension. If no offer was forthcoming, it was clear the club were prepared to let you leave. It was a system that worked and had kept many of the senior players together for a long period of time. Everyone knew where they stood and few players were unsettled.

The new chairman, Eddie Ashton, didn't quite grasp the importance of keeping the players secure and preferred to keep them guessing which, inevitably, led to them being 'tapped up' by other clubs. It was a huge mistake; after running Wigan so close all season, we had a real chance of challenging them for years to come. All we needed was a three-quarter and a back-row forward. I knew it, JJ knew it and most of the rest of the team knew it as well, but the board just wouldn't, or couldn't, provide JJ with the money he needed not only to sign those players but to retain the players we already had. Rather than strengthening the side, Richie Blackmore, Tony Kemp, Tawera Nikau, Tony Smith and Singe Ellis all ended up leaving over the next few years and the club's fortunes have never really recovered since.

Unsurprisingly, the following season was an anti-climax and we played in fits and starts. We had one stretch where we went unbeaten for nine games, before losing six out of the next seven. Our inconsistency frustrated everyone and we also missed the cup finals and semi-finals we had grown used to. I always liked those big games and, for me, the highlight of the 1994-95 season was the fixture against the Australian touring team.

The Cas supporters were still on a high after the previous season and fancied our chances of giving the Kangaroos a real contest. There was massive interest in the game and the kick-off was delayed by ten minutes to allow enough time for the fans to get into the ground. There were over eleven-thousand packed in, more than double our average crowd.

At that stage of my career, I had just about accepted that I might not play for Great Britain again. I was just looking forward to getting in a few big hits and letting them know Lee Crooks wasn't finished yet. But who knows? A stunning performance might just rattle a few cages one last time.

Because it was played midweek, the Australians only named a handful of their regular Test side but there were still a few big lads in there and I was really looking forward to the challenge. For some reason, I took exception to Paul Harrigan early on and gave him a smack the first chance I got. It was great, just like being nineteen all over again, taking a shot at an Aussie forward to rattle him and let him know who I was.

I was pissed off when he didn't rise to it, to be honest. I guessed it was a sign of the times; he was more concerned with not conceding any penalties than having a pop at a Pom. But when I found myself with ball in hand and saw him coming out of the line, I knew he was going to have a go. He couldn't resist it, after all.

I've always had good spatial awareness, peripheral vision or whatever you want to call it, so I can usually read situations quite well. I knew that, with the ball in my hands, I wouldn't be able to defend myself if he hit me, so I stepped to one side, bringing a team-mate into the game and slipped out a pass. There was nothing on and Rich Russell was surprised to find the ball in his hands, but I was only concerned with getting my arms free to defend myself against Harrigan.

As soon as the ball left my hands, I brought my arm up and managed to block the worst of the 'tackle'. It was high, it was late, but it was fair enough. I'd smacked him first and I knew that, for a while at least, he had been more focused on having a go at me than following his game plan. He hadn't really caught me and I wasn't hurt. Or not, at least, until I lost balance and fell over. As I put my hand out to break my fall, my middle finger bent beneath me and took my weight as I hit the floor. The impact flipped my knuckle out of its joint and caused a spiral fracture right through the upper finger bone. It hurt like a bastard but I felt bloody daft to be going off with a finger injury after I'd traded blows with one of the biggest blokes in the Aussie team.

The next day, I went to A&E who referred me to a BUPA clinic in Leeds for an appointment with a finger surgeon. He obviously knew what he was doing but he was as camp as anything and like a character from *Carry on Nurse*. When he took a good look at my hands, gnarled and scarred after fourteen years as a professional rugby league prop forward, he couldn't believe the state of them. He shrieked and yelped as he ran his soft little hands over my battered knuckles and digits. He was starting to annoy me. I hadn't come for a bloody manicure.

'Just what would you like me to do with these blooming fingers, Mr Crooks?' he asked.

'Just fucking fix 'em, soft cunt,' I barked back at him and he didn't say much after that.

*****

As the season came to an end, the Super League war in Australia was intensifying and both sides of the dispute were more and more desperate to sign up the best players, wherever they came from.

Many of the top English players made a lot of money around that time, and quite a few average players made a fair bit as well. While the ARL was offering big bucks to those willing to play in their league down under, Rupert Murdoch's men were offering even more money to players not to switch to the ARL. It seemed, for a while, as though almost everyone was being offered money for one reason or another. But if ever I needed reminding that my career had more yesterdays than tomorrows, it was the fact that my phone never rang once and I never got a penny.

Events moved quickly and, although the players knew something was going on, we were as surprised as anyone when it was announced that Super League would start in the summer of 1996 - less than a year away.

There were lots of protests and arguments over the next few weeks but, as players, we tried our best to put it out of our minds and focus on playing rugby. The game had barely changed in a hundred years and suddenly it was being turned on its head in the space of a couple of weeks. The biggest change was the switch to summer and that's what caused most controversy at first. The Castleford supporters were generally against the move although many of them were relieved when the prospect of a merger with Wakefield was

quietly dropped and we learned that we would be playing in
Super League in our own right. On a personal level, I liked the
planned changes. I just hoped I could continue to play a part
at Castleford and get the opportunity to play in the new
competition.

I was out of contract at the end of the 1995 season and
knew, as did the club, I didn't have many more seasons left
in me. I had fifteen English seasons behind me, plus three in
Australia and three GB Lions Tours and my body could feel
it. My knees had been giving me problems for a couple of
years and I was playing against opponents every week who
were full-time professionals. There was more intensity and
speed in every game, which left me feeling off the pace.

Nevertheless, I wasn't ready to call it a day just yet. I had
no intention of moving anywhere else, so I was pleased to be
able to negotiate another two-year deal with the chairman. I
was very happy with the deal. It was structured to pay me
fifty grand in the first year and up to fifty grand in the
second, depending on the number of appearances. At the
age of thirty-two, with a couple of busted knees, I would be
earning far more than I had ever earned at any stage of my
career. It was quite ironic and I suppose it summed up how
much the game had changed over the years.

*****

With a new contract settled, I began to prepare for the last
shortened winter season, but the 1995-6 centenary season
was a bit of a waste of time. We were disappointed with our
form at Castleford and finished mid-table. Wigan totally
dominated and won the league by a mile. For many weeks,
it felt like most sides were just going through the motions
and counting down the weeks until Super League started.

In the break before Super League, the Challenge Cup

competition continued as normal throughout the spring, which meant that for some teams the season never ended. For Castleford, it didn't matter all that much; we were slaughtered at home by St Helens in the first round of the Cup and earned ourselves an extra six weeks off.

Meanwhile, John Joyner was struggling to put together a strong squad. Frano Botica was an excellent signing but Tawera Nikau decided to head back down under before Super League began. 'T' had been massive for Cas, both on and off the field. Not only was he an outstanding player, he had a big impact on the rest of the players and the club as a whole. It was always going to be impossible to replace him and John's hands were tied to a large extent by the financial constraints at the club at the time. When 'T' left, JJ brought in Brendon Tuuta who, to be fair, was never going to have the same impact 'T' had.

John relied heavily on an Australian agent called Mick Robinson, but I don't think Castleford were very well served by the arrangement at all. John was persuaded to take a punt on the Samoan forward Junior Paramore, who had played some decent games in the World Cup. Paramore never made much of an impression at Castleford but it was no surprise when he went on to be relatively successful in rugby union.

The early weeks of Super League went well. Our crowds were up and, as the pitches hardened, the rugby became faster and more intense. The game was changing, there were more tries and any errors in defence didn't seem to matter much. The momentum became all important; once a team got on top it was very difficult to stop them. I found the pace hard but not impossible and still felt I had something to offer, particularly as we were lacking experience.

In early June, we played the glamour game of the season, away in Paris, which happened to coincide with a heatwave in France. It was over ninety degrees for the whole time we were there which made it difficult for us to train properly. The game was played on a Friday night but it was still steaming hot when we kicked off at about nine o'clock. We hoped the Aussies and the likes of Junior would cope with the heat better but, if anything, they suffered even more. All three of them went off with one injury or another while the English lads were left toiling in the heat.

As ever, the Cas fans had travelled in large numbers and, after the game, most of the players went out for a beer with some of them. I headed back to the hotel with JJ quite early, but the lads had a good night out in Paris and enjoyed the novelty of it all.

We did well to win in Paris but struggled for most of the rest of the season, and with the team underperforming it gave some fans an excuse to turn their back on the new competition. After a burst of interest at the start, our crowds fell and there were less than three thousand at Wheldon Road by the end of May.

Nevertheless, I had really enjoyed the first Super League season and thought that most of the changes were good for the game. I'd no particular passion for winter rugby. Playing in cold weather wasn't too bad but I don't believe anyone who ever said that training on cold, dark winter nights was much fun.

Playing in summer with harder grounds and a dry ball was bound to lead to a more expansive style of play and it was no surprise that the first season saw a lot more points being scored. It was great for the Sky broadcasters and for the new fans, but it didn't always impress the traditional types of whom there were many in Castleford. I have always found Cas fans to be some of the most knowledgeable in the world. Every fan is like a coach and playing in front of them always added extra pressure because you knew they were scrutinising everything you did. Once Super League began, the new fans who came along were interested mostly in the tries and big hits. The atmosphere began to change.

*****

JJ was already under pressure after a disappointing start to Super League and he continued to struggle to keep the team together. Tony Smith grew unsettled and we were resigned to losing him. It was clear that Wigan wanted to sign Tony. Although JJ was disappointed to lose him, he was hopeful we could at least swap him for Nigel Wright. The deal rumbled on for weeks but, in the end, our board couldn't sort out a deal and Wigan got their man. Smithy got a big pay rise and the opportunity to play for the best team in the country, while we got a lousy £80,000, which was paid in instalments so we couldn't even go out and replace him. It thoroughly pissed me off because I knew it would seriously weaken us and put an extra burden on everyone. It was going to be a tough year. A lot would depend on myself and Graham Steadman who, at 35, was even older than I was.

I was up for the challenge but when an approach came suddenly from Hull FC, I was tempted to change course. The move was appealing for two reasons; as a lifelong Hull fan, I had always hoped to return one day but, on a more practical level, the pace of Super League was getting away from me. I knew I might not make it through another season. A drop down to the First Division, Hull's level at the time, might extend my career by a year and be an opportunity to move into coaching. I was still an important player for Castleford, though, and knew that JJ was reluctant to give me permission to speak to them at first. In the end, he saw that it was a good chance for me and didn't stand in my way.

I had a meeting with Stephen Ball, Hull's chief executive. Initially, he only wanted to offer me a one-year deal but I managed to persuade him to come up with a two-year offer. There were one or two other issues I wanted to discuss but Stephen suggested I speak to the coach.

I knew Phil Sigsworth from one of my spells in Australia and when we met again we got on well. We both knew what I could bring to the team but, at first, he wasn't happy to give me the central role I wanted. I told him I wanted to be captain and have a role off the pitch as well. I would be the most experienced player by a long way and didn't want to drop down a division to play second fiddle. It was probably quite an arrogant approach but I knew that I wouldn't be able to give my best for Hull if that wasn't the case. Phil was quite loyal to the captain he already had, Gary Divorty, but we managed to come to something of an agreement.

Everything seemed to be in place until Stephen Ball went on holiday. He assured me it would all be sorted out but, while he was away, nothing happened. I got the impression the club was having second thoughts about the contract they had offered me. After a couple of weeks of getting nowhere, I told JJ that I had decided to stay at Cas after all. It was disappointing but I just got fed up of being messed around and, at that stage of my career, I had quite a low tolerance threshold for anyone who didn't do things professionally.

Hull took their league by storm that year and it would have been great to help them get promoted and possibly even play for them in Super League. But it wasn't to be and so I started preparing for the new season at Castleford again.

*****

There's no doubt JJ was under pressure as the 1997 season began. We started badly and knew that the Easter fixtures against Halifax and Bradford would be crucial, but we lost both and were hammered by the Bulls in front of our own fans. We were rock bottom of the competition and John paid with his job.

JJ was and still is a very good friend of mine and I backed him completely as Castleford coach. I couldn't understand how the club could come to the conclusion that he was no longer good enough to be in charge after he had been so successful just a few years earlier. He hadn't become a bad coach in that time but the circumstances in which he had to work had changed massively in terms of the resources he had at his disposal. I made it clear to the directors what I thought of the decision, which didn't go down too well.

The new chairman, Philip Hindle, wasn't happy that I had criticised the decision to sack JJ and nor did he like my suggestion that Graham Steadman and myself should run the team until a new head coach could be appointed. Once again, my tendency to be outspoken had ruffled feathers and he made it clear he expected more loyalty from the club captain. Meanwhile, Mick Morgan was asked to stand in as caretaker coach.

Mick had been at the club for years and had been assistant to Darryl van der Velde. Recently, though, he had been the club's commercial manager, so he was an odd choice as coach. Nevertheless, Mick did make an immediate impact. We got worse. He was only in charge for four games and we lost the lot.

The new man proper was an Australian, Stuart Raper, son of Kangaroo legend Johnny. As soon as he took over, he pulled me into his office for a chat. He told me he had worked with Tawera Nikau down under and, through 'T', or more accurately his wife, Letitia, he had got the impression I would be difficult to manage. I think Letitia had always felt that her husband ought to be the captain of Castleford rather than me and we never quite saw eye to eye. I assured Stuart that, although I had been unhappy that John Joyner had been sacked, I still wanted the club to be successful and that he had my full support. The meeting ended amicably and I just got on with things.

Stuart's first game in charge was at Liverpool FC's Anfield stadium against St Helens, which was a bit weird but quite a routine game, because we lost yet again. We lost the next couple of games under Stuart too before finally winning our first game of the season in round ten. I was finding it difficult to keep myself positive and motivated. All around, the team was struggling but, as much as I wanted to help turn things around, I was struggling more than anyone. Everything was getting quicker and I was getting slower. I got caught out a couple of times and remember one occasion when someone stepped around me in a game at Oldham. As soon as that happened, I knew it was all over. I was finished.

*****

Calling time on my playing career was a tough call to make. I didn't like to admit I wasn't young enough or fast enough any longer, so I never said anything to anyone, even though I had already begun to look for a way out.

Around the same time, I was waiting for an operation to clean up my knee. The cartilage was in need of a further trim but when the club doctor looked at it he found there was hardly any cartilage left to trim. He advised me to retire or risk serious long-term damage; he even mentioned I could end up in a wheelchair. As shocking as that was, in a way, it was what I wanted to hear - it gave me a reason to retire other than being 'past it'.

I spoke to Stuart and told him what the doctor had said. The fact that I was being forced to retire on medical advice made it much easier to accept and meant I couldn't be talked out of it. Stuart accepted my decision but I still played one final game; in the World Club Championship against the Hunter Mariners.

I wasn't really in any kind of state to help my team against the Mariners and we were beaten 42-14 in my last game. Although I knew it was the right decision, I was devastated to call time on my career. I asked Stuart if I could give the news to the players myself and told them one night after training, in the Tiger Bar at Wheldon Road. It was one of the toughest things I have ever had to do and there was a tear in my eye as I spoke. There was quite a bit of shock from their point of view too; I had been a part of the furniture for seven years.

There was no doubt that Cas were struggling and I was gutted I couldn't help them out. But I couldn't deny what my body was telling me every single day as I struggled out of bed. It was over.

11

Made in Hull

As an eight-year-old, on a Friday afternoon, I would come home from school, have something to eat, sit in front of the telly and wait. On any other day, I'd be out in the street with my mates. But Fridays were different. Friday was the one day of the week when I might - just might - get the chance to go away for the weekend with my dad.

Dad was always working away, delivering fish from the docks of Hull to the South West of England. He would set off from Hull on a Friday afternoon and sometimes take me with him. I'd hear his lorry pull up in front of the house at teatime and his footsteps as he walked up the path. I would convince myself that, if I didn't expect it too much, then he would be more likely to ask me to go, so I sat there trying to put the thought out of my head.

Sometimes he would come into the house and say, 'I just popped back for my flask, Joan,' and my heart would sink. More often than not, he would pop his head around the door of our front room and say: 'Are you coming with me then, or what?' I would leap off the settee, grab some things and be down the front drive and climbing into the front cab before he knew it. Those weekends were the happiest times of my childhood. All I did was sit in the cab of his lorry for a day and a half but, for a lad who didn't often get to leave Hull, it was the most exciting thing in the world.

I loved it when we stopped at a service station for something to eat or, better still, the truckers' cafes that lined the A1 and other roads south. Dad knew every one. Once we reached our destination, which was usually Taunton in the early hours of Saturday morning, Dad would hand his lorry over to a mate of his called Jock, who would make all the local deliveries while Dad slept through the rest of the night at Jock's house. I could never sleep so I would jump in with Jock while he did the rounds of markets and fish shops around Exeter and Plymouth.

Eventually, we'd pick Dad up and we would head back to Hull. Dad might have a present for me that he would have bartered for a box of fish, but spending so much time with him was always the best bit of the trip. I barely slept for the whole weekend except for nodding off occasionally in the cab while Dad was driving. I was as happy as a young boy could be and I never got tired of those trips away. I only stopped going when I was thirteen and started playing for Hull Boys on a weekend instead.

By then, I had grown up quite a bit and was expected to do my share of chores around the house. With Dad away so much and Mam also working full-time, I took responsibility for looking after my brother, Richard, who is six years younger than me. I would tidy up, make a fire and do some tea for when Mam got in from work. I didn't mind doing my share of jobs but it often felt like I was doing far more than most lads my age. At the end of one particular day, when I had been doing everything while Mam sat around resting after a day at work, I asked her: 'Mam, why do I have to do all this?' I was a bit frustrated and knew she would probably tell me off but her reply shocked me. I have never forgotten what she said. 'Why have a dog and bark yourself?' She probably meant it as a throw-away line, a joke, but I didn't see it that way. I had already started to feel like Mam wasn't very interested in me and her comment made me start to feel a bit of resentment towards her.

I had to look after myself in lots of ways. When I trained with Hull Boys I made my own way there, which meant taking a bus from school into Hull city centre and then another bus all the way up to Bransholme High School. It was a hell of a journey for a thirteen-year-old but I didn't mind. I was quite happy to be independent and doing my own thing and that's how I first ended up at the Boulevard.

*****

I didn't come from a rugby league family so I don't know what first prompted me to want to go. I suppose I just caught the bug and started going with a group of mates. We used to sneak in around the back of the Threepenny Stand. There was a strip of wire meshing topped with barbed wire which someone had ripped a hole in. Providing you waited until the game had kicked off and there was nobody around, you could climb through and get into the ground for free.

The club had fallen on lean times by the mid-seventies and were relegated from the First Division in the first season I started watching them. But the following year was a record breaker. We won every single one of our twenty-six league games that year and I saw every one, home and away. By then, I was big enough to hold my own in the middle of the Threepenny Stand. I hadn't always stood there. Like most young fans I preferred to stand on the edges of the stand at first and watch, from a safe distance, what was going on in the middle. It was very noisy, passionate and quite scary for a young lad. Over time, I gradually moved closer to the middle until I had a regular spot close to the halfway line, but at the front against the fence. As I got bigger and madder, I stood among the hardcore fans in the middle and at the back.

The Threepenny Stand was full of characters; one that I remember particularly well was a teenage lad who everyone called Marcus. He used to ride his bike up and down along the front of the stand shouting 'Ivan Mauger, Ivan Mauger' after the Kiwi star of the Hull Lada Vikings speedway team. It was the late 1970s, so obviously it was a Raleigh Grifter. I have no idea how he got his bike into the ground, or even why, but someone on the turnstile obviously had a soft spot for him, as did most of the Threepennystanders.

I was in the middle of that stand for the Floodlit Trophy final just before Christmas in 1979. Hull had beaten some top teams on their way there but we were still underdogs against our local rivals, Hull Kingston Rovers, who were First Division Champions. The Boulevard was packed on a freezing Tuesday night as we beat Rovers 13-3 to win our first trophy for years.

In those days, whenever we played Hull KR some fans would bring a red and white scarf into the ground, tie it to a wooden stanchion and set fire to it while we chanted Rovers' 'Red, Red Robin' anthem back at them, ending the song with a chorus of 'Shoot the bastard! Shoot the bastard!' On that particular night, it seemed that hundreds of fans had brought Rovers scarves. I spent the whole game dodging chunks of burning wool.

The first time I went to the Boulevard, I loved it and knew I would keep coming back. But the first time I went to a live game of sport was to see Hull City play at Boothferry Park. I was taken by our babysitter's boyfriend and was about ten years old. He was nineteen and a big City fan. It was the season that Manchester United were in the Second Division and he decided to take me along for one of the biggest games Hull had played in years.

He didn't want me to get in the way, though, so he shoved me down to the front of the South Stand while he joined his mates in the middle of the terrace. We must have arrived early because I can remember watching the trains pull up on the hill behind Boothferry Park and thousands of United supporters pouring out. I'd no idea what to expect and was completely over-awed by the size of the crowd and how they behaved.

As the tension built before kick-off, a Man United fan jumped out of the Kempton Stand, ran across the pitch towards the City fans' end, with his red and black scarf tied to his wrist, and dived over the fence into the crowd. A huge hole appeared where the United fan could be seen punching away at anyone who wanted to take him on. He took a real kicking before he was thrown back to lick his wounds.

Soon after, a City fan did the same, racing across the pitch and diving into the Kempton end for an inevitable kicking. I couldn't believe what I was seeing; there were fights breaking out all over the place. I kept looking for the lad who had brought me but couldn't see him anywhere; he was lost in the middle of the crowd of City fans as the mob surged backwards and forwards. I decided I didn't want to be there any longer. I could just about remember how we had come in so I went looking for the exit. The crowds were still pouring in, but I was heading in the opposite direction.

I managed to persuade a steward to let me through one of the turnstiles and I was back out on North Road, the street next to the ground. There were Manchester United fans everywhere and I realised that the black and amber scarf around my neck marked me out as a home fan. I took it off, threw it over a hedge into someone's garden and ran home as fast as I could. I hadn't liked the experience one bit.

*****

The babysitter's boyfriend was quite a lad. He started to come round to our house when I was about eight or nine and I didn't like him much. Every time he came round, I was packed off upstairs so he could snuggle up with the babysitter on our settee. When I got a bit older, I told him I wasn't going to my room and would sit on the floor in front of the telly while he and his girlfriend wriggled around under a blanket, doing God knows what to each other.

I was quite naïve. Before Janet, I hadn't really had a girlfriend or spent any time chasing girls. I do remember having a crush on a girl called Michelle at junior school. I was good friends with her but she had no idea I fancied her like mad. I thought that if I could invite her to a party I might be able to make my move. So I persuaded my Mam to let me have a Christmas party when I was about thirteen and invited three or four mates, along with Michelle and some of her friends. I was nervous as hell and thought I would show off by drinking some of my Dad's home brew and getting a bit drunk. I had no idea how much you needed to drink to get drunk, though, and ended up making myself ill. I spent most of the party in the toilet, while Michelle got bored and went home. I gave up on her after that.

To be honest, I preferred the parties my parents used to have. They would often come back from the pub on a Friday or Saturday night with their friends and have an impromptu do at our house. I didn't really know who their friends were but I was often allowed to come downstairs and join in as they sang along to songs like 'The Old Rugged Cross' and a local tune that was popular at the time called 'Hessle Road'.

It was always a good laugh and I felt quite grown up joining in with their jokes and pranks. That was until one of them decided to de-bag me (an odd prank popular in Hull when I was a kid, which basically involved picking on someone and ripping their trousers and pants off to embarrass them). After that, I tended to stay upstairs when anyone came back.

As I got more and more serious about my rugby league, Dad started to come and watch me play. He never took an active role in what I did; he didn't know much about the game so preferred to watch in silence. But I always knew I had his full support and encouragement. Mam, on the other hand, was never really interested in what I was doing until I signed professional and she realised that I was obviously quite good and wasn't just wasting my time. It didn't bother me too much at the time, but I had noticed and it came to affect our relationship later. Nevertheless, between them, they always found a way to make sure that I had a pair of boots to play in. My first were a pair of George Best football boots made from the best moulded plastic, but I always wanted some Adidas Flankers and Mam and Dad got me a pair for Christmas when I was sixteen.

I didn't give much thought to whether we were poor. We were no worse off than most families I came into contact with; just a typical working class family growing up in the Hull of the 1970s. Like most working men connected to the fishing industry, Dad would have had his worries about job security and paying the bills, but he worked as hard as he could to make sure he kept a decent lifestyle for his family.

When I was about nine, we moved out of our council house on Orchard Park Estate and into another council property, a bigger home, on Aylesbury Grove in West Hull. To make sure they could pay for it, Mam went to work at Hull Infirmary in the laundry department and also did one or two other part-time jobs. Between them, they made sure that Richard and I had the things that most kids wanted; toys, clothes, trips and so on. Finances must have been okay because, when I was thirteen, we went on our first family holiday to France.

Mam, Richard and me got a lift down to Plymouth with one of Dad's lorry driver mates and met Dad there. It was a great adventure but I felt sick on the ferry from Plymouth to Roscoff. We stayed on a campsite in Brittany which was great for Richard and me; we loved it. We even thought it was hilarious when it poured down and the rainwater almost washed away our tents and all of our gear. It was the first time any of us had been abroad and we poked around the campsite and the surrounding beaches and villages with real curiosity. Then, one day, the Welsh woman who was camping a few yards from us, came out of her tent in tears. From everyone's reaction and behaviour, I sensed that something awful must have happened. I started to hear music coming out of tents all over the campsite. It sounded familiar and when I asked my Mam what was happening, she told me: 'Elvis is dead.'

I knew who Elvis was but didn't understand why people were so upset. We heard nothing but Elvis Presley music for the next few days and, even when we got back home, people seemed to be talking about it for ages.

We went back to France a couple of years later, to the same place, I think, but it wasn't the same. I was going out with Janet by then and probably felt I was too old to be going on holiday with my parents. Even though we had upgraded to a caravan (in case it rained), I didn't want to be there and moped around. I spent quite a lot of time on my own and I soon realised that I didn't actually mind my own company. I think Richard liked having me around, though. He would swim out to the diving platform at sea and then be too tired to swim back, so I had to go out and rescue him. He did that a couple of times. I think he liked it.

On one occasion, the four of us settled down for a day on the beach and, after a few minutes, I turned around and my Mam had taken her bikini top off and was sunbathing topless. I was shocked. She had never done anything like it before. I wasn't happy and had no intention of sitting next to her all day. 'Fuck this,' I said. 'Come on Rich, we're off.' And me and my brother went off in search of something else to do. I was quite moody all holiday. Dad got fed up of me at one point and gave me a bollocking and told me to cheer up, which was understandable. I was fifteen, though, and just wanted to be with my girlfriend.

*****

Mam didn't like my choice of girlfriend mainly because she was six years older than me. One of my team-mates at Ainthorpe was a lad called Andrew Taylor. I spent lots of time with Andy and his family and that's how I came to meet his older sister, Janet.

I was quite a baby-faced teenager and slow to develop physically, so there was absolutely nothing about me that she could have been attracted to when we first met. To me, she was just Andrew's big sister who was always knocking around with her mates. They were probably quite amused by us and nothing more. But, from the age of fourteen, I shot up in height rapidly and started to stand out on the rugby pitch as the biggest, strongest and most mature. By the time I was fifteen, I had changed quite a bit and Janet and I became good friends in spite of the age difference. Shortly after she had split with a boyfriend, we got chatting at a family Christmas party and, before I knew it, we were kissing. We kept the relationship secret for a while, unsure how people would react, but I was soon infatuated.

Our daughter, Emma, now tells her Mum it's 'disgusting'

that we started courting when I was just fifteen and Janet's family felt exactly the same way at the time. But we were pretty headstrong in our determination to see each other. I suppose it's understandable that they would find it a bit odd that their twenty-one year old daughter had hooked up with a schoolboy, but there wasn't much they could do about it. They soon accepted me as part of the family. They were all obsessed with rugby league and I found myself spending more and more time with them.

Mam had never met Janet or her family before we started going out but she still decided she didn't approve. It seemed to me that she just wasn't interested in what I was doing and, when she did show any interest, it was only to disagree with me. There had been comments but it didn't really kick off until one New Years Eve party at Janet's aunt's house, to which Mam and Dad had also been invited. For a while, all was okay but, at some point, Mam said something about Janet and I reacted. I had a real go at her, saying all kinds of things that had been building up for months. Dad was quite old-fashioned and stepped in to defend Mam, telling me off for the way I had spoken to her. I turned on him as well and ended up storming off in tears.

After a while, they realised they weren't going to change my mind, so they stopped trying and even began to get along quite well with Janet and her family. It helped when I started to break into the Hull FC team and there were always lots of diversions. Soon after, we got married and moved in together. By that time, it was obvious this wasn't some stupid childish infatuation but a proper relationship.

I was still only eighteen years old when Janet told me she was pregnant. It didn't come as a shock though; we had started to think about having kids as soon as we were married the year before. To many, we were too young to start a family but, to Janet and me, it seemed like the next step.

We were married, I was earning quite a lot of money and both of our families had by now accepted our relationship.

I had grown up very quickly during the previous two years and the prospect of having a baby didn't faze me at all. If anything, it would show - to anyone who still had any doubts - that our relationship was serious and for keeps. I totally doted on Janet and would have agreed to anything she suggested. I think she also felt a bit broody when her older sister, Christine, announced she was pregnant a few months earlier. We decided we wanted to have kids at the same time so they could all grow up together.

It was good for Janet to be pregnant at more or less the same time as her sister and we were there in the hospital soon after Christine had Becky. In fact, we went into the delivery room within minutes of the birth, which meant that the nurses were still clearing up and I made the mistake of being nosey and looked around the room. When I saw the remnants of the placenta on a tray by the side of the bed, I had no idea what I was looking at, so I asked Christine's husband, Trevor. When he told me what it was and where it came from, I nearly passed out. I told Janet there and then that, as much as I wanted to support her and be there for her, there was no way I was going to be at the birth of our baby.

When Emma was born, Mam was just like any other grandparent, besotted, and she was the same when we had Stuart a couple of years later. She also started to take a bit of an interest in my rugby career as I became successful and began to want tickets to come and watch, particularly when I was in a Cup final or playing for Great Britain.

Ironically, she then became my biggest fan. She had never been to any kind of sports event so she had no idea about how crowds behaved. She couldn't understand why supporters criticised players they didn't know. She thought it was rude and would react furiously when someone had a go. She'd jump to her feet and tell them: 'That's my son, how dare you say that about him!' Funny, really, since she never gave a toss about me until I started playing for Hull.

*****

In June 2008, I was working as assistant coach to Justin Morgan at Hull Kingston Rovers. On the day we were due to play St Helens in the quarter-finals of the Challenge Cup, the phone rang at five o'clock in the morning. At that hour, a phone call can only mean bad news. It was my brother, Richard, to tell me that our Mam had died.

She had undergone an operation a few days earlier to fix a problem with a valve in her heart, but it hadn't gone as well as they had hoped and she had needed another shortly afterwards. She was sixty-eight and not in the best of health. As a result, her body wasn't strong enough to cope with the surgery and, one by one, each of her organs just shut down and she passed away.

The last time I had seen her was a couple of weeks earlier at the wedding of my son, Stuart, to Kate. I had gone to the wedding with Megan and Ben but, as the evening reception began, they went home, leaving me there on my own. I didn't know many of Kate's family and felt a bit awkward. Maybe that's why I started having a go at my Mam. I was annoyed to see her drinking when she knew she had an operation coming up. After a few white wines, she was also quite argumentative and we had a bit of an argument.

To be honest, my relationship with Mam was always difficult. It took a long time for her to accept my relationship with Janet until I decided to leave her and the kids, at which point, she became much closer to Janet and was very hostile towards Karen.

Not long after that I moved to Castleford and, whenever

I came over to Hull to spend time with Emma and Stuart, I always made a point of taking them over to see their grandparents. I don't know why but, as the years went on, I began to take the kids to McDonalds instead and so started to see less and less of Mam and Dad. I suppose there was fault on both sides but it got to the point where I would go months without seeing them.

When Karen and I had Megan in 1989, I didn't even tell my Mam at first. I was quite worried about how Emma and Stuart would react too, so I just chose not to tell anybody. It was stupid really because I knew they would find out from someone else, but I suppose I still felt guilty for having left them in the first place. Eventually, I took Megan over to meet them and they were thrilled which was a massive relief.

The situation mellowed a bit but Megan and Ben were never particularly close to their Nana, which upset Karen. The situation bothered me for years and I knew that I ought to do something to properly make up with my Mam. I still loved her but things had happened which meant we weren't close any more. Rather than sort those things out, I just let it drift. I should have made a point of sitting down with her and clearing the air, but I didn't.

And then she died and I didn't know how I should feel. After Richard gave me the news, I rang Justin Morgan and he told me to take as much time as I needed to sort things out. But Richard was already making the arrangements and I felt useless. I was the older brother and had a sense of duty that I ought to be helping out, but there was nothing for me to do so I just got back to work as if nothing had happened. I was a bit more emotional at the funeral where it started to sink in that my Mam was dead, but the whole episode was very strange.

Over the following weeks, I thought about it all a lot and started to blame myself more and more for the way that I had drifted away from my parents. I spent twenty-two years living in Castleford and, in that time, never made much of an effort to be with either of them.

After Mam died, I spoke to Emma my eldest daughter, and that caused me to stop and think as well. After Emma had given birth to my grandson, Sonny, she suffered quite a bit from post-natal depression. Emma reminded me that my Mam had suffered from that condition after both Richard and myself were born. It had been so bad she spent time in De La Pole Hospital being treated for depression. It was a part of my childhood I was aware of but hadn't really understood or spent much time thinking about, but it may well explain the way that my Mam acted and behaved at times.

I had always thought of her behaviour as quite erratic and unpredictable but I never stopped to think that there might have been a medical reason. With all of that in mind, I feel guilty that I didn't do more to resolve some of the issues we had. The whole messy episode was down to my own inability to be more open. I tried to bury things rather than confront them head on and, for that, I blame myself.

12

Is Pat on the Bus?

I was head coach of York in the Northern Ford Premiership and things weren't going well. We hadn't won in weeks and in February 2001 suffered our highest ever defeat, conceding ninety points at Widnes. There had also been a player exodus when wages weren't paid. So short of players were we that I had even been forced out of retirement myself.

There was only one team below us in the league; Chorley Lynx. Chorley were routinely getting hammered even more than us, so when we set off to Lancashire in the middle of March, we went in confidence, hopeful we could come away with a comfortable win to give us a boost.

We started badly, conceding a try after just three minutes. Shortly after, we had a player sent off for using his elbow in the tackle. Nevertheless, Chorley were poor and we fought back to draw level at 8-8 halfway through the first half. As I watched from the stands, I realised I had overestimated my players and stopped thinking about a comfortable win. I was just hopeful we'd beat them any way we could. Even that seemed optimistic when they scored a couple of quick tries and we were 16-8 down. Our confidence collapsed and they scored another three tries before half-time.

At 32-8, I doubted our ability to come back and I have no idea what I said in the changing room. We were poor but Chorley had been dreadful all year, walloped by everyone. And now here they were beating us! I couldn't think of anything that would make the slightest difference. Chorley scored nine times in the second half and it was only because their goal kicker was as shit as everyone else on the pitch that we lost 78-8 and not by an even heavier scoreline.

Fortunately, there were only a couple of hundred people there to witness the massacre. I couldn't believe what I had seen. There were a small number of reporters but none of them could bring themselves to come over and talk to me. They only had to look at my face to see how I felt.

It wasn't supposed to work out like this. When I retired in 1997, I had great visions of myself as a successful head coach in Super League, following in the footsteps of Arthur Bunting and Malcolm Reilly. How had I finished up at Chorley watching a bunch of hopeless amateurs hammer my bunch of even more hopeless amateurs? How did it all go so wrong?

*****

Throughout my playing career, I always imagined myself as a coach. I never planned for anything else and as soon as I decided to hang up my boots I wasted no time looking for my first job. As things turned out, I still had four months left on my contract with Castleford, so Stuart Raper asked me to coach the Academy side. I shared the job with Tony Marchant and thoroughly enjoyed it. I was learning new things every day, loved working with Tony and felt that we did a decent job. I knew I still had a lot to learn but was hopeful that the experience would help me to achieve my ultimate goal.

You only need to look at the numbers to see how difficult it is to reach the top in coaching. There are over three hundred professional players in Super League and only fourteen head coaches. Most of those are Australian, so it doesn't take a rocket scientist to figure that it was never going to be easy for me to reach my aim. Nevertheless, that didn't put me off. Coaching was what I wanted to do. I had confidence in my ability and I was determined to get there. It was only a matter of time. Or so I thought.

At the end of the 1997 season, my contract ran out with Castleford. I was hopeful I might get the job as Stuart Raper's assistant for 1998 but missed out to Graham Steadman. Steady still had a year's contract with the club so it made sense, but my outspoken reaction to John Joyner's sacking may have also been a factor. Whatever the reason, after nearly eight years I left Cas and began the search.

I was still out of work when the next season began. The only job offer to come my way was from Oxford Cavaliers in the RL Southern Conference. Although I was very flattered that they wanted me to join them, I declined and hoped that a professional club might come in for me. In the meantime, I accepted invitations to do a bit of media work.

I had done one or two spots on Sky Sports alongside Eddie and Stevo at the back end of 1997 and thought it went quite well. I also had some radio work lined up and was looking forward to spending my weekends getting paid to watch rugby while still knocking around with old mates.

In some ways, punditry is quite similar to coaching in that you spend hours watching rugby league matches and then you have to analyse and explain what you've seen. The main difference is that - if you get it wrong - there isn't anything like as much pressure on you.

That was quite appealing to me and it also meant that I wouldn't have to deal with the man-management side of the job, which was the area where I knew I lacked experience. Being a pundit was the best of all worlds and when I was asked to join the Sky team as a summariser on their coverage of the 1998 Academy competition, I accepted straight away. Nevertheless, I still thought of it as a temporary position while I waited for the right coaching vacancy to come along.

*****

Keighley Cougars had lost their first four games. Financial problems meant they had a weak squad and had struggled to field a team in some games. Once their current coach John Kain got the sack, I applied for the job and had no hesitation in accepting when it was offered to me.

Coaching was what I really wanted and I was thrilled to have an opportunity to show what I could do, but it meant I wouldn't be able to take the job with Sky Sports. Academy games would be broadcast on Sundays, when I would be busy with Keighley, so I had to turn it down. It was a tough decision because, in the back of my mind, I knew that the broadcasting job might be just what I needed. It might have helped me to develop new skills, meet people and move in another direction. It was certainly a safer proposition. That seemed sensible but I couldn't help being drawn to the prospect of becoming a coach. I desperately wanted to stay involved in the game on a day-to-day basis and wanted to put into practice many of the ideas I had picked up over the years playing for coaches I admired.

Sky turned instead to another recently-retired player, Phil Clarke, while I took up the helm at Keighley in March 1998, with a contract until the end of the season.

I was delighted to have landed a head coach's job so soon

after ending my playing career and the challenge was right up my street. I couldn't wait to get started and headed up to Cougar Park with real enthusiasm on my first day.

My mind was buzzing with ideas but I didn't really know what to expect. When I took over, Keighley hadn't won a game and were bottom of the league so, in some ways, the only way was up. I took the view that it couldn't get much worse and that it would be relatively easy, if we could win a couple of games, to show that I had made a difference. I had a clean slate and decided that the first thing I had to do was get the team fitter than they currently were. I had seen their last match and wasn't impressed.

I extended the length of the training sessions and really got stuck into the players. They worked exceptionally hard that first week, although some weren't happy at the length or intensity of the sessions. Nevertheless, after winning our first game, I was pleased with the improved work ethic and it was nice to get off to a positive start.

I continued the tough approach in training. I gradually brought in a few variations to how we played the game as well but still focussed hard on technical skills and fitness. To support my vision, I brought in my mate Grant Anderson as assistant coach. I knew he shared my values and attitude and felt that he would help me communicate my message.

That was my first mistake. There were already two assistant coaches, Neil Harrison and Frank Punchard, and I didn't really give them a chance to show what they could do. Neil decided to leave which immediately had a negative and unforeseen impact. I misunderstood the importance of having an assistant coach who acts as a buffer between you and the players. Bringing in Grant and losing Neil meant the players felt that they had no one to talk to if they were unhappy. Even so, our performances improved and the rest of the season went quite well. We finished mid-table and just outside the play-off spots, but my second big mistake came when I agreed to handle the players' contracts.

I had never wanted to do it and made it quite clear that I thought the chief executive should be the man who deals with a player's livelihood, leaving the coach to get on with the job of making him a better player. Not only was it a bad allocation of roles, I had no experience of doing it either and managing a budget of £360,000 was quite a responsibility.

There's no doubt I made mistakes; losing players I should have kept and keeping those I should have let go. In order to bring in the experience we needed, I decided to recruit some overseas players, which brought me into contact with the player agent Mick Robinson. Mick was a nice bloke but you had to be on your mettle when it came to some of his suggestions. At Cas, he got Stuart Raper to sign Adrian Vowles as a stand-off, but it was only when Stuart played Adrian at loose forward that we started to get good performances out of him.

I told Mick we needed a scrum-half, he recommended a young lad called Nathan Antonic. We duly signed Nathan and it wasn't until we were a third of the way through the season that he told us he had never played scrum-half in his life before coming over to England. He was a hooker.

Nevertheless, we also took Dave Chapman and Andrew Shtick. Both were Mick's players and, having played with them at Castleford, I was confident we had made a couple of important signings. Unfortunately, Chappy was carrying an injury when he came over and I don't think Andrew had the same mentality as he had at Castleford. I can't blame Mick for those two. I knew them as well as he did - we just didn't get that one right.

Having had a very good pre-season and overcoming the contract problems, the season got underway. I was confident 1999 would be a good year but things didn't go to plan. Our results weren't great and, by the time I made my third big mistake, I was under a bit of pressure.

We were playing at home one day and comfortably in control when I decide to take our half-back, Christian Tyrer, off the field. He was having a very influential match but I wanted to see if the other players could raise their game and step up if one of our key players wasn't in the side.

It was a gamble but one I was confident would pay off. However disaster struck. Our opponents fought back and we soon found ourselves behind. The obvious thing to do was put Christian back on the field, but my stubbornness wouldn't let me. As I watched the players struggle I became more determined that it was up to them to get out of trouble. They couldn't, we lost, and afterwards everyone laid the blame on me for taking Tyrer off. On reflection, my decision was a nail in the coffin.

When we were beaten at Leigh shortly afterwards, my fate was sealed and I was called into the office and sacked. Failure is something I don't take kindly to and, fortunately, I haven't come across it too many times. But being sacked by Keighley was a hurt it took a while to get over.

*****

Coaching was much more frustrating than I had thought it would be. Watching from the stands while the players tried to put my game plans into practice caused me real anxiety. I found it difficult to contain my emotions when someone made a mistake.

I also wanted to stamp my mark on the place right away and let everyone know I was going to be strong. I wanted to make things happen immediately but it came as a real shock when I attended my first session at Keighley and realised just how different the set-up was. It was a bit of a wake-up call; Castleford were a well-organised club on a sound financial footing with a full-time bunch of players whereas Keighley…. weren't.

One of the worst effects of being fired was that I actually started to doubt my own values. I have always believed in hard work and positive mental attitude but, at Keighley, I could feel myself compromising those values in order to try and work with the players. It was only later that I realised I still needed to hold onto those values but just find a better way to communicate them. Man-management was key and the area I needed to work on.

In hindsight, I wasn't ready for a head coach's role. I'd have been better advised to take a job as an assistant coach somewhere, but I was up for a challenge and prepared to learn on the job. I had a long way to go.

*****

After leaving Keighley, I worked as a representative for a local pub company for a while, along with coaching Lock Lane ARLFC. But I was constantly on the lookout for the next opportunity. When a vacancy came up at York Wasps in the summer of 2000, I felt the time was right to have another crack. York had always struggled to support a rugby league team, but there was enough potential for me to give it a go.

Although I was keen, there were plenty of people telling me to stay clear. The club had a bad track record, poor crowds and a history of financial problems. But all that mattered to me was that it was a job as a rugby league coach, which was exactly what I wanted to do. After the experience at Keighley, I ought to have given it more thought but I was stubborn. I ignored the advice and took the job.

I knew now that a strict approach wasn't always the best way to start, so my first aim was to try and establish some sense of togetherness. I thought that might be achieved by building a team around some of the York-based players who had been at the club for years, such as Mick Ramsden and Alan Pallister. I also managed to sign up some players with experience of Super League, such as Michael Smith from Hull and a couple of players from Castleford. By the time we started the season, I was confident we'd be competitive.

My first game in charge was a pre-season friendly at home to Hunslet who were, at the time, coached by one of my old team-mates, David Plange. Dave had more coaching experience than me but coming up against someone like him reminded me of just how many blokes there were, some of them mates, in exactly the same position as I was. Plangey had the upper hand that day and we started our season with a defeat, although I was pleased with the effort of my team.

The following week, we headed to Hull to take on Hull KR. Facing the Robins as a coach was a big occasion for me and I was desperate to get something out of the game. Once again, we fought well and I was quite pleased, even though we lost, 2-0. We had faced two tough opponents and played well, but there was still no denying the fact that my second spell as a coach had started with two straight defeats.

Meanwhile, off the field, I started to hear rumours that all was not well. The club had come close to going bust just before I arrived, with money owed to the Inland Revenue. I had been assured that the debts were under control and that there were no other financial problems lurking around the corner. But, in reality, their finances were an absolute mess and, just before Christmas, York entered into a Creditors' Voluntary Agreement (CVA) to avoid going bankrupt. It was then that the extent of the debts became public and I realised I had been badly misled when I was asked to take on the job.

*****

From Hull to Hell and Back

The club had debts of over £180,000 and, after the CVA was agreed, I was told the players weren't preferred creditors, which meant that they wouldn't get the wages they were owed. Their contracts were basically worthless. I hadn't gone into coaching to deal with contracts, CVAs or anything like that.

I was pissed off and I suppose I should have just walked away right then. I owed York nothing and they had let me down as well as their players. Nobody would have blamed me if I had just turned on my heels but something held me back. I had an opportunity to turn the situation around if I could put a decent team on the pitch. Although everything seemed stacked against me, I couldn't resist the challenge.

It soon became obvious, though, that there was far more to the job than coaching the team. A week before Christmas, I had to meet each of the players to explain the situation and try to persuade them to accept reduced contracts. It was one of the worst things I've ever had to do. Many had families to support and you could see them agonising over how the club's problems would impact on what they could buy their kids for Christmas. I was pissed off as well, but there was no point me moaning and complaining; I just had to get on with it and do whatever I could to help the club and its players.

Not surprisingly, most players chose to leave but one or two stuck with us and I began the job of assembling a brand new squad with the season already in full swing.

As the players drifted away, my job became a nightmare. There was barely any time to think about training patterns or tactics and I spent most of my time just trying to find new bodies. I scoured the amateur leagues and student competitions searching for lads who were good and keen enough to play for us.

I barely had enough players to make up a team and the

last thing I needed was an injury crisis, but that's exactly what we got. Eight players picked up knocks in our first five games. It seemed I was forever on the phone to Stuart Raper, asking him if there were any players he could loan me for a couple of weeks. He helped out when he could. At one time, I had nine Castleford players in my side.

I couldn't knock the commitment of the blokes I brought in; I had huge admiration for their bravery but they simply weren't up to it. We had a team that would have struggled in the Conference. Consequently, some started to pick up injuries. We were hammered at Dewsbury in early January and a couple of young trialists got badly beaten up, literally.

The following week, the players and their advisors met with the club to discuss new deals. They hadn't been paid for several weeks and there was still no guarantee of any regular wages. Instead, they were offered a share of the gate receipts. Understandably, it was too much of a risk for some and there was yet another flow of players out, including Michael Smith, who had been our star player.

After that, the wheels came off in spectacular fashion. A couple of Cas players decided not to stay on after their loan spells ended and Alan Pallister was banned for seven games after a tackle that broke the jaw of Jamie Rooney in a game at Featherstone. It could have been worse; I'd been warned to prepare for him getting three months. By mid-February, we were desperately short of confidence and chronically short of players. We were knocked out of the Challenge Cup by Villeneuve which at least meant we wouldn't be distracted by a cup run.

And then we played Widnes, our toughest game of the season. I feared the worst in the build-up. With half of my out-of-contract players leaving plus the injury crisis I was seriously struggling to field thirteen players. As a result, the spirit wasn't great and some of them started to wonder whether there was any point in carrying on. Yet I wasn't giving up and I made sure the players knew how committed I was. My frustration and disappointment was obvious but I began to realise how lucky I had been as a player not to have to put up with what these lads were having to deal with. The fact that they were all there, training on a freezing Thursday night, meant that they were committed as well. That made them bloody heroes in my book.

Nevertheless, a few told me they were struggling to juggle playing with work commitments and I had been quite lenient in allowing some players flexibility. But when the bus arrived in Cas to pick up the West Riding-based players and myself, I was surprised to find three blokes missing.

Nobody had thought to telephone ahead so, with no time to spare, I had to find three players from somewhere in order to fulfil the fixture. If we didn't we would be fined, probably be the final nail in the club's coffin. Besides, I had too much pride than to cancel a game so, along with assistant coach, Frank Punchard, I set about trying to raise a side. While I made calls, Frank nipped into the Lock Lane clubhouse and a couple of local pubs hoping to find someone available to pull on a pair of boots. Don't forget, that this wasn't an amateur game we were trying to salvage, but a professional rugby league match against Widnes. A few blokes seemed to be interested in a run out but when they found out it was Widnes we were going to play, they suddenly remembered they had to take the wife shopping. Fearing the worst, I made a quick call to Karen and asked her to drop my boots off just in case I needed them.

By now, we were running short of time and had to set off with just thirteen fit players. I still had to name seventeen, though, so I had no choice but to pick myself on the bench, four years after my last professional game. I was sure I'd have to play; there weren't any other options. The only other blokes on the bus were Frank, Steve the kitman, Pat the physio and one of our injured players, who had a pot on his leg. I still needed another three names on my team sheet so 'pot-leg' was named second substitute. Steve's name also went down after he assured me he had played a bit at school. At this point, Frank started sweating and twitching in his seat.

'Lee, I'm fifty-six,' he said. 'Some of them Widnes lads have played for Great Britain. If you put my name on that team sheet, I'm getting straight off this fucking bus.'

I took another look at Frank and then looked over at Pat. Pat was a fireman who had never played a game of rugby in his life. He wouldn't stand a chance against the likes of Martin Crompton and Karle Hammond. On the other hand, he wasn't fifty-six. Pat the physio became my final substitute.

I laced up my boots after one of the most bizarre warm-up speeches of my short coaching career and wondered how the hell I had got myself into this. I tried to convince myself that maybe it wouldn't be quite as bad as I feared. Widnes were one of the big names in the Northern Ford Premiership but their form so far hadn't been that good. We just might be able to give them a game. Or at least keep it respectable.

*****

Widnes scored their first try after twenty seconds. As they kicked off, two of our blokes went for the same ball, bumped into each other and fell over. Martin Crompton picked up the ball, passed to Steve Gee and he walked over for the easiest try he ever scored. There were two more tries before we touched the ball and, after twenty-five minutes, we were losing 42-0. I figured that I might as well suffer along with my players, so I brought myself on at half-time to see if I could help us turn it around. I had to accept that my best days were firmly behind me but I managed to give the lads a bit of a lift and I was proud of the way the young lads kept plugging away in spite of the non-stop flood of Widnes tries. I came off ten minutes from the end and was surprised and touched by the standing ovation I got from the Widnes fans when I came off. We managed to score a good try ourselves and I was almost relieved that we managed to hold them to ninety points to six. Even so, it was a record victory for Widnes and a record defeat for us.

The heavy defeats kept coming and when Leigh came to play us, I was so desperate for players that I was forced to ask Frank Punchard's son, Frankie, to play at short notice. Frankie Punchard was a decent player who had played for one or two semi-professional clubs in his day so his ability wasn't in question, but his sobriety was on the Thursday evening that I asked him to make his York debut at the age of thirty-four. He had been out drinking for most of the afternoon and was a bit worse for wear when I bumped into him. I told him I only needed him to keep the bench warm and eventually managed to persuade him to go home to get his boots. Providing there were no injuries, he could snooze on the bench and sober up. That's more or less how it panned out, until we got an injury ten minutes from the end. I'd no option but to send Frankie on for the last few minutes.

I wasn't too worried about having to pick Frankie, there were bigger problems to deal with. I'd been forced to draft in even more new players in the build-up to the game. Four blokes made their debuts and most of the players hadn't even met each other prior to the match, let alone trained with one another. It was a brave effort but it didn't stop us getting hammered, 84-12.

The following week came the trip to Chorley and - without doubt - the lowest point in the season. Afterwards, I went to see the chairman, John Stabler.

I was very tempted to quit. I have never been a quitter in my life but I just couldn't see how I could do anything to make things better. There were several times when I thought it would be better for the club to just pack up and fold. I was battling every day to try and find new players. They were training to the best of their ability, only to be embarrassed every weekend in front of a handful of supporters. It seemed totally pointless.

A few options were discussed and a few promises made but, to be honest, John wasn't too bothered about what was happening on the pitch. He was more concerned with trying to attract the sponsorship that would give the club some financial support. I could understand his position but I still faced the problem of trying to fulfil our fixtures.

The heavy defeats kept coming and, after conceding seventy in consecutive games, I prepared for Rochdale by challenging the players to keep them to less than fifty points. Given how badly we'd been doing, that would be some kind of an achievement. By half-time, it was 54-0 and I felt like going home.

The final score was 98-0, another record that shouldn't have been a great surprise. I only had three recognised professionals to call on; Allan Pallister, Mick Ramsden and Gareth Dobson. The season was only just past the halfway stage and I had already been forced to use over fifty players, most of them amateurs, students from York University or blokes recruited from the local Army team. I couldn't even recruit decent amateur players - they earned more in expenses with their amateur clubs than we could pay them. The attendances were now so low that their share of the net gate receipts meant they would be lucky to come away with a tenner each. It's quite funny to look back at now, but it was a living nightmare for someone trying to prove he should be taken seriously as a rugby league coach.

And the situation just kept getting worse. As Easter approached, a couple of young players I recruited from York University and Leeds Met said they wouldn't be available for a couple of weeks as it was their Easter break and they were going home for a holiday. I couldn't blame them. I was tempted to ask if I could go with them.

I was well aware that I still had much to learn if I was to make it as a head coach. My experience at York was stretching me but not in ways I had anticipated, so I paid a couple of visits to some Super League clubs to watch how they trained. I spent time at Hull and at Castleford and tried to keep myself up to date with current training methods. Afterwards, I would return to York and try to implement some of what I had learned, but it was never easy working with amateur players, however enthusiastic and committed they were.

After Easter, I managed to field a fairly settled team for a few weeks and we found some stability. I also tried to get the players to train more frequently but that never worked out. At Keighley, I had taken a very tough stance with the players, not fully realising that their priorities as semi-professionals were different to mine. At York, I was forced to be much more flexible and, quite often, was just grateful if they turned up. Some players were more than willing to turn up for extra training on a Monday, Wednesday and Friday, but there wasn't much I could do about those that couldn't make it. Consequently, training often took place with only half the team present. There were no set moves, no fancy plays. I just tried to put a team on the pitch, give them a gee-up and hope for the best. It wasn't what I had in mind when I set off on my coaching journey.

*****

The defeats continued and we conceded our thousandth point of the season at home to Hull KR in May. The next week we travelled to Gateshead. Unbelievably, at this stage of the season, we still weren't bottom. Having beaten Gateshead at home in February, we were a point above them. This time around they turned us over and dumped us to the bottom of the league. Despite our defeat, we hadn't done too badly and the following week we put up a good show in the first half at home to Dewsbury. The score was six-all at half-time and I gave the boys a big rap for their efforts, convincing them that this could be their best result of the season by far.

It had been a tough year, I told them, but they had showed character I would never forget. They were playing for the future of the club and had not been found wanting. I was thankful to have something positive to say. It was a proper Winston Churchill speech and I probably overdid it a bit, but I felt I had given them what they needed as they took to the pitch for the second half. Being level at half-time with one of the best teams in the league was a great achievement. This could be a massive result for us, if they could just keep it up for another forty minutes.

The twelve tries we conceded in the second half was yet another club record.

There were only five games left of the season by now and I was resigned to finishing bottom. I just hoped we could fulfil our fixtures and start to plan for the following year. It hadn't gone well at Keighley, it plainly wasn't working out at York and I wasn't sure what to do next. I concluded that I had definitely chosen the wrong route into coaching. I had figured that I could take charge of a small club and gain my experience there before moving on to bigger things, but I had been naïve. There was far more to the job than I had imagined and there were many occasions when I just didn't know how to deal with a particular situation. I realised that I should have looked for an assistant coach's role first so I could learn more about the man-management side of the job from someone with more experience. I was still committed to York Wasps but I knew that my future as a coach would probably require a spell as a right-hand man.

We continued winless for a few more weeks and, as we approached the final three games of the season, there was light at the end of the tunnel. On the other hand, those three games were against the top three teams in the league, Featherstone, Widnes and Leigh. There was a possibility that the club record defeat could be broken for the next three weeks in succession. At 18-0 down after fifteen minutes at Featherstone, anything seemed possible.

After a decent set of six, we found ourselves in a good attacking position and were awarded a penalty. The players were aware that they hadn't scored a single point for a couple of weeks, so they all agreed that they should go for goal. Even when losing heavily, I would expect my players to stay positive and try to score tries. To take a kick at goal when you're losing 18-0 was futile and beyond the pail as far as I was concerned. I was watching from a seat just in front of the press box and my reaction to the decision was widely reported in the *York Evening Press*. I went mental at them. The players could argue that they at least got on the score sheet, but by the end of the game the score was 92-2.

With just two games to go, all thoughts were on the next season and I was pleased to be called in to a meeting with John Stabler to discuss our plans. I'd wanted a meeting for a while and was sure John was avoiding me. Nevertheless, I went in hoping to find out how much money would be available to attract new players to the club. I had rehearsed what I would say about my plans for the team and where I would search for them. In spite of the chaos, I was still fully committed to York and looking forward to better times. John had made me lots of promises and I was hopeful that some substance would come out of the meeting.

What I didn't expect was for John to ask me to re-apply for my own job. He told me the club couldn't make any promises about contracts for 2002 and that included my own. He was hopeful there might be better news over the summer but, in any event, he couldn't guarantee I would be in charge next season.

I was furious. I couldn't believe my ears. I had worked like a dog all year just to be able to put a team on the pitch every week. I had even come out of retirement to enable us to fulfil our fixtures and called in all the favours I could in order to keep the club going. There was little doubt that if I had walked away during the season, York would probably have folded. And now I was being told that none of it was valued and they hoped someone else might come along to take over. Who, exactly? Brian Noble? Wayne Bennett?

There was no way I could continue to work for a chairman who could do that to me, so I resigned immediately. I told the players after training that night and their warm reaction amazed me; they were so upset at the way the club had treated me they considered refusing to play their next game against Widnes. I was horrified the club might not - after all - complete its fixtures and told them to stay professional. It goes without saying that Widnes hammered them. And then they lost 84-1 at Leigh (an injury-time drop-goal).

*****

Once again, I was out of work but, worse still, I'd now had two coaching spells that had ended badly. I could accept my mistakes and that I had been naïve in the first place to expect to be able to pick up the reigns at a club and make things better overnight. I also felt I had been badly let down and wondered why it was that that kept happening to me. Why, for instance, had John Joyner turned down the job at Keighley? What had he known that I hadn't? Not only did I have lots to learn about coaching, it was clear my decision making wasn't great either.

Furthermore, I'd been so busy dealing with the problems at York that I had given up the radio work and it seemed like Phil Clarke was settling nicely into the Sky Sports' studio. If I was to stay in the game, I had to be prepared to change my expectations and to effectively reinvent myself. Somehow.

13

On the Right Path

Four years had passed since I'd stopped playing; a lifetime in the world of rugby league coaching. The game had moved on and there was every danger that I would soon become a forgotten man. The prospect frightened me. There weren't likely to be many coaching opportunities but I was desperate to stay in the game so I decided to give my friend, Nick Halafihi, a call. Nick was the RFL's performance director and a man who I hoped might point me in the right direction. I laid my cards on the table and told Nick I was willing to consider whatever role he might feel I was suited for.

Fortunately, the RFL was undertaking a review of its youth development structure and had decided to use the Wakefield area as a pilot project. Nick asked me to do some research so I spent eight weeks investigating the youth set-up there and compiled a report on the options available in terms of coordinating what was going on. The task was different to what I had been used to and got me outside of my comfort zone, but I found it very interesting and rewarding.

I asked Nick if there would be any opportunities to work with the RFL on a more permanent basis and he found me a part-time position talent spotting. Alongside that, I managed to get some funding from the local council for a part-time role as service area co-ordinator for Wakefield, Featherstone and Castleford. For eight months, I split my time between the RFL and Wakefield Council working on youth development and learning a great deal along the way.

Over the next few years, I gradually worked my way up the ladder at the RFL working closely alongside David Waite to monitor the scholarship programmes being run by the professional clubs, as well as developing and guiding the club's player performance managers.

I had wanted to stay in the game and thought that a coaching job was the only way to do that, but my work at the RFL showed there were other pathways to follow. After a while, I developed lots of new skills and gained experience. Before long, I was a youth development manager.

*****

I have always been very impressed by David Waite. He was a successful coach in Australia before moving to England in 2000 in the role of Great Britain coach. He was also the RFL's technical director but neither title does justice to the impact he made in the four years he was here. Not only did David bring over lots of exciting new ideas which had a big impact on our youth structures, he had the leadership skills to push through change. He breathed new life into the governing body and, as soon as I met him, I knew that he was one of those blokes it would be good to know. I wanted to build a future in the game and I guess that David became something of a mentor.

By 2005, David had begun to work behind the scenes to

help Catalans Dragons prepare for Super League. He knew he wasn't going to be staying at the RFL much longer and he asked me to join his staff on what was called the Talent Identification programme, with the intention of taking it over when he had gone. Once again, I worked closely with David and learned a lot.

In essence, I managed a group of people whose job it was to identify the best players up to the age of eighteen and to do as much as we could to ensure they progressed to the top of the game. That involved a wide range of tasks such as overseeing the selection process for regional and national teams at various age groups. We watched games, spoke to coaches and staff at the amateur clubs, talked to the players themselves and their parents, and generally made sure that they had advice, support and guidance. Talent identification is always a matter of opinion and you can never always get it right. You can never please everyone but as long as you don't just say 'he's not good enough', most people accept that there has been a rationale behind the decision. That kind of analysis and support was new to the English game until David Waite joined the RFL and I was very satisfied with my contribution to the system we were putting in place.

It wasn't coaching and it wasn't Super League but I was working with good colleagues and helping young people to reach their potential. I took a lot of satisfaction from the job.

*****

The biggest problem facing rugby league in this country is that we don't produce enough good quality young players. We seem to have no problem producing good players up to the age of eighteen but then struggle to convert them into world class players at twenty and twenty-one. In Australia, they don't seem to have any trouble doing that but, in this country, too many fall by the wayside. As a consequence, at full international level there is more competition for places in Australia. If any of our top players get injured or lose form, there aren't many blokes to take their place. So we continue to struggle to compete. I believe there are several reasons why this happens.

Firstly, the Australian junior competition is much tougher than ours and provides great preparation before lads are promoted to the NRL. Good players improve by playing good players. That hasn't always been the case in the UK where under-18 and under-21 competitions have not been the ideal preparation for Super League. The introduction of an under-20 competition in England, with dispensation for over-age players, is a good move and may go some way to providing the same level of intensity that our players need.

In truth, nobody really knows whether the under-20 competition will be the best way forward, but I believe it has much to offer and we now need to stick with it for a few years and have some stability. For too long, we have changed the way we develop our young players to the detriment of the game as a whole.

The second big area for development is at the grassroots level. There is a massive responsibility on community rugby league teams to develop young players' skills. This puts great pressure on amateur coaches, most of whom are only in those roles because they are enthusiastic and want to help out. I'm full of admiration for those blokes and would like to see the sport do much more to support them. But the biggest challenge is to try and recreate the conditions in which I learned to play the game - on the field at the back of my house! At the moment, youth teams are under too much pressure to win games. We need to take that pressure away and give them time to just play, try things out, get things wrong and learn naturally.

I also think that kids start to play the game too early. Some start at just six or seven and can soon lose interest if they start getting hurt or aren't involved enough. By the time these kids reach the age of sixteen they're often bored of the sport. The modified version of the game which is played at junior level also stops the development of key skills of the game; for instance there are restrictions on players kicking the ball, which is daft. Kicking skills are crucial for success in rugby league and it's important that young players have the freedom to experiment with these skills at junior level.

Funding at the grassroots level is also a bit of a lottery, literally. Many clubs have secured National Lottery funding and built clubhouse facilities that help to bring in more income. That's a great idea but there are many more clubs that can't get access to sufficient funding. Because of that, there are parts of the country where the facilities aren't good enough to support the development of the sport.

In Australia, the sports facilities are far better than what is available in this country and that doesn't just apply to rugby league. The climate helps them but they have also invested heavily in community sports facilities. In the UK, you often find parks and sports fields locked up once it gets dark, leaving kids to hang around on streets with no opportunity to play sport. Where there are facilities, the quality is uneven. I am a great believer that if you expect junior players to adopt professional attitudes you have to give them professional facilities and that is a huge problem, especially for rugby league. In 2009, I spent months trying to find a suitable location for the Hull FC Academy team to train through the winter. We ended up using school fields, gyms and parks across the city. It's not ideal and it's hard to get the kids motivated to aim high when that's all we can offer them.

Finally, the most obvious way to guarantee more GB-eligible players is to reduce the number of overseas players in Super League. I grew up in a Hull FC team that included the likes of Peter Sterling and Gary Kemble, current internationals. Playing alongside them made youngsters like Garry Schofield and myself better players. Nowadays that's not always the case. There are too many overseas players in Super League who will never play Test rugby or whose best days are far behind them. I'm not knocking the commitment they show, but we all know they are filling places that could just as well be occupied by English lads.

To help with that, I would reduce the limit on overseas players to three, rather than five. This would force clubs to choose the best ones. If they want to recruit a mediocre player so be it. They'll probably pay him less and have more money to pay English-born players.

Unfortunately, the problem comes from the layers of rules and laws covering who is eligible and who isn't. The outcome is that Super League clubs can fill their teams almost full of non-British players if they really want to. And, let's face it, it's the clubs who run the game in this country, not the RFL. But I'll come back to that one! Too many overseas players means the England coach doesn't have as many players to choose from as his Australian counterpart.

*****

I still think we can beat the Australians again on a regular basis, but it won't happen unless we help to make it happen; stability in our junior structures, more money into grassroots facilities, more support for community rugby coaches and, once those talented young players start to come through the system, fewer overseas players to hold up their progress through the game and into the GB team.

For all of that to happen, though, the sport needs a strong, single governing body. BARLA have achieved great things in the past, but they have lost sight of why they primarily exist: to allow players of any age and gender to play at whichever level they are capable of achieving. Organised rugby league at the amateur level is also very effective in promoting healthy lifestyles and community involvement, but that doesn't give them the right to act against the interests of young sportsmen who want to play professionally. I think that's what often happens.

BARLA would deny it but I believe they've become more concerned with building up the amateur game at the expense of the interests of young players. Over the years, BARLA has continuously expanded its range of competitions and, as a result, extended the length of the season. With the amateur season lasting well into May for the most successful clubs, it makes life very difficult for young players on scholarship schemes with professional clubs. Young players don't want to turn their backs on their amateur clubs when they need them, but they shouldn't be put in that position if their future lies in the professional set-up.

At the same time, professional clubs must try and understand the amateur clubs' predicament and try to work with them. I have spent years involved with BARLA teams and I understand the issues that bother them. No wonder many amateur clubs feel like poor relations to the rich clubs of Super League when they only get £500 in compensation if one of their players is picked up by a pro club. That's not much for six or seven years of care and development of young talent.

To have two different organisations running the game is daft and I fully agreed with the Genesis Report in 2004 which advocated a single governing body. I was disappointed when the RFL decided not to adopt the recommendation.

*****

Working for the governing body also gave me a perspective on the issue of expansion. When I first started playing rugby league, there were thirty professional clubs, all of them based in the north of England. But within a couple of years new clubs were established in Cardiff, Carlisle and Fulham. For the fans, it was all a bit of a novelty. The first time I played against Fulham at Craven Cottage, I couldn't believe it was an away game, there were so many Hull FC fans there. In a crowd of around 11,000, half of them must have been from Hull, having taken the opportunity for a good day (or weekend) out.

That was also the attitude of most players at the time; we just turned up and played and, if we got the opportunity for a night out somewhere different, so much the better. We played in Cardiff one season and the club flew us down there in a charter jet from Humberside airport. We loved it.

Nowadays, expansion is a much bigger issue because for every club fast tracked into Super League from France or Wales, there is a club from within the game's heartland that misses out. I have mixed views on this. I am totally in favour of spreading the game wherever there might be a demand for it. The sport is too good for us to keep it to ourselves in the north of England, but there is a limit to how far we should persevere when it becomes obvious it isn't going to work.

The experiment in France has, for me, been a success so far. The idea of playing in Paris was daft because there is no rugby league interest there. The best place to set up a rugby league club was always going to be in the south of the country. I played for Great Britain in places like Carcassonne and Avignon lots of times and have seen the appetite for the sport in those parts. Since Catalans joined Super League in 2005, they have been successful both on and off the field and I think they deserve another licence to develop the club further.

The expansion into Wales could also work for the same reasons eventually; the Welsh love their rugby. But there is a much greater appetite for rugby union in the south, whereas, in the north, football is dominant. I'm not sure what the point was of moving to Wrexham in 2010 and, although they did better on the pitch, their support has so far not taken off. At the time of writing, they are bottom of the competition again and, although they may well get a new license, I would be surprised if there is a long-term future for the Crusaders.

*****

I have no doubts, however, about the future of Super League in London - there shouldn't be one!

I have played against Fulham, or London, or whoever, lots of times and have never been able to understand how the whole venture works. They still can't draw decent crowds after nearly thirty years on the go and I don't think they ever will. Londoners have no interest in rugby league despite millions of pounds being spent to persuade them otherwise and I can't understand how the club manages to survive on such tiny crowds. Either someone is bankrolling them or the RFL are subsidising them but they can't be paying their own way.

In recent years, there has been growth in community rugby league but that has largely been funded by Sport England. One or two local players have come through into the Harlequins team and the coaches working down there have down a superb job. The outcomes, though, don't really justify the money being spent. If I had my way, I'd cut the handouts and let them fold. There's a much stronger argument for having a team in Cumbria where there's a decent supporter base and where the amateur game is strong.

However, it looks to most people that Harlequins will be

given further opportunity to establish themselves in Super League. With Widnes set to make the step up in 2012, it now looks likely that Wakefield will be the team to miss out when the next round of licenses are allocated, although time will tell. That would be a real shame for a club with such a history in the sport and with such great people associated with it. Nevertheless, the Wildcats haven't managed to build up their support or find the financial backing they need. It will probably be in their long term interests to take some time out to regroup away from the pressures of Super League.

Don't think that I'm a traditionalist, though. I believe that clubs must be able to stand on their own two feet and that means, unfortunately, there will probably never be a place in the top flight for the likes of Featherstone, Dewsbury, Keighley, Rochdale or any other team based in towns that are too small to enable them to pay their way. What Featherstone have achieved is incredible but there is no way that a town of 10,000 people can support a team in Super League even if they can persuade 2,000 of them to watch their team every week (which they probably can't). We can't have a fast, open sport played in decent stadiums with some of the best players in the world and expect Featherstone to be able to compete at that level; it just won't happen. I don't expect everyone to agree with that view, especially supporters of Featherstone Rovers. Their coach Darryl Powell has brought a lot of professionalism and a fair amount of success to the club recently. But those are my opinions.

Having said that, I would love to see all of those clubs survive outside of the elite competition without feeling that they have to aim for Super League. I like the fact there is so much choice in the sport. On a weekend, I like how I can still go and watch the likes of Featherstone on a Sunday afternoon, have a pint in the clubhouse and not have to worry about whether I need a ticket for the game, although, given what I've just said about them, they might not let me in any more! Then again, I'd be just as likely to go and watch Lock Lane play in the National League and would enjoy myself just as much.

There is still a natural hierarchy to the English game, but if we are to challenge the Australians on a regular basis we have to be pragmatic and make sure the elite competition produces high quality young players. To do that, we need strong clubs with good finances and solid foundations and have to accept that, unfortunately, this means no place for the likes of Featherstone and Dewsbury, as well as Harlequins.

14

Crossing the Divide

My time at the RFL flew by. I was based mainly at Red Hall in Leeds; a good working environment, especially in the early years. The staff were well looked after and there was a feeling that all the departments - performance, commercial, refereeing and so on - were working towards the same aim: pushing the game forward. It wouldn't stay that way. After a while I noticed subtle changes. Some people became more interested in their own work areas and job security. I wasn't the only one pissed off, but I was the only ex-rugby league player and often felt my objectives were at odds.

Then, towards the end of the 2007 Super League season, David Howes made me a very interesting proposition.

*****

Like most Hull FC fans, I had watched with interest as Hull Kingston Rovers, under Justin Morgan, took the National League by storm in 2006 and were promoted to Super

League. They did okay in their first season too, securing their position. There was no doubt about their ambition.

David Howes had been giving me advice since the early 1990s and also acted as agent to my son, Stuart, when he started to play rugby league. David would occasionally ring with an invitation to a dinner or function, or a bit of media work. He would also pick my brains and ask me what I thought of certain players he was trying to find a club for. So it wasn't a great surprise when he rang and told me that Hull KR were looking for an assistant coach. He asked if I could think of anyone who might be interested. I certainly could, although I was reluctant at first to reveal my own interest.

After seven years at the RFL, I felt that I had learned as much as I was going to and was starting to go a bit stale. If I stayed, I didn't think it would benefit my career in the long run. My main goal hadn't changed; I wanted to be involved in club rugby. I looked upon my time at the RFL as further preparation for achieving my aim of one day becoming a head coach. Nevertheless, I was comfortable in the job and it was fairly secure. I hadn't been actively looking for a return to coaching but the moment that Howesy mentioned the Rovers job, I knew it was the right move. After the disastrous spell at York, I reached the conclusion that I needed a spell as an assistant coach. The opportunity to work with Justin was one I suddenly found myself desperate to take, so I told David I was interested in the job myself. I'm sure Howesy knew that all along but didn't want to come right out and ask.

Just as I could never see myself leaving Hull FC all those years ago, I had never imagined for one minute that I might end up working for Hull KR. But I was very keen to be involved in Super League and in order to make my move back into coaching I needed to work with a good coach with lots to offer me. Hull KR ticked all of those boxes.

I met Justin at the Xscape venue near Castleford. I felt that the meeting went well; we were on the same wavelength in many ways. At the end of the meeting, Justin told me that if I still wanted the job it was mine. He advised me to sleep on it and let him know the next day.

I knew it would raise eyebrows in some parts of the city but also knew it was the right job for me. I had no doubts about accepting it. There were bound to be some who would doubt my commitment to Rovers when I had never made any secret of my loyalty to Hull FC, but I don't think Morgs gave it a moment's thought. Chairman Neil Hudgell was a different matter though.

Neil is a passionate Rovers fan, which is great, but he can allow his support for the club to cloud his judgement and I have often wondered how he privately reacted to having me work for his club. On one hand, he might have felt he had a traitor in his camp but, knowing Neil, I suspect that he might have taken pleasure from it, in a funny sort of way.

After accepting the job, I called my brother, Richard, as I tend to do when I am about to make a major decision in my life. He didn't care that I was joining Rovers; he was more concerned that I was giving up a secure job and taking a bit of a risk. He had a point. It was a big decision and my track record in that department wasn't great. I had already turned down Sky in order to coach Keighley and stepped away from another steady job working for a pub company to take over the mess at York. Now I was preparing to leave yet another secure job for the uncertainty of club rugby once again.

I suspect that if the opportunity had come up a few years earlier I wouldn't have taken it. Karen would have talked me out of it. But by 2007 my personal situation had changed. I wasn't with Karen any longer and my kids were just about grown up. I was in a position where I could make a decision for myself and not have to worry about what other people thought or how they might be affected.

*****

The more I thought about the job, the more appealing it became. I wanted to get back on the training ground and the position at Craven Park gave me plenty of opportunity to develop my coaching credentials. I had spent a long time dealing with young players and now I was really looking forward to working with Super League players again.

That said, I had been out of club rugby for a while and had to admit to a few nerves before I joined up for the first training session just before Christmas. The players, though, were great towards me and I was certainly helped by the professionalism already in place at the club. The pre-season training programme impressed me a great deal and Morgs, in particular, was a huge presence around the place.

At the end of January 2008, the squad flew to Portugal for warm weather training. We stayed at the Browns complex on the Algarve, which was quite ironic as the Hull FC squad was due to stay there the following week. Both groups of players bumped into each other at the airport.

The players worked hard for the whole trip but, in the middle of the week, Morgs gave the players a day off to go out for a beer. I decided to join them and we went into the nearest town and had a good laugh over a few drinks. Some of the lads headed on to a club but I decided I'd had enough and went back to the room I was sharing with conditioner Billy Mallinson and physio Stuart Leek.

When I awoke the next morning, I realised there was no one around. They had both already left and I realised I had overslept. Worse still, I had missed the bus taking the team to the beach for training and had to make my own way down there. You can imagine the stick I got when I turned up, walking along the beach while all of the lads were having a game of football on the sand. It wasn't the best start to my time at the club. Even though Morgs saw the funny side, I was still pissed off with Billy for not waking me up.

Once the season got under way, the team did very well and there were some great wins I was proud to be involved with. We got off to a terrific start by beating St Helens in round two and the following week travelled to France. The game against Catalans Dragons was a big one for Justin; he had spent time coaching in France and knew a bit about French rugby. More importantly, he saw it as the kind of game we had to win if we were serious about challenging for a place in the top six. It was there that I saw just how passionate Justin could be about his rugby.

Despite good preparation, Rovers never really got going in the first half and came in at half-time trailing 14-6. I was intrigued to see how Morgs would deal with things and what he would say to try and improve the performance. He was usually fairly composed, but on this occasion he couldn't contain his anger. He was particularly frustrated with scrum-half James Webster who he felt wasn't involved enough. As James came through the door, Morgs screamed: 'And when are you going to take your fucking dinner jacket off?' It was a real eye-opener. I had never seen him lose his temper in that way but it certainly worked and the players went on to win in the last minute. Morgs rarely lost his cool but when he did he became one of the angriest men I have ever seen.

The first derby of the season was in March and it was a game I was really looking forward to, even though I knew it would be strange to be plotting the defeat of Hull FC. The match took place in terrible conditions and Rovers won with a late drop-goal. When the hooter went, to my surprise I celebrated like everyone else associated with the club. I had played my part in preparing the team so it was only natural that I should take pleasure out of being on the winning side.

Nevertheless, I was reminded of my affinity for the black and whites wherever I went that year. Hull FC made it the Challenge Cup semi-finals in 2008 and I took my son, Ben, to Doncaster to watch the game. Ben was a bit worried that we might get some abuse from the Hull fans, but that couldn't have been further from the truth. As soon as they saw us, they started to give me a bit of friendly stick about working for the enemy. It was great banter and I loved it.

*****

At the end of the season, I felt that it had all gone very well. I had a good relationship with Morgs and like to think that over the course of the year I managed to establish myself as a credible member of the coaching squad. Morgs, though, felt the club could have done better. We had finished seventh but he wanted us in the top six and was determined to make sure we did better the following year.

Justin is a very passionate, hands-on manager who has great tactical awareness as well as a very strong character. I was always impressed by his work ethic and he would leave no stone unturned in order to give his team an edge. Like most good coaches, he would spend hours working on detailed preparations that many people would never see.

Morgs is a very good man-manager who expects players to take responsibility for themselves. As a player, he liked to have the odd drink but, when he did, he would be the first in the gym the next day working it off. That was exactly what I did, especially towards the end of my career, and I admired how he tried to instil that kind of approach.

When Rovers were promoted, Morgs stayed loyal to most of the players who got them there but, over the next couple of years, he managed to recruit some genuine quality and one or two signings in particular stand out. Clint Newton has been one of the club's most important signings in recent years. Newts' work ethic is tremendous and, like Morgs, he is a very strong character with lots to say. Occasionally, Clint probably has a bit too much to say for himself but, when you work as hard as he does and have such a positive influence, then you are probably entitled to speak your mind.

I always felt that Clint, and possibly Ben Galea as well, had the ability to leave a real legacy and Clint certainly had a massive impact on the development of Rovers' younger players while I was there. When he first started out, Liam Watts had some bad habits which frustrated Clint and he wasn't afraid of letting him know. But it was all designed to make Liam a better player which he has certainly become, thanks, partly, to Clint.

Stanley Gene was another talismanic figure; an enigma and a huge character. I got on very well with Stan and we talked for hours about Papua New Guinea, a place that has always fascinated me. Nobody is really sure of Stan's age. Although he claims to be in his thirties, I don't think anyone believes him. I would often joke that I was sure I had played against him during my first tour of PNG in 1982.

Another player to intrigue me during my time at Rovers was Paul Cooke. Cookie had signed the previous season but struggled to settle. During 2008, he had a number of issues off the field which caused him to struggle for form. I had a lot of sympathy for Paul and could see that a lot of what he was going through was very similar to some of the problems I had struggled to deal with.

I really wanted to help Paul. When I was going through a bad time in my career, what I needed more than anything was for someone to sit me down and talk about what I was going through. When Darryl van der Velde took the time to do that after yet another misdemeanour at Castleford, it effectively changed the course of my life.

There were many times when I offered to do that for Paul but it never happened. It can be very hard to admit that you need help from someone and, like Paul, I always felt that I could sort out my own problems. Paul is no longer playing, which is a real shame. He has made some bad choices but it's not too late to find a way back into the game. I wish him well.

There were some big characters at Hull KR but none bigger than Justin himself, except perhaps Neil Hudgell. I have a great deal of respect for both men. What they have achieved with Hull KR is impressive. After a year working with Justin I came to the conclusion that he was as good a coach as any I have worked with.

*****

While the rugby side of the club looked healthy at the end of the 2008 season, the recession had bitten deep and there were financial problems behind the scenes. A number of backroom staff were made redundant and the club was looking at ways to save money.

At the same time, Neil Hudgell was aware that the club needed to appoint a head of youth development in order to comply with Super League criteria. Since I had undertaken the same kind of role for the RFL, he approached me and asked who would be best suited to fill the position. I told him that, in all honesty, the best person to do the job was me but, of course, I was already very busy as assistant coach.

The obvious solution was for me to do both. Neil knew I was the right man and that he could save quite a bit of money if he could avoid hiring someone new and just pay me a bit more. He said it was a good idea and that he would discuss it with his chief executive, Paul Blanchard, who would sort out the detail.

A few weeks passed and I heard nothing from Paul

confirming my new role but, in the meantime, I started doing the job anyway. As usual, the money wasn't that important, but I don't like being treated as a mug and, as time went on, that's how I started to feel. Over Christmas and into the New Year, I continued to email Paul and left messages but I was never able to pin him down for a meeting. I got the impression he had no intention of sorting it out.

Early in the New Year, the club made some more back office staff redundant and I wondered if they were hoping I would just quit and save them more money. If that was what they wanted, I decided, then that's what I would do. I drafted a letter of resignation, told Justin what I planned to do and sent the letter to Blanchard.

Paul never acknowledged the letter. I also sent further emails to let him know what I had done; all of which were ignored. It wasn't long before the story emerged on fans' websites that I had left and most drew the conclusion that I was another casualty of Rovers' financial problems, which was only partly true.

Paul himself resigned as chief executive in mid-January amid all sorts of speculation, so I tried to get Neil Hudgell to acknowledge my resignation. Not only did Neil refuse to speak to me, he also denied I had ever sent a letter of resignation to anyone at the club. News of my resignation became public on 19th January, but I had actually resigned some time prior to that. That detail is important because, soon after resigning from Rovers, I had gone in search of what I hoped would be my dream job.

*****

I had always hoped that one day I could go back to work at Hull FC. Mel Harman, a very good friend of mine, had been the club's head of youth development for years but he had always told me he would step aside if ever I wanted to return to Hull in that role.

As far as I was concerned, having resigned from Rovers I was free to look for another job. The fact that they hadn't acknowledged my resignation was up to them. So once I had sent my resignation to Paul Blanchard in early January, I gave Mel a call and asked if the offer still stood. He said he would speak to the Hull FC chief executive, James Rule.

A return to Hull FC would be a dream for me but I was also wary of placing too much emphasis on just a couple of conversations. I had often been very naïve when it came to contract negotiations and there was a danger I could end up with nothing if I wasn't patient. Mel was the go-between but it didn't happen overnight. Four more weeks passed through January and February while I spoke to Kath Hetherington, James Rule and other staff at the club about the role I would play. Eventually, they came up with an offer and it was the easiest decision I'd ever had to make. It had been twenty-one and a half years since I left Hull FC and I'd long since given up on any chance of returning. But once the deal was done it was made public on February 19th.

The decision to leave Hull KR wasn't easy, despite what some might think. I enjoyed my twelve months there and I'd like to think I got on well with everyone on the football side, especially Justin Morgan. It was Morgs who gave me the opportunity to return to coaching and I was determined to do a professional job. He was a great bloke to work with and it came as no surprise to me that Rovers did so well during the 2009 season, when they finished fourth in Super League. Unfortunately, the rest of the club lacked the same level of professionalism. Once they started to mess me around, I knew I couldn't work for them any longer.

Although leaving Rovers was a bit of a disappointment, turning up for work at the KC Stadium was a great feeling. I spent the first couple of weeks just savouring being back at the club where it all started. Every now and again, I would turn a corner at the KC Stadium and spot a photo on the wall of some of the players from the 1980s and it would remind me of those days. It felt good. I was back home.

*****

Things hadn't gone very well for Hull FC in 2008, on or off the field. And the board was quite sensitive about the lack of local people involved with the club, so bringing me back did no harm. Soon, they also brought back another ex-player, Jon Sharp, as football operations manager. Together with Steve Crooks and Andy Last we made up a nucleus of people who had a bit of history there. On top of that, the team had kicked off 2009 well with a couple of early wins, so there was an air of optimism around when I started work. But, while most fans had their eyes on the progress of the first team, my job was very much about making sure that Hull FC had the best youth development structure they possibly could.

It was a broad remit that gave me responsibility for everything affecting the development of the young players. It was very fluid and not a nine-to-five job by any means. There was always the odd day when there wasn't much to do but, more often than not, there weren't enough hours in the day. There was lots of administration involved which I didn't mind and the variety of tasks kept me on my toes.

One of my responsibilities was to co-ordinate the junior teams' training programmes. Hull FC has always had a good youth structure and I would like to think I added something to the programme. With Brent Dickinson working incredibly hard as the youth team conditioner, I was able to put in place a programme that provided our young players with the basic skills and knowledge needed for future development. As well as technical skills, we covered tactical knowledge, sessions on athletic development, core stability and mental attitude. With these bases covered, the players are much better equipped to adapt smoothly to the type of coaching they will receive when graduating to the under-18s.

I also had to make sure we used appropriate facilities. My base was at the KC stadium but the club's training facilities are scattered all over the city, which creates quite a logistical problem. I soon realised some of them just weren't suitable.

The first team trains at Brantingham Park, home of Hull Ionians RUFC. It's a decent facility but it's ten miles away from the KC and only used by the first team squad. There isn't the capacity for junior teams to train there as well and so they train at various other locations, including a gymnasium at the old Boulevard ground, school fields and parks. It's not ideal and the quality of the facilities is outside of our control which means that, on the whole, they aren't good enough. The need for a single training facility is vital if Hull FC are really going to move forward.

*****

The most important element of my role was one with which I was quite familiar; identifying the right players to sign. This is a key job and one that I took very seriously. Not only did I have to make important decisions for the club, I was always aware that the choices we made had a massive impact on the lives of the young lads.

Selection is always a complex task; you have to make sure the players brought into the club are going to add something to the set-up even if you think they might not make it all the way to Super League. It might surprise some that coaches sign lads who we don't actually think will make it, but that's how it works. Not every young player will go on to play for the club and, in actual fact, a very small percentage of the lads we signed to our scholarship will go on to be successful. Even so, we operated a squad of around twenty to twenty-five in each of our under-18 and under-20 teams, while also running a successful scholarship scheme for fourteen to sixteen year olds. When kids were signed up for those teams we looked for them to have a certain level of skill, but we also wanted them to have the right attitude so that they could challenge their team-mates and help them improve as well.

While the goal for everyone is to sign professionally for Hull FC, there is still a lot to achieve if that doesn't happen. Super League clubs nowadays are, ironically, the feeder clubs for many of the game's semi-professional and amateur teams and if a lad doesn't make it there he may go on to have a decent career in the Championship, where lessons learned are passed on to more young players. Alternatively, he may decide to go into coaching or personal training. What we did with the young kids, therefore, is important in preparing them for a career in sport, one way or another. For that reason, I have always been very keen to work with young players on their mental attitude, so they can deal with disappointment if it happens and continue to learn and be prepared to take new opportunities.

*****

I remember one occasion while working at the RFL when I went on a tour of France with an England Schoolboys' team. It was around 2004 and there were some good young lads in the side, such as Tommy Lee and Scott Moore. I wasn't the coach, I had just been asked to keep an eye on things and see which players impressed.

Once we arrived in France, I gave the lads a little pep talk. I wanted to speak to them about what it ought to mean to represent their country, how they should take it seriously and be proud of what they were doing. I think I might have called them 'ambassadors'. It was that kind of speech and, while I was speaking, I could see out of the corner of my eye that one of the coaches was chuckling to himself.

Twenty-five years earlier, I had been in their position and got pissed on cheap wine at the after-match reception and broken curfew to find a bar in the town. It was quite ironic that it should be me, of all people, who stood there giving them this message. Or maybe I was better suited because I've been there, made the mistakes and paid the price.

Steve Crooks no longer works at Hull FC but he used to tell the young Academy players about all the great tries he scored at the Boulevard. They knew he was only joking and thought it was funny. Once I arrived though, he started to tell them that I really had done those things, not only for Hull but also for Great Britain. It was very nice of him but, to be honest, I was never comfortable talking about myself and so, whenever I spoke to the lads at Hull FC about discipline and professionalism, I never talked about my own experiences unless they asked me to.

In any case, as far as most of Hull's young players were concerned, I was just another member of staff. They weren't even born when I played for the club so the worst thing I could do would be to harp on about the old days to a bunch of lads who just wanted to make their own mark in the game. That said, Steve Crooks and I did try to make them aware, for their own sakes, of the history of the club they'd joined and what it meant to the supporters and the community. If they are able to take that on board, I think it gives them a bit of humility, makes them appreciate things a bit more and makes them nicer kids to have around.

*****

I threw myself into the role at Hull and really hoped that I could see out the rest of my career there. Working there also gave me the opportunity to see more of my kids and their own families. After a few months, I decided to go one step further and, in July 2009, I moved into a flat in Hessle with my youngest son, Ben.

Having lived in Castleford for so long, I didn't know too many people in Hull any more and so spent most of my time working. I wanted to make a difference and be very hands-on but, right from the very beginning, I realised I was going to have problems. The club had one of the biggest backroom staffs in the game and my duties and responsibilities overlapped quite a bit with those of Jon Sharp. Jon likes to take control of things in much the same way I do and quite often we found ourselves taking different views on how things should be done. I felt I had the greater experience when it came to youth development, but I also recognised that Jon had lots of other relevant experience in the game. It became difficult for us to do our jobs properly.

I was also irritated by one or two other things that I felt were getting in the way of progress. One day, I put my frustrations down in writing and emailed it to James Rule. It wasn't well received and I learned that, to get things done in an organisation, you sometimes have to be more diplomatic than my usual gung-ho approach.

The 2009 season was another poor one for Hull FC on the pitch and there was tension behind the scenes and amongst the coaching staff. The lack of success also hit the club in the pocket. As the season came to an end, there were one or two rumblings that there might be cutbacks. At the end of November, I was called in to see James Rule.

I'm not one for small talk and when I'm involved in a meeting I just want to get straight down to business. James is the same and it didn't take him long to get to the point. He explained that the club intended to restructure its backroom staff. They had decided to let me go.

It was a real shock; I hadn't seen it coming. Although, given the amount of staff the club employed, I shouldn't have been surprised. They definitely needed a clear out and since I had only been there for nine months, it was also much cheaper to get rid of me than someone that had been there longer. I'm not trying to make excuses for why I was fired; they obviously didn't want me to continue in the role and I think some people at the club were a little afraid of me and the way I conducted myself. I wanted to discuss and debate things and try to reach a consensus about how we might move forward in terms of youth development, but nobody else seemed to want that. The club wanted me to do my job and not challenge things.

To be honest, I was more embarrassed than anything. To be fired within a year of being hired doesn't look great on anyone's CV. Having got so excited about rejoining Hull FC, I now had to deal with the fact that they had rejected me for a second time.

Yet if there is one thing I have learnt in life it is how to deal with disappointments. There were no tantrums this time around. I had made a conscious decision to stay involved in professional sport and had to accept that these things happen. I had left behind a secure job at the Rugby Football League in order to return to club rugby. Within two years, I was out of work again. Where I was going next?

15

Back to the Future

In spite of being made redundant by Hull FC, I was still convinced that I had plenty to offer the game. As well as my achievements as a player, I had twelve years' experience of coaching, talent identification and administration which had given me a wide set of skills. I wasn't expecting to walk into a top coaching job but I was fairly confident it wouldn't take me long to find another role. I couldn't have been more wrong and had no idea that I was about to experience one of the worst periods of my life.

The years since I retired hadn't always been hugely successful but I had never spent much time out of the game and had always been able to find work of some kind. But for eight or nine months during 2010 I really had no idea what I might do next. After a while, I had no idea whether I was going to be able to pay my bills or even where I might end up living. It was a nightmare and caused me to make some tough choices about the future.

Whatever I ended up doing, I decided there wasn't a lot

of point living in Hull any longer. So in January 2010 I gave up the flat in Hessle and moved back to Castleford. I was very grateful to my mate Frankie Punchard for giving me a place to stay and was keen to help him out with the pub he runs. After a few weeks, I started to think about getting back into the pub business myself.

At the end of March 2010, I took over the management of The Malt Shovel in Glasshoughton, near Castleford, but it only took a couple of weeks for me to realise that the combination of long hours and uncertain income meant it just wasn't for me. I still had a lot of contacts in the game and had been back in touch with the RFL in the hope that there might be a job for me at Red Hall. They were able to give me one or two bits of work which kept me occupied, but there was nothing long term and nothing permanent.

As the months ticked by, money worries started to creep in. When I was a player, I always managed to live a decent lifestyle and, although I was never flash, I got used to being able to look after myself and my family. I had always earned enough to get by and spent whatever I earned. I was never really a saver and it was only when I found myself out of work that I realised how nice it would have been to have put some money aside for my future.

All the same, I have no regrets about that and nobody to blame but myself. Finding myself short of money did come as a bit of a shock though and the day I first went to the dole office to sign on was absolutely horrendous. One of the worst days of my life.

I have always prided myself on my mental strength and ability to bounce back but I can't deny there were times when I was totally miserable. It was hard to stay positive about the future. Gradually, I began to accept that there might not be a role for me within rugby league any longer and I had plenty of time on my hands to think about why that might be.

From Hull to Hell and Back

*****

I've always tried to be honest with myself and one of the reasons why I have struggled to stay involved in the game is because some people think I'm difficult to work with.

I have always had strong views but been quite happy to back up my opinions with facts and explanation. That's what I expect other people to do as well but, unfortunately, I have found that there are a lot of people who aren't prepared to discuss things. Instead, they just make a decision and refuse to explain themselves. I guess, if they're the chairman or the chief executive then they can do that, but I find that very frustrating and difficult to accept.

I don't know why that should make me difficult to work with. I expect to be challenged in whatever I do and I can't see why anyone else in a position of responsibility shouldn't feel the same way. Nevertheless, the harsh reality of being unemployed caused me to reconsider. When I was a player, I could get away with having strong views because I was valued and clubs didn't want to lose me. Since I've retired I've discovered I'm not so indispensible. I need to be more diplomatic, which is something that doesn't come easy to me.

I'm not on my own in finding it difficult to stay in the game though. Rugby league struggles to utilise the players who have served it well. Over the years, I have seen many ex-players drift away from it completely. If you look around, there aren't many people around who played the game in the pre-Super League era like I did. Brian Noble and Jon Sharp are probably the only ones to successfully make the transition.

Obviously, there are lots of blokes who would like to stay involved but are not prepared to work at it and think the sport owes them a living. Yet you can't rely on the skills and knowledge you once had as a player because time changes

320

everything. The only way to stay relevant is to reinvent yourself continually and ensure you have something to offer.

A few of my ex-team mates have become very successful in rugby union, such as Shaun Edwards, Graham Steadman and Mike Ford. I admire them for that; it can't be easy to adapt to a new sport as well as make the transition to coaching. On the other hand, there are lots who have been allowed to drift out of the game, either because they couldn't keep up with what was needed or because the game itself didn't work hard enough to keep them involved.

The sport of rugby league is a great family, one that I am very proud to belong to and I think we're usually quite good at looking after one another. But the question does need to be asked: why aren't there as many ex-players involved in the same way as there are in football, rugby union or even rugby league in Australia? People like Alfie Langer at Brisbane will probably be at the Broncos in one capacity or another for the rest of his life. We don't value that kind of relationship.

One of our sport's greatest assets are the players, but I don't think we invest enough to help them develop the skills they need to help the next generations. It is a huge waste of talent and I know from personal experience how frustrating it is to be an ex-player desperate to make a contribution, but needing a bit of help to know how best to use your skills.

There are very few ex-players working at the RFL and that is a real shame. We need people who have played at the elite level involved in running the game. At the moment, there are too many people at the RFL who come from an academic background and whose sporting experience comes from another sport, usually rugby union. I appreciate there are transferable skills which can be utilised across all sports, but I think these are only helpful on the logistical and administrative side. To develop young players and coaches properly, I really believe you need a background in the game;

and to develop elite players and coaches, you need elite experience.

In my view, we need to encourage players to get involved in this kind of work when they retire rather than just look for careers in coaching or the media. We just can't afford to lose their expertise and knowledge.

*****

It's not particularly easy to stay involved through the media either, firstly because the press and TV coverage isn't very extensive and, when it is, the media tends to prefer to use coaches as pundits rather than players or ex-players. It's only recently that ex-players have started to appear on the telly, possibly on the back of Phil Clarke's success. Nowadays, people such as Robbie Paul, Brian Carney, Barrie McDermott and Terry O'Connor pop up on the box from time to time. All of them are bright, intelligent and entertaining and it's quite refreshing to see them rather than Martin Offiah!

I have probably missed the boat in terms of securing TV work and the decision I made to turn down the offer from Sky Sports back in 1999 ranks as one of the worst I have ever made. But I still enjoy the occasional radio work I do.

I first acted as a radio pundit when I finished playing. Radio Leeds invited me to work for them and I have done it on and off ever since. In the past, I just used to roll up to the game and chip in with an opinion whenever I was asked. Now that I have a bit more time on my hands, I have tried to make myself better at it. Last year, I did some summarising for KCFM, one of the local radio stations in Hull and, having a bit of time to do some preparation, hopefully made my comments a bit more interesting and informed.

Aside from working for the radio, I wasn't idle after leaving Hull and spent a lot of time thinking about what I needed to do next in order to get back into the game. Not only did I carry on studying for my Level 3 coaching badge, I also started to learn French. I don't really have any intention of living across the Channel but with the game expanding there I just thought it might give me something which other coaches or administrators might not have. I found it quite difficult to start learning something new at my age and I might never use it, but it shows how determined I am to keep learning and how keen I am to stay in rugby league.

As the months rolled by, I tried to stay patient, hopeful that something would come up to get me back into the game. Or at least give me a bit of financial security. It was hard to stay positive at times and there were occasions when I wondered if I would ever get any good news. And then, in the space of a few weeks, things started to pick up.

*****

In July 2010, I was pleased to be asked to help out with the coaching of the Castleford scholarship programme. Having lived in Castleford for nearly twenty-five years, I feel very much part of the community and it gave me a lift to know that I would still have a productive role to play there.

Currently, I coach the under-15 team and would like to continue with the role, possibly moving up to coach the under-18s at some point. Castleford are a terrific club, very close to my heart and, at the start of the 2011 season, they were briefly top of Super League with a tight-knit team made up of lots of young local players. It's great to be involved with the club again and the offer came at a good time for me.

Around the same time, the RFL also asked me to do some coaching for the Ladies' talent development squad. That was an interesting assignment but one I enjoyed and, if nothing else, it kept me involved and made sure I wasn't being forgotten about. With each and every job I took on, I hoped it was adding to my CV and moving me a step closer to the kind of permanent job that I wanted. I tried to keep in contact with as many people at the RFL as I could and, eventually, it paid off. Vinny Webb is the RFL's head of coach development and he approached me with a very interesting offer.

There are a number of countries in Europe such as Italy, Russia and Serbia, where there is real potential for rugby league to develop and take off. They are a long way from being competitive with the likes of Ireland or Scotland, let alone England, but in October 2011 they are scheduled to take part in a qualifying competition that will see one of them going on to participate in the 2013 Rugby League World Cup. One of Vinny's roles is to develop the coaching structure within these countries and part of the plan was for their national teams to have an input from English coaches. Vinny asked if I would be interested in helping to coach Serbia and that's how I found myself on a flight to Belgrade at the start of August, 2010.

The RFL flew me out there to take a look at the state of the game and discover what level of support they needed. I have to admit that, before I went, I knew very little about the country, its history or even its precise location. But during the week I spent there, I thoroughly enjoyed the place and couldn't have been made more welcome.

Belgrade is a strange city. The war has clearly left its mark. There is still a very old part to it which I enjoyed seeing, but there is also a lot of redevelopment taking place in those areas that were badly affected by the conflict. That said, it is still a modern European city with most of the distractions you would expect anywhere else. I was well looked after and got on very well with Marko Jankovic, the current Serbian coach.

Once we got out of Belgrade and travelled up into the

mountains, it changed dramatically and was like going back in time. The countryside is very rural and quite undeveloped but the people were wonderful, very friendly and hospitable and also very patient when trying to communicate with me in English. Most of the blokes associated with the team spoke quite good English, but I soon realised that I would need to gain a grasp of at least some of the language if I was going to take on the role.

I was being asked to consider taking on the job of coach but another idea popped into my head while I was out there. It seemed a shame that I would only get the chance to work with the national team, particularly since I would only be able to meet up with the players occasionally. I decided that a better idea might be for Marko to keep his position as head coach and for me to take up a different role as a technical director, guiding him and helping him out. That way, he wouldn't be pushed aside and I could take a wider remit and look at the game as a whole in Serbia rather than just the national side.

Most of my ideas were quite strategic and I had already met up with some regional coaches with whom I was keen to work in the future. It made sense for me to be involved in a wider role and, when I put my ideas to Jovan Vujosevic who works for the European Federation and to the people back at the RFL, I was pleased that they accepted them.

When I came home, I was given a twelve-month contract as technical advisor to the Serbian RL. It's only a part-time post but the idea is that I visit the country six times in the build up to those World Cup qualifying games in October 2011. In between, I'll stay in touch with Marko and the other coaches via e-mail and telephone. Marko will also send over DVDs of games so I can keep tabs on the players out there.

*****

The game in Serbia is played at a very basic level. There are ten teams, most of them based in Belgrade. The quality of play, I soon learned, is poor by international standards. I would probably equate it to about Championship One. What is missing more than anything is any kind of game sense and awareness of how rugby league ought to be played. That's largely down to the fact that most players have not grown up watching the sport. That will change but, in the meantime, one of my priorities is to help the coaches teach the players the basics, such as the particular roles and responsibilities that exist. Without such awareness it's hard for the players to improve. Nevertheless, within the small rugby league community, there is a real passion for the sport and a genuine desire to improve and prosper.

I went back out to Serbia in October 2010 to watch the end-of-season play-offs and Grand Final. The final itself, between two Belgrade-based teams, Red Star and Dorcal, was played at an amateur football club ground in the capital. The crowd of around 500 suggests it is going to be some time before the game can start to generate the kind of profile and income it needs to grow. But there are some promising players there with a fair bit of technical skill. I would love to bring some of them over to play in this country, perhaps to play in the Championship or as part of Super League's under-20s competition. It is going to be difficult for their elite players to improve unless they play regularly against tougher opponents and I would really like to help facilitate that. Unfortunately, with Serbia not being in the European Union, they would be classed as quota players and no club is likely to want to use a quota place on a player from Serbia. I have asked questions about that situation but can't see it changing in the short run.

The details of the World Cup qualifying tournament were

released early in 2011. As it stands, there are four teams involved and Serbia are due to play Lebanon away and Italy and Russia at home. It will be a huge challenge to try and steer Serbia to the World Cup and there is no doubt we won't be favourites. One thing we could do to improve the national team immediately would be to go looking for players in Australia and England who are qualified to play for Serbia. There are one or two high-profile players we could go for but, to be honest, even if there were more, I wouldn't want to go too far down that road.

There's no doubt we would benefit from a small number of players with top-level experience and I would have no problem with picking a couple of 'foreign' players in key positions. They would have a massive impact on the team and the native players would really benefit from playing with better, more experienced players. But on the whole I believe the best way for the team to improve in the long run is for Serbs to play together, so I certainly won't be looking to field a team full of Australians.

*****

The opportunity to work with Serbia came at a great time for me. But by the time the job arose, I had already come to the conclusion that I could no longer rely on rugby league to earn a living. Fortunately, another opportunity was just around the corner.

A friend of mine, Terry Maxwell, is involved with the recruitment company Aqumen. They sponsor the hospitality suite at Castleford and I had met a few of their key people. I was aware they were a very successful, ambitious company but didn't know Terry was trying to persuade them to offer me a job. I started working for them in early 2011.

I had never worked for a recruitment company before but

they were very patient and gave me the training I needed. I currently manage a couple of accounts but I'm also involved in developing a pilot programme which will help to prepare players at Castleford for employment outside the game. At the moment, we've managed to organise work experience for some lads on the scholarship programme but, in the longer term, I'd like to develop a programme to help players who are coming towards the end of their careers, to gain the skills and knowledge they need to enter the 'real' workforce. It's a theme that is close to my heart and something the game really needs for many of the reasons I have explained earlier. It's early days yet but if it works out at Castleford, we would like to offer it up for more clubs to take advantage of.

Alongside that, the company is also looking to expand into Hull and I'm involved with that as well. It's supposed to be a nine-to-five role but I've had barely a minute to myself since I started, not that I'm complaining. After months out of work and being uncertain of where to go next, it's a great opportunity for me to move in a different direction while also getting a bit of financial security.

Because they are so heavily involved with rugby league, Aqumen are very keen for me to carry on working with the Castleford scholarship programme, as well as with Serbia, which means that the job is a great fit for me.

After an horrendous nine months, suddenly in the space of a few short weeks my whole future was looking a lot rosier. But the year had still taught me some harsh lessons. The experience of unemployment had humbled me a fair bit and made me realise that I couldn't rely on rugby league any longer. It also made me realise that working for a living isn't like playing rugby. You have to tolerate things and put up with people you might not like. I don't think I'll find that easy, but it'll be a damn sight more tolerable than being on the dole!

*****

While my job prospects were beginning to look up, I couldn't believe my good luck when I received an invitation from Wests Tigers to fly out to Sydney in September 2010. A reunion dinner had been organised to celebrate Western Suburbs' 'Team of the 1980s' and I had been selected. That was an incredible honour since I only played twenty-odd games for the club in 1985 and 1986. As a result, they had arranged for me to fly out there and spend a couple of weeks attending some club functions.

The invitation was for two and I decided to take my son, Ben, along for the ride. We were very well looked after by Wests and I managed to catch up with a lot of my old mates such as John Ribot, Steve Roach, Benny Elias, Ian Schubert, Brett Clark, Herbie Smales and Graeme Bradley.

While we were there, we were also invited to a New South Wales RL dinner where I found myself seated with Max Krilich and Ray Price. Well, you can imagine what we talked about! Nearly thirty years earlier, I had been sent off for smacking Max in a Test match and Ray and I had traded blows on the same tour. We pissed ourselves laughing at the memory of it all and, because they are much older than me, they still looked on me as a bit of an uppity young lad, I think. Unfortunately, we weren't able to stay long enough to watch the NRL Grand Final, but we did manage to catch the preliminary semi the week before when Wests were beaten by St George-Illawarra.

The trip reminded me how lucky I am to be a part of the great family of rugby league. I always enjoy meeting up with old mates from Australia and it gives me a real buzz that I can call some of the great legends of the game mates and enjoy a beer with them.

From Hull to Hell and Back

It's a shame we're not able to do it more often but one of the best reunions I have ever been involved with was when a guy called Peter Banner organised the Legends of League competition in 2001, between teams of ex-Great Britain and Australian internationals.

When I got the call to play I didn't hesitate to accept, particularly since a lot of my mates were also called up, such as Garry Schofield, Tony Marchant and Andy Gregory. Unsurprisingly, Schoey took it very seriously indeed and appointed himself captain straight away on the basis that he was determined to lead his country to win a series against the Aussies at least once in his career.

Playing against and battling with Australians has been one of the defining characteristics of my career and I relished taking them on again. The first game was played at Widnes and the five-thousand fans who turned up loved it as we stormed into a big lead in the first half. I thoroughly enjoyed myself as well and managed to put Schoey through a gap early in the game with a lovely pass that I doubt I ever bettered in my prime.

In the second half, it was clear that the Aussie lads had looked after themselves better than we had and their superior fitness told as they came storming back. When they scored a try in the 75th minute to lead 28-22, it looked like yet another defeat for GB. By that stage, we were relying more and more on the amateur players who had been drafted in as our substitutes. It was one of them, Johnny Bowles from Simms Cross, who managed to sneak over for the final try of the game in the last minute. The score was 28-26 with just enough time for the conversion. Step forward Lee Crooks!

Referee Fred Lindop had made it clear that it would be the final kick of the game. Sixteen years earlier, all eyes had been on me at Elland Road as I prepared to kick a penalty that would tie the scores and draw a Test series against New

Zealand. The situation was almost identical. Identical, except that the conversion was from in front of the posts, there were only five-thousand inside the Autoquest stadium and the prize was a bit of fun rather than a fully-charged Test series. Consequently, instead of being given encouragement from my team-mates as I lined up my kick, most of them were taking the piss. There was plenty of stick from the Aussies behind the posts as well, but I held my nerve, went through my kicking routine as I had done thousands of times before, and saw the ball fly between the posts to level it 28-all.

Someone suggested we play extra-time but thirty-odd panting and wheezing ex-pros treated that idea with the contempt it deserved and trudged off for a well-earned pint.

The second game was at Headingley the following week but, in between, both sets of players had a great time mixing over a few beers. I was particularly keen to spend time with Cliffy Lyons, with whom I played at Leeds, and Steve 'Blocker' Roach, who was my team-mate at Balmain.

After giving up a healthy lead at Widnes, we were determined to pace ourselves better in the return game but it unfolded in almost exactly the same way. We went into a big lead before they came back and, again, the game ended in a draw. Once again, the players were invited to play extra-time to try and settle the two-match series. And once again the response was: 'Fuck off.'

Although we drew the series, it had felt like a mismatch at times. The Aussies had been much fitter than us and I'm sure the average age of their team was much lower than ours, particularly since we had Dave Topliss and Mick Morgan in our side. Although Morgan must have been in his sixties, it wasn't just the older blokes who struggled; Andy Gregory looked like he was going to have a heart attack at the end of the first game.

For the players, the series was a great success. The games

were well organised and we were well looked after. We got into a routine that many of us had missed since retirement. We met up, trained, stayed over in a hotel, prepared for the game, drank beer afterwards and then did it all over again.

*****

But, for me, the most enjoyable get-togethers I still take part in are the Hull FC player reunions. They are organised in aid of the Roy Waudby Foundation and bring together most of the lads I played with at the start of my career. I think the first one was a reunion of the 1982 Challenge Cup-winning team and there have been several others since. Whenever the word has gone out that a reunion is afoot, everyone starts buzzing and looking forward to seeing one another. The highlight is usually a sportsman's dinner but, as you can imagine, the partying doesn't end there. We usually spend most of the week together one way or another.

The first time the players were brought together, I was a little nervous before I met up with them at the Holiday Inn in Hull. I had no idea what to expect and was a bit worried I would have nothing to say. I needn't have worried. Within five minutes of seeing those old faces and saying 'hello', it was like nothing had changed and no time had passed at all. I'll never forget my time at Hull. The reunion events are some of the best days I've had in retirement.

*****

A little over thirty years after I made my debut for the Hull FC first team, my youngest son Ben made his own first team debut for the club in a pre-season friendly at Doncaster. Like me, Ben was just seventeen and I was there to watch, of course.

With Lee Crooks as his dad and Steve 'Knocker' Norton his uncle, it was no surprise that Ben would play rugby at some time or another, but it was never inevitable that he would be so successful. Firstly, Ben overcame some serious medical problems as a youngster which meant that, even now, he dehydrates much more quickly than other players. Although I always wanted him to give rugby a try, he spent some time playing football and competing in gymnastics as well before returning to rugby league.

While I was at the RFL, Ben was just coming through the junior levels at Lock Lane and was involved in some of the training camps I managed. In fact, I occasionally coached Ben myself when he was playing for Lock Lane. It would be unfair to Ben, though, to say that my involvement had any impact on his progress and, to be honest, he has done even better to overcome the pressure that goes with having a dad who has played the game.

Nevertheless, I have always tried to give him as much support and feedback as I possibly can and, if anything, I have probably been quite critical of him over the years. At least he knows that when I tell him he has played well I mean it and that I'm not just trying to make him feel better. Ben and I have an excellent relationship and I think he knows how to use my experience and knowledge to his own advantage. I do occasionally find it difficult not to get too involved with his career, though. As a member of the Hull FC playing squad, his coaches are Andy Last and Richard Agar, depending on which team he is playing for or training with. It's not for me to start interfering with his game.

Ben is a smart boy; he could have achieved far more at school if he had wanted to, but he had already decided he wanted to make a future in rugby league. At the age of 15, his studies became secondary to his rugby. If he had shown as much dedication towards his GCSEs as he has done to his rugby, he would have done very well, I'm sure. He uses his intelligence well, though, and knows what it will take for him to achieve his goals. Ben is still developing physically but I have no doubt that, within the next few years, he will play in Super League for Hull FC and that will make me incredibly proud. After that, how far he goes will depend on the size of his own ambition and how much he wants to achieve. I will be there for him throughout that journey. In any kind of weather.

*****

Few people are aware that I already have one son who has played for Hull FC. Stuart was just eighteen when he played for Hull FC in a pre-season friendly at Featherstone and, for a while, there was a lot of hope that he could go all the way. As a young lad, he was very good indeed and was much sought after within the amateur game, before signing on for Hull FC's Academy team in 2001.

I was extremely proud when I saw him play his first game in the black and white hoops and even happier when he was selected to represent Yorkshire Academy. Stuart came through at the same time as Scott Wheeldon who went on to play for Hull before joining Hull KR. Stuart was a different type of player to Scott; he liked to pass the ball and make things happen and he drew comparisons with the way I used to play the game. He wanted to try and create things as well as just do the yardage. Unfortunately, that kind of player wasn't what Hull were looking for at that time.

Stuart also had a lot of problems with his knee and was out of the game for quite a long time, which ultimately cost him any chance of a professional career. He continued to play and coach a bit for West Hull and is now carving out a niche for himself as a professional cage fighter.

Stuart is a family man as well these days. He married Kate a couple of years ago and, in 2009, they had their first child, Georgia. I'm incredibly proud of how Stuart has overcome the adversity of his injuries and found a new focus and lots of happiness.

*****

Georgia isn't my first grandchild. I became a grandad for the first time in 2007 when Emma gave birth to Sonny. Emma is my eldest child and I have always looked on her as the rock of the family. She wasn't really old enough to understand what was going on when her mum and I split up, but she was incredibly mature in how she dealt with it all and how she welcomed Megan and Ben into the family. She has always been extremely level-headed but she was really quite nervous before telling me that she was expecting a baby.

She called me up and told me to sit down as she had some news. When she told me I was going to be a grandad, I was elated. When Sonny came along, it was wonderful to see him for the first time and then, in 2009, after she married her partner Mikey, they had their second child, Beau. Beau and Georgia were born within a couple of weeks of one another and I am very pleased to see both of my first two children happy with families of their own.

*****

In contrast to Emma, Megan is the quietest of my four kids. In a sports-mad family, there was always the danger that she could be squeezed out, but Megan has proved to be a determined and quiet achiever. Few of her teachers expected her to do particularly well at school, but she surprised them all when she came away with eleven GCSEs. She is now at

University studying Psychology, which might help her to understand what makes her old man tick.

I remember how determined she was to learn to drive and how disappointed she was when she failed her test. She passed eventually and Karen, her mum, rewarded her by buying her a car for her eighteenth birthday. I will never forget the look of joy on her face when she was given the keys, just as I will never forget how happy Ben was when he learned he had been selected to play for England Schoolboys or when Emma and Stuart had their children. If ever I feel disappointment or frustration with my career, my children and grandchildren give me all of the pleasure that I need.

*****

At the start of March 2010, I was travelling over to Hull when my brother, Richard, called me to tell me that our dad had been rushed into hospital. Richard found him slumped on his bed and called an ambulance right away. Dad was rushed into hospital but, by the time I managed to get to the hospital, he had died.

I knew that Dad had been struggling with his health for a few years and, deep down, I suppose it didn't come as a huge surprise. His breathing was laboured and difficult and his quality of life can't have been very good. He had stopped going to rugby a while earlier due to his health and Richard had even got him a mobility scooter to try and help him get around a bit better. Nevertheless, he struggled to get out of the house and had even stopped going to his social club. A few months earlier, his dog had passed away and, even though it was a mangy, scruffy little thing, Dad would have been lonely without it. Fortunately, he had Richard close by who would visit regularly with Sue and his son, Liam.

After the funeral, we sprinkled his ashes under the same

tree where we had placed Mam's ashes a few years earlier. After thirty-odd years of marriage, Mam and Dad had actually split up late in life. Richard and I commented that they could now continue their argument underneath that willow tree in Western Cemetery in Hull for evermore.

*****

Losing your parents is a sobering experience and, for me, a humbling one. Over the years, I had drifted away from them both and never really reconciled with either before they passed away. In some respects, writing this book has been my way of offering an explanation for why I have behaved in the way that I have. That regret will stay with me for the rest of my life and makes me all the more determined never to let it happen with my relationship with my own children.

I suppose that Dad's passing means I am now the head of the family but, to be honest, it was always Richard who was there for them. I am glad that he was and proud of him for being so.

Losing both parents and having an enforced break from rugby league has caused me to take stock of my career and my life and so, I suppose, this is where the story ends for now. As a rugby league player, I was good enough and fortunate enough to play in over twenty major cup finals. I lost more than I won but still managed to collect two John Player Trophy medals, a Challenge Cup, a League Championship and a handful of Yorkshire Cup medals. I played at Wembley four times, twice as captain, and also played in a famous Challenge Cup replay. I represented Great Britain on nineteen occasions in a twelve-year international career and there were many other representative honours along the way as well.

It has been said that I was one of the best ball-playing prop forwards this country has ever produced and, with that in mind, some have asked whether I ought to have achieved more with my career.

I have always tried to be very honest with everyone and, most importantly, with myself. Because of that I have to admit that I didn't reach my full potential. I know how hard I worked at the end of my career in order to sustain it into its seventeenth season - twentieth, if you include, as I do, the three seasons I spent playing club rugby in Australia. If I had always prepared so professionally in my early and middle years, there is no doubt that I would have earned many, many more Great Britain caps and might also have gained more domestic success as well.

So do I have regrets? Of course I do.

I regret that I didn't make the best of the opportunity I had at Leeds and I regret that I turned down the opportunity to work for Sky Sports and rushed into coaching at Keighley. But, career-wise, that's about it, to be honest. Of course, I could have looked after my money a bit better and there are one or two scrapes I could have avoided along the way, but that's just what comes with the kind of lifestyle I've had. Like anyone, I regret those occasions when I have behaved like an arsehole but, on balance, I think I have always tried to treat people well and with respect. More than any of my possessions, I am immensely proud to have so many true friends within and without the game all over the world.

Of course, there are many things I wish I could have done differently in terms of family relationships. But there's nothing I can do about that now. It's in the past and I'll just have to live with it. Where my kids and grandkids are concerned, I'm determined to play a full, active and positive role in their lives for as long as they want me to.

Am I a happy man? Well, that's difficult to answer. The price that many professional sportsmen pay for their success is that they have to live with it for the rest of their lives.

I was catapulted from a normal working class family in Hull to incredible success almost overnight and, trust me, I had an unbelievably enjoyable time for years, doing some crazy, crazy stuff with some of the best mates a bloke could ever have. Had I not been so keen to maintain those friendships, I could have written a far more scandalous book!

The party lasted for seventeen years and then it all ended. I had to find my way in the real world and come to terms with being Lee Crooks. Not the nineteen-year-old Lee Crooks who played for Great Britain; or the twenty-four year old Lee Crooks, the most expensive player in the world. Lee Crooks, the ex-player with two dodgy knees struggling to find his way back into the sport he loves.

As I write, in the past few months, I'm pleased to say that things have started to go my way, but that hasn't always been the case since I retired from playing. When I feel a bit down and bemoan my bad luck, I try to think of those worse off. Some of my old mates aren't around any longer: Singe Ellis, one of the fittest men I ever met, who died of a heart attack aged 41; Mike Gregory who was just 43 when he died after a long illness; and three of my old team-mates at Hull who passed away long before their time - the great Clive Sullivan, my old mentor Dave Topliss and brilliant Ronnie Wileman.

When I think of them and their families, and when I see my kids and my beautiful grandkids and how happy they all are, I realise I am a very lucky man indeed.

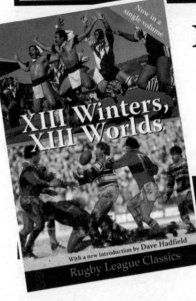

The definitive history of Northern comedy

ISBN: 978-0956007568
HARDBACK
656 PAGES

'...colourful & fascinating...' -
The Yorkshire Post

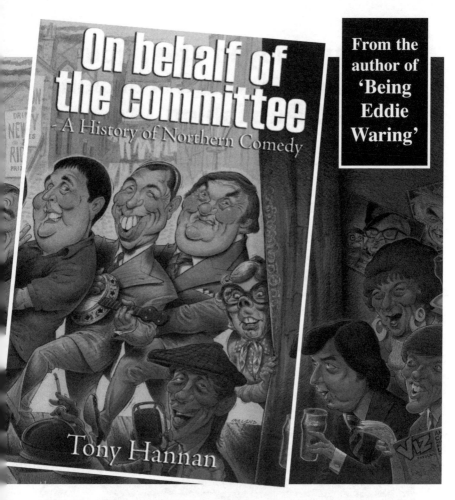

On behalf of the committee
- A History of Northern Comedy

Tony Hannan

From the author of 'Being Eddie Waring'

From the Industrial Revolution to our own comfortable 21st century digital age - via music hall, Variety, working mens clubs, radio, cinema & television - Northern-born comedians have consistently been at the heart of popular British comedy culture, tickling the funny bone of the entire nation.

This witty and informative book questions why that should be so, all the while charting an entertaining course through the careers of George Formby, Tommy Handley, Gracie Fields, Frank Randle, Al Read, Jimmy James, Hylda Baker, Jimmy Clitheroe, Les Dawson, Morecambe & Wise, Bernard Manning, Alan Bennett, Monty Python, Victoria Wood, Ken Dodd, Chubby Brown, The Young Ones, Vic and Bob, Steve Coogan, Caroline Aherne, the League of Gentlemen, Johnny Vegas, Peter Kay and many many others. Along the way, it also wonders why such a huge contribution to the British entertainment industry should be so often under-appreciated.

Mostly, however, it is a rich celebration of British comedy history & confirmation that you really do have to laugh - or else you'd cry...

If you enjoyed this, you'll love these from Scratching Shed Publishing Ltd...

Scratching Shed Publishing Ltd

Scratching Shed Publishing Ltd is an independent publishing company founded in May 2008. We aim to produce high-quality books covering a wide range of subjects - including sport, travel and popular culture - of worldwide interest yet with the distinctive flavour of the North of England.

Scratching Shed Publishing Ltd - Bringing history to life

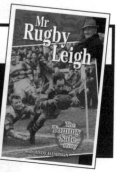

Scratching Shed Publishing Ltd

Scratching Shed Publishing Ltd is an independent publishing company founded in May 2008. We aim to produce high-quality books covering a wide range of subjects - including sport, travel and popular culture - of worldwide interest yet with the distinctive flavour of the North of England.

A sports autobiography like no other....

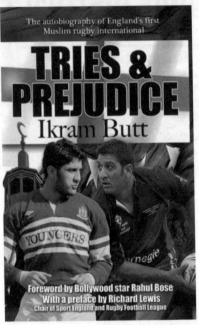

The autobiography of England's first
Muslim rugby international

TRIES &
PREJUDICE
Ikram Butt

Foreword by Bollywood star Rahul Bose
With a preface by Richard Lewis
Chair of Sport England and Rugby Football League

In February 1995, Ikram Butt became England's first Muslim rugby international in either code - blazing a trail for British Asians.

Since then, the former Leeds, Featherstone, London, Huddersfield and Hunslet rugby league star has continued to campaign for wider Asian involvement in sport and in 2004 was a prime mover in the formation of BARA - the British Asian Rugby Association. From the start, BARA had a vital social as well as sporting function. How could it not, in the wake of such 'War on Terror'-related atrocities as 9/11, 7/7 and the reported alienation of Britain's disaffected Asian youth?

Now, for the first time, Ikram Butt has his say, telling of his upbringing in Headingley; his own experiences on the wrong end of the law; the potential conflict between personal ambition and religion; racism in sport; run-ins with coaches and short-sighted officials; and, most recently, his regular visits to the House of Commons and pioneering development work in the UK, India and Pakistan.

Tries & Prejudice is by turns amusing, controversial, humane and eye-opening. It provides long overdue food for thought for politicians, the public and sports governing bodies alike.   ISBN 978-0956007537

THE STORY OF FOOTBALL:

via the Moors, Dales and Wolds of England's largest and proudest county

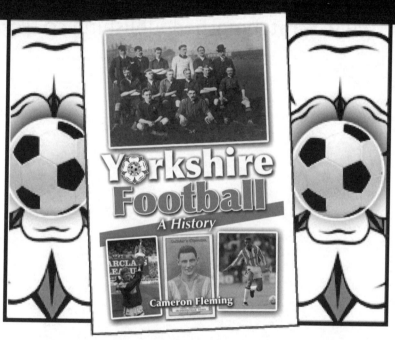

YORKSHIRE FOOTBALL - A HISTORY

Cameron Fleming

ISBN: 978-0956252654

Scratching Shed Publishing Ltd

Stay up to date with all our lastest releases at
www.scratchingshedpublishing.co.uk